CULTURAL LITERACY AND THE IDEA OF GENERAL EDUCATION

CULTURAL LITERACY AND THE IDEA OF GENERAL EDUCATION

Eighty-seventh Yearbook of the
National Society for the Study of Education

PART II

By

THE YEARBOOK COMMITTEE
and
ASSOCIATED CONTRIBUTORS

Edited by

IAN WESTBURY AND ALAN C. PURVES

Editor for the Society

KENNETH J. REHAGE

19 NSSE 88

Distributed by THE UNIVERSITY OF CHICAGO PRESS ● CHICAGO, ILLINOIS

The National Society for the Study of Education

Founded in 1901 as successor to the National Herbart Society, the National Society for the Study of Education has provided a means by which the results of serious study of educational issues could become a basis for informed discussion of those issues. The Society's two-volume yearbooks, now in their eighty-seventh year of publication, reflect the thoughtful attention given to a wide range of educational problems during those years. In 1971 the Society inaugurated a series of substantial publications on Contemporary Educational Issues to supplement the yearbooks. Each year the Society's publications contain contributions to the literature of education from more than a hundred scholars and practitioners who are doing significant work in their respective fields.

An elected Board of Directors selects the subjects with which volumes in the yearbook series are to deal and appoints committees to oversee the preparation of manuscripts. A special committee created by the Board performs similar functions for the series on Contemporary Educational Issues.

The Society's publications are distributed each year without charge to members in the United States, Canada, and elsewhere throughout the world. The Society welcomes as members all individuals who desire to receive its publications. Information about current dues may be found in the back pages of this volume.

This volume, *Cultural Literacy and the Idea of General Education*, is Part II of the Eighty-seventh Yearbook of the Society. Part I, which is published at the same time, is entitled *Critical Issues in Curriculum*.

A listing of the Society's publications still available for purchase may be found in the back pages of this volume.

Library of Congress Catalog Number: 87-062791
ISSN: 0077-5762

Published 1988 by
THE NATIONAL SOCIETY FOR THE STUDY OF EDUCATION

5835 Kimbark Avenue, Chicago, Illinois 60637

First Printing, 6,000 Copies

Printed in the United States of America

Acknowledgment

The subject of this volume is again the focus of much discussion today, as indeed it was in 1932, 1939, and 1952 when the Society published yearbooks addressing the theme of general education. In authorizing the preparation of the present volume, the Board of Directors recognized that important societal changes in the last three decades more than justify a new look at the pervasive issues that arise when questions are asked about general education.

The several authors contributing to this yearbook have taken a fresh look at many of the questions that lie at the center of discussions concerning general education. Their thought and effort have resulted in a provocative set of essays and interesting insights to enrich those discussions. The Society is grateful to each of them.

We are especially indebted to Professors Alan C. Purves and Ian Westbury, editors of the book. They were responsible for drawing up the initial proposal that was presented to the Board and for soliciting contributions from a distinguished group of authors. Mr. Westbury has assumed major responsibility for reading proof and attending to all the tasks that come up when a volume is in the final stages preceding publication. In addition to their work as editors of the volume, both Mr. Purves and Mr. Westbury have contributed chapters to it.

We see this book as a significant contribution to the literature on general education and a worthy addition to the Society's series of yearbooks.

Table of Contents

Section One
Introduction

Section Two
The Idea of General Education

Section Three
Cultural Literacy and the Curriculum

Section Four

Curriculum "Reform" and Its Problems—Higher Education

Section Five

A Pessimistic Conclusion—General Education and the Public School

Section One
INTRODUCTION

CHAPTER I

General Education and the Search for a Common Culture

ALAN C. PURVES

Turning and turning in a widening gyre,
The falcon cannot hear the falconer;
Things fall apart, the center cannot hold.

W. B. YEATS
"The Second Coming"

General education might best be defined as the purposeful attempt to provide a particular group of students with a common core of knowledge, skills, and values. The term "general" refers not to the people who will undergo that education, but to the substance that is imparted. Paradoxically, general education, in many cases, is "caviar to the general," and is not to be equated with common schooling or basic education. At times it has been equated with "liberal education," that which traditionally includes training in the modes of thought of the humanities, including foreign languages, the natural and physical sciences, and the social sciences. At times it has been seen as encompassing a broader set of studies. General education, as applied to colleges and universities, appears to be a peculiarly American conception. It is often viewed as also the province of secondary schools, particularly by those who recall the fact that many universities ran their own preparatory schools to provide students with sufficient "general education" to be ready to begin specialized university training. Such schools no longer exist, but the very idea of university entrance or high school graduation requirements may be seen as vestiges of this earlier state of affairs.

1

General Education and Cultural Literacy

The idea of general education is related to the idea of culture, which is something to which people are affiliated as opposed to their natural filiation. General education has come into the news during the 1980s, thanks to an article by E.D. Hirsch, Jr.[1] and the addition of a measure of cultural knowledge in the National Assessment of Educational Progress. The idea of culture goes back at least as far as the eighteenth century and was spurred in the nineteenth century by the nationalist impetus. Culture may best be defined as Edward Said has defined it: "[C]ulture is used to designate not merely something to which one belongs but something that one possesses, and along with that proprietary process, culture also designates a boundary by which the concepts of what is extrinsic or intrinsic to the culture comes into forceful play."[2] Anthropologists tend to see culture somewhat differently from literary people, but this root definition of possession and being possessed seems to apply both to those societies that operate through what might be called natural filiation (a system of intergenerational and familial relationships), and those that operate through affiliation to some arbitrarily instituted set of relationships. Current "American" culture is a culture of affiliation, whether it be the culture of Hawthorne and Harriet Beecher Stowe, the culture of Black Studies, the culture of feminism, or the culture of "hard science." Some have argued that the idea of general education came to America in its attempt to define itself as America and to define American culture. Others have seen general education as an attempt by American educational institutions to ensure that the European heritage remained part of the American culture.

Any culture serves to isolate its members from other cultures and any culture is elitist in some senses. As Said points out, "What is more important in culture is that it is a system of values saturating downward almost everything within its purview, yet paradoxically culture dominates from above without at the same time being available to everything and everyone that it dominates."[3] Cultures are exclusionary by definition; people who have a culture see others as outside or beneath them, and certainly very few people transcend cultures or are full members of more than one culture, although they may be members of several subcultures, such as that of mycologists, joggers, or film aficionados as well as of the broader culture of "generally educated" Americans.

To be a member of a culture, one must possess a fair amount of knowledge, some of it tacit, concerning the culture: its rules, its rituals, its mores, its heroes, gods, and demigods. This knowledge lies at the heart of cultural literacy, and such knowledge is brought into play when people read and respond to a text that comes from the same culture. It is such knowledge that, in fact, enables them to read that text and is brought into play when we read and write as social beings within a particular community. The lack of such knowledge keeps us outside, as witness the problems of visitors to a national or disciplinary culture who often suffer trifling embarrassments or serious misunderstandings.

Cultural literacy may be thought of as language learning, for the study of any discipline or field of knowledge involves the learning of a language which represents a mode of thought culturally appropriate to the discipline. Judit Kádár-Fülop[4] has written that there are three major functions of the language curriculum in school (and by extension the curriculum in any discipline) that accord with the definitions of language functions proposed by Uriel Weinreich.[5] The first of these functions is the promotion of cultural communication so as to enable the individual to communicate with other members of the culture or discipline. Such a function clearly calls for the individual to learn the cultural norms of semantics, morphology, syntax, text structure, and pragmatics and some common procedural routines so as to operate within those norms and be understood. The second function is the promotion of cultural loyalty or the acceptance and valuing of those norms and routines and the inculcation of a desire to have them remain. A culturally loyal literate in physics, for example, would have certain expectations about how texts are to be written or to be read as well as what they should look like, and would expect others in the culture to follow those same norms. The third function of language education may be the development of individuality. Once one has learned to communicate within the culture and developed a loyalty to it, then one is able to become independent of it. Before then, independence of those norms and values is seen as naive, illiterate, or childish. As Lev Vygotsky wrote (1956): "In reality a child's thought progresses from the social to the individual not from the individual to the socialized."[6]

When writers such as Hirsch speak of cultural literacy they are clearly advocating the first two goals set forth by Kádár-Fülop and restrict the sense of the term to literacy in a particular culture, as did William Bennett in his report, *To Reclaim a Legacy*,[7] or that segment of general education which is defined as "the humanities" or "American classics." Hirsch and other advocates of cultural literacy refer to a definite body of knowledge (although Hirsch might not include specific titles, the National Assessment suggested that specific titles are necessary) that enables readers to read certain kinds of texts—notably texts that are shared by a group that one might define as "highly literate Americans." These would be people, for example, who can read the *New York Times* with understanding and can also read books and such journals as the *Atlantic Monthly*.[8]

The argument for this sort of cultural literacy is the argument that supported the Chicago Great Books Program, Harvard's General Education proposal, and Columbia's Humanities and Contemporary Civilization program in the early part of this century: such literacy brings together a disparate immigrant population and helps the melting pot do its job.[9] Such proposals bore with them the arguments of Matthew Arnold that a common culture based on the western heritage forged society into unity through affiliation and prevented anarchy and mobocracy. It does so not without cost. Again to cite the comments of Edward Said: "When our students are taught such things as 'the humanities' they are almost always taught that these classic texts embody, express, represent what is best in our, that is, the only, tradition. Moreover, they are taught that such fields as the humanities and such subfields as "literature" exist in a relatively neutral political element, that they are to be appreciated and venerated, that they define the limits of what is acceptable, appropriate, and legitimate as far as culture is concerned."[10]

The Limitations of the Equation of General Education and Cultural Literacy

But it is at this point that the similarity between the concern for general education and the current definitions of cultural literacy begin to break down, for those who advocate cultural literacy appear to think of the culture primarily in belle-lettristic terms. Such a conception seems hardly appropriate in an age of American culture in which science and technology play so large a part. One must consider the nature of American culture in broader terms. In part it is those terms which this volume sets out to consider and debate. Some of the points raised in the debate include the following:

1. Given a comprehensive secondary and initial tertiary educational system, more diverse groups with their distinctive cultural

heritages are now passing through the system and we must attend to the needs and values of those groups. The current conception does not adequately address these minority groups.

2. Education should meet the functional needs of the students and the workplace; there is little room in life for the sort of culture that is implied by any of the definitions of general education.

3. Any concept of general education must recognize the technological and scientific nature of our society. The emphasis on the humanities must be lessened, otherwise American society will lose out to the technologically more sophisticated nations.

4. In current academic practice, general education exists in the curriculum of both higher and secondary educational institutions. It is often defined in terms that resemble a menu in a mediocre Chinese restaurant; a person has attained a general education if the requisite number of hours have been spent in certain portions of the course catalog, instead of particular kinds of knowledge, skill, or attitude. It is also generally defined in terms of a limited number of academic fields (literature and history, with the social, natural, and physical sciences playing a secondary role). Yet one could easily make the argument that the fine arts, physical education, and the practical and technical arts should be included in general education. These areas, too, are constituents of our culture.

5. At the same time the very notion of the culture that a general education was to support has come to be challenged on a number of fronts: the culture appears too "Western" and too masculine and in defining itself has excluded much of the world in which Americans play an important but perhaps small part; the culture appears to have excluded the tremendous flow of information and the social and intellectual changes brought about by the new technologies; the culture has neglected the fact that people in various occupations have had to become so specialized in order to keep up with the occupation that they have "no time" to be cultured, and in many cases it has tended to see people in those occupations as without culture.

These are but some of the challenges to those planning general education for the students of the next century. To meet these challenges, educational planners and policymakers must face issues that are intellectual, political (both nationally and within the various educational institutions), and practical. This volume explores the challenges and the issues arising from them.

The volume contains five sections. This introductory chapter is Section One. The four following chapters comprise Section Two in which Sheldon Rothblatt, Herbert Kliebard, Hazard Adams, and Thomas Popkewitz explore various facets of the idea of general education. Rothblatt looks at the history of the idea and its implementation in schools and colleges. Kliebard devotes much of his chapter to the effect of Huxley and Spencer on the disintegration of the humanistic assumptions concerning general education along with the rise of the importance of practical studies. In his chapter, Hazard Adams explores the issue of what is it that is to be known in general education, citing that "knowing that" has turned to "knowing knowing," and more recently to "knowing language." The call of various proclamations to go back to a simpler view of knowing may be appealing but impossible. Finally, Thomas Popkewitz explores how the very debate over general education curricula masks the underlying social stratification inherent in the school system. To refer to general education at all serves as a way by which a power group can stay in control.

In the Section Three various issues are explored regarding general education. The first pair of essays, by William Plater and William Reid, pursue some of the points set by Adams and Popkewitz and particularly examine the ways by which the impact of the new information technologies manifests itself on general education. Plater compares the influence to that of written language and sees our society as going through the same sort of epistemological revolution that Plato discerned to be associated with literacy, whereas Reid sees it as equally pervasive in modifying how we conceive of schooling and raises questions about the conservative calls for general education. Arthur Efland and Murray Thomas take up respectively the role of the arts and of values in general education. Efland explores the political questions associated with the exclusion of physical education and the arts from the canon of general education and suggests how they might be reincorporated into general education. Thomas shows how the affective domain of general education is given short shrift and how it might better be seen as an important aspect of the curriculum. Finally, Ian Westbury explores the role of general education in the secondary schools, how they have been forced to anticipate but not duplicate the colleges and universities. He shows that the secondary schools have changed roles in the course of this century, but not curricula, and that if they are instruments of mass education, they have somehow to rethink their mission and their definition of general education.

Section Four contains two chapters concerning the problems surrounding curriculum "reform" in general education. Phyllis Franklin examines the various pressures confronting colleges and universities as they attempt to implement changes or modifications in general education programs. She shows how the Reagan administration has called for educational reform and then has both attacked and not supported educational institutions, particularly those of higher education, and explores the possible consequences of those attacks. Lawrence Mann shows the complications of this reform effort as it comes against the demands for professionalization and professional education, which have come to be so important in our society and which have almost destroyed the idea of general education.

In Section Five, Mark Holmes speculates on the possibilities and prospects for the very idea of general education in a time when it would appear that there is no such thing as a common core of knowledge or a defined border to that which should be the general knowledge of all people regardless of culture, gender, or profession. The very notion of a single society has crumbled in the United States; we have not the chance for a commonality that we once had and that we believe we see in the schools of Japan. Nor do we have a sustaining myth to provide a common core beyond the ABCs. What the future will bring is unclear.

The volume, then, explores the possible collapse of general education and of the broad cultural literacy that Hirsch proposes for our schools. This volume is in one sense a somber one. The high hopes for general education and the bringing together of a diverse people into a broad educated culture appears to be diminishing as the century wanes. It may be that we are in a *fin de siècle* mood, a point in our history where we find the lines of Yeats which began this introduction to be even more apposite than they were when written over sixty years ago. Yeats raised the question of a second coming and wondered "what rough beast [was] slouching towards Bethlehem to be born." In our world of schools and colleges, the shape of the rough beast is yet indistinct and may remain so for years to come.

FOOTNOTES

1. E. D. Hirsch, Jr., "Cultural Literacy," *American Scholar* 52 (Spring 1983): 159-69.

2. Edward Said, *The World, the Text, and the Critic* (Cambridge, MA: Harvard University Press, 1983).

3. Ibid., p. 9.

4. Judit Kádár-Fülop, "Culture, Writing, and the Curriculum," in *Writing across Languages and Cultures: Theory and Method in Contrastive Rhetoric*, ed. Alan C. Purves (Beverly Hills, CA: Sage Publications, in press).

5. Uriel Weinreich, *Languages in Contact: Findings and Problems* (The Hague: Mouton, 1963).

6. Lev Vygotsky, *Izbrannye psikhologicheskie isseldovaniia* (Moscow: RSFR Academy of Pedagogical Science, 1956), quoted in A. K. Markova, *The Teaching and Mastery of Language* (London: Croom Helm, 1979).

7. William J. Bennett, *To Reclaim a Legacy: A Report on the Humanities in Higher Education* (Washington, DC: National Endowment for the Humanities, 1984).

8. It is important to note that in his reworking of that article into a book, *Cultural Literacy: What Every American Needs to Know* (Boston: Houghton Mifflin, 1987), Hirsch has extended his view of cultural literacy to include much in science and the practical arts as well as current events and popular culture. It would seem that he is no longer in the same camp as Bennett.

9. Daniel Bell, *The Reforming of General Education* (New York and London: Columbia University Press, 1966).

10. Said, *The World, the Text, and the Critic*, p. 21.

Section Two
THE IDEA OF GENERAL EDUCATION

CHAPTER II

General Education on the American Campus: A Historical Introduction in Brief

SHELDON ROTHBLATT

May not the ardent humanist still cry (and not in the wilderness): Let us be well-balanced, let us be cultivated, let us be high-minded; let us control ourselves, as if we had passions; let us learn the names and dates of all famous persons; let us travel and see all the pictures that are starred in Baedeker; let us establish still more complete museums at home, and sometimes visit them in order to show them to strangers; let us build still more immense libraries, containing all known books . . ., and let us occasionally write reviews of some of them, so that the public, at least by hearsay, may learn which are which.

GEORGE SANTAYANA
The Genteel Tradition at Bay

Means and Ends in American General Education

Whether we attribute the origins of the idea of the love of knowledge being its own reward to Aristotle or to Plato and Pythagoras, the fact must be that all education, including general education, is by definition practical. How it is practical is the operative question. Is it broadly or narrowly useful, general preparation for life in the world or for a specific career? Even this polarity hardly exhausts the possibilities of utility. General preparation for life presupposes some kind of life, some kind of social role, and the word "career" covers occupations as diverse as soothsaying to the writing of software manuals. Furthermore, some occupations require more general preparation than others; some demand only rudimentary instruction.

The important point is that education must have a purpose or an objective, an end, and the correlation between that objective and the means to achieve it is usually best, that is, most "fitting," when education is undertaken with a specific objective in mind, when the curriculum has been constructed for a definite set of career objectives and skills. The fit is weakest and most ambiguous where the means of education do not presuppose a precise end. It is not difficult to train an engineer for a career designing hydraulic systems. It is not difficult to educate a civil servant in Latin, if Latin is essential to a career in administration (or Cherokee, said Lord Macaulay, if Cherokee is needed), and it is also not hard to train a poet for a career in the writing of poetry. The fact that the demand for engineers may in certain societies be greater than the demand for poets does not alter the direct relationship that can exist between education and career, although it may well affect the attitude that poets have to the market.

Disagreement exists over how engineers should be trained, and doubtless some disagreement exists over how poets are to be educated. But these disputes hardly compare to the quarrels that characterize discussions about general education; for where the means are not designed for very specific ends, where the utility to the individual seems to be at odds with social utility, where ultimate objectives are stated in the largest terms, or where no test of competency can be devised to prove the success of a particular course of studies, there we are likely to find acrimonious debate and stubbornly held opposing views. This has been true throughout the history of general education, but it has been especially true of the United States in the twentieth century when the phrase "general education" came into widespread use.

The Origins of Breadth, Coherence, and the Common Core

The attributes of a general education curriculum are usually said to be breadth, coherence, and a common compulsory core. Breadth and coherence are at one level antithetical. The narrower the view, the more coherent the perspective; the broader, the less coherent. The object, therefore, is to bring the two attributes together, as in Matthew Arnold's dictum that the purpose of culture is to see life clearly and to see it whole. Coherence restrains the centrifugal tendencies of breadth, while breadth controls the centripetal propensities of coherence. How did these notions come to play so important a part in American higher education?

American ideas of general education, of the unity of knowledge, derive from the colonial college of the seventeenth century, heavily influenced by the curriculum of the Cambridge University colleges, and the Scottish Enlightenment curriculum which supplanted it in the course of the eighteenth century. The core of both—and it was a common core—was classical languages: grammar, syntax, translations, and composition. A curriculum composed of the study of classical languages, particularly the study of Latin, is neither broad nor narrow. That judgment requires us to know more about the subjects studied, the spirit and manner in which they were interpreted, and the purposes for which they were undertaken. The classical heritage is and was vast. Portions of it could be taught without reference to the others, for example, Latin without Greek, the Hellenistic writers in preference to Hellenic ones, the Church fathers but not the pagan tradition, medieval scholasticism but not Byzantine scholarship or Italian Renaissance humanism, poetry but not history, comedy but not tragedy, philosophy but not astronomy. The study of classics could elevate the mind or lower it, depending upon whether one read Sophocles or Apuleius. The emphasis in the colonial period was on those portions of the classical curriculum most conducive to the specific ends of general education as then conceived: to promote fidelity to the precepts of Protestant Christianity and to advance regard for piety and religious obligation. Since most graduates were intended for positions in the churches, there was even a direct connection between a general curriculum and a career.[1]

The ends of the eighteenth-century general curriculum were similar to those of its predecessor, but there were some differences in the means. The colonial college was more tradition-minded and still labored under the spirit of scholasticism, which meant that classical languages were studied with the methods and objectives of rhetoric, but the eighteenth-century curriculum was broadening or "modernizing" in response to the discoveries of the Scientific Revolution. The problem of how to restrain the new propensities for breadth was solved with the adoption of the Scottish School of Common Sense, a comprehensive framework of ethics and metaphysics which provided an explanatory basis for understanding past and present behavior and institutions. Since neither Scots nor Americans of the Age of the Enlightenment were secular-minded or anticlerical, there was no likelihood that the collegiate curriculum would be distorted in such directions.[2]

Social and Institutional Dimensions
of General Education

The history of education is as much a story of culture and institutions as of ideas. It is therefore necessary to emphasize some well-known and some relatively neglected features of the history of general education. The realities of social existence—a scarcity of resources, and, until recently, the relatively short life span of most people—imposed limits on the length, extent, and possibilities of schooling, that is, education outside the home or guild. Hence formal education was limited to the few, the wealthy few, for it is easy to see that any kind of general education not specifically related to the occupational structure would be considered a luxury rather than a necessity. The historical practice was therefore to confine the period of general education in a young person's life to the period of schooling, the years before age fourteen or sixteen, and to regard any subsequent education—tertiary or postcompulsory education today— as training or career preparation. The years following school were reserved for more specialized studies. This accounts for several institutional characteristics of the history of schooling, such as the prevalence of corporal punishment, the emphasis on language study as a means of discipline (or as a puberty rite),[3] and the interpenetration of skills, homilies, and exempla. Young persons had to be watched and restrained. Their natural inclination to fidget, to be defiant, and to seek relief from the tedium of study had to be brought under control in order to awaken the adult in the child.[4]

Because the majority of undergraduates in America (and Scotland) were very young in past centuries, that is, below the age of eighteen, semantic confusion existed over the use of words like "college," "university," "school," and "academy." These institutions were not highly differentiated one from the other and performed similar and certainly overlapping functions. A college, it may be suggested, was closer in spirit and teaching to a high school than to what we understand a university to be.

Specialization

It is tempting to describe changes in a curriculum as historically sequential, but that would be misleading. Attempts to break away from the ideal of the unity of knowledge, to bring in more specialized examples of study sometimes related to occupations or careers have a history virtually as long as that of general education itself. This took the form of hiring specialized "professors" to replace tutors or "regent masters" in the Scottish universities of the seventeenth century or establishing wholly separate institutions, for example, military academies, but the degree to which this occurred in the past depended upon the capacity of outsiders—individuals, governments, municipalities—to challenge existing monopolies. The relatively open environment of the American continent, the constitution of federated states, the absence of established status hierarchies, the plural religious settlement of the colonies and early Republic, and the strength of the market and private sector of the economy produced a highly differentiated educational environment early in the nation's history. The signs are already present by the end of the eighteenth century. The old collegiate curriculum, embodied in the famous colonial liberal arts foundations and their offspring in the midwest and south, was challenged in the earliest days of the Republic by such institutions as the College of Philadelphia, the University of Virginia, and by numerous private "academies" which, like the non-Anglican dissenting academies of England, but also like the colonial colleges and their clones further inland, largely served an adolescent population.

The second quarter of the nineteenth century is the period in which general education, with coherence provided by the study of classical languages in the general framework of Scottish moral philosophy, competed for national attention with newer private and public institutions anxious to promote greater variety in the curriculum in response to market challenges and to ideas of university as opposed to college education starting to arrive from Europe. On the continent the system of professorial chairs and the competition for talent among the post-Napoleonic German states was producing innovation in the pantheon of university subjects, although philosophy was the higher or integrating study until the second half of the nineteenth century. In England a movement that had commenced in the latter part of the eighteenth century with the establishment of the specialized honors degree at Cambridge University, represented in the first instance by the mathematical tripos, very slowly challenged the supremacy of the older less specialized ordinary degree program of studies. The movement spread to Oxford in 1800 but resulted first in the establishment of what today must be regarded as a form of interdisciplinary studies, albeit based on the classical languages, philosophy, and history, *literae humaniores* or "Greats." In the middle of the nineteenth century the Scottish universities adopted the English honors degree, and a century of specifically Scottish influence on American collegiate education was brought to a close.

Americans studying abroad, especially in Germany, began to bring back a conception of university education demarcated from collegiate education. Supporters of the first stressed the knowledge function of universities, supporters of the second the educational or ethological function, that is, the character-forming purposes of colleges where knowing was subordinate to being or doing. Colleges, to adopt a familiar distinction, were for students, universities for knowledge. "Knowledge" did not necessarily mean what it does today, new knowledge or discovery. This is a radical conception, opening the door to relativism and to the idea of "outmoded" or superceded forms of knowledge, throwing into doubt and question past practices and beliefs. For many, "knowledge" simply meant the greater dissemination of existing knowledge or new knowledge that had been discovered outside the college or university.

However, the research mission also had its supporters. From the earliest days of the Scientific Revolution in Europe, and from the founding of the Republic in America, they had sought an appropriate institutional means of livelihood, sometimes locating in government-supported or chartered academies, botanical gardens, naval and military establishments, ordnance surveys, astronomical observatories, and chemical laboratories. The medical sciences tended to cluster within medical schools, which was only to be expected, except that medical schools were most often associated with hospitals, and hospitals were clinical rather than research in orientation. From the standpoint of the researcher, the difficulty with all these institutions was the absence of support for what today is thought of—if somewhat ambiguously—as pure or basic research. The solution to the problem lay in access to the considerable resources of universities, which possessed capital, endowments, established teaching positions, libraries, buildings, and relative isolation from government and in some cases from the market. The Dutch universities of the eighteenth century were hospitable to research. Gradually at first, and with more momentum later on, the research ideal entered universities in the nineteenth century, either capturing established ones or influencing the creation of new ones.[5]

The diversity of the American market, actual and potential, the "natural" curiosity that produces research, and the institutionalization of research in the form of academic departments carried universities and colleges toward specialization. Discoveries of the first rank could not be made without close attention to detail, facts, changes in methods, and the exploitation of new information and sources. Inevitably the curriculum was forced to adjust, and specialized programs of study began to replace more comprehensive ones, if not without struggle, disagreement, and compromise. New influences and interests could no longer be contained within a broad philosophical outlook such as Common Sense supplied, nor could they be linked directly to a particular religious heritage and outlook.

School and College

Differentiation within the collegiate and university structures was not possible without systematic differentiation throughout the body of existing networks of education. These were not and had never been regularly interconnected. Historically, there was not a neat progression from elementary or primary to secondary and then higher education. The phrase "higher education" was in fact late in arriving. A more common expression to distinguish the later from earlier stages was "superior education" (as in the famous Yale Report of 1828). Specialization had little opportunity to penetrate teaching institutions as long as undergraduates were virtually adolescents. In order to succeed, specialization required students who had received necessary preparation in the earlier stages of a particular subject of study. In the absence of extensive existing publicly or privately supported systems of secondary education, universities and colleges were sometimes compelled to establish lower or preparatory schools.

It is therefore worth remarking that one of the most truly significant changes in the history of higher education is the expansion of secondary levels of education and with it (and largely because of it), the rise in age of students at the time of matriculation. This enabled American colleges and universities to experiment with changes in the undergraduate curriculum, and the university ideal of specialized study began to replace the collegiate ideal of the unity of knowledge. But ironically this possibility was not as fully realized in the American context as elsewhere. Whereas in Europe, high school teachers in the advanced secondary sector valued their ties to universities and identified with the academic community above them, taking pride in their interinstitutional associations and common professional interests, in the United States the identity of high school teachers remained closer to that of teachers in the lower schools.[6]

The implications for general education at the collegiate level were therefore two-fold. Since the schools looked outward rather than upward, becoming entangled in the wider issues of American politics and society and finding themselves drawn into local and community affairs, universities and colleges could not always depend upon them as feeder institutions. Higher education, especially in the public or weakly endowed private sector, was therefore forced into the politics of remedial education. The establishment of community colleges in the twentieth century provided some relief, but the problem of the underprepared undergraduate remained as the higher education system expanded. At the same time, the failure of the schools to provide a reliable combination of skills, proficiencies, and general knowledge essential for advanced academic work kept alive a belief in the necessity for some version of breadth at the tertiary level, especially in the first two years where problems associated with weak preparation were most acute. This situation was further complicated by the history of the single course or credit-unit system which had ridden into the modern period on the coattails of the late nineteenth-century introduction of electives, itself a by-product of efforts to break down the supremacy of the old collegiate core curriculum. The independent course was an effective means of promoting innovation in the curriculum, but the autonomy of the single course made coordination of teaching awkward. It also brought with it the problem of maintaining uniform standards of teaching and learning, and quite possibly no other purely "academic" feature of American higher education has remained so conspicuous or disturbing.

Incomplete Combustion

The problem of the schools, caused by American patterns of social integration and its democratic ideology, meant that the shift from some kind of general education to some kind of specialized education could not follow the same pattern in the United States as in England or Scotland. The characteristic change was from the old prescribed collegiate curriculum of general education to a variety of hybrids combining some general education with some specialized education but without adopting the principles that lay behind, let us say, the British honors degree. A multiplicity of programs of general and specialized education existed in American universities and colleges in the last three decades of the nineteenth century. The principle of breadth was represented by a mixture of partial electives, compulsory first or second-year courses, quasi-specialized courses, or what were called "parallel courses." Majors and minors were created to represent the principle of specialism; and wherever the collegiate faculty or college presidents were reluctant to experiment with specialized studies, new degree programs or separate schools were established as options and alternatives. In both the distribution and the majors courses there was normally opportunity for choice or electives. Furthermore, the choices were sometimes such that relatively specialized courses could be chosen in satisfaction of distribution requirements and relatively broad courses selected in satisfaction of major requirements. The variations on the themes are quite bewildering and resist adequate summary.

Just before, and just after World War I, the American higher education curriculum settled into the elaborate pattern of compromises which in most institutions has prevailed to the present day. The long-term effect of this has been profound and accounts for what is today not exactly an exclusive but certainly a peculiar (comparatively speaking) American interest in general education at the postsecondary level. In Europe general education ended at the secondary level, even to some extent before the upper secondary level, and the student who went on to university was expected to have mastered the skills and general knowledge essential for acquiring education at an advanced level. One may well dispute how general the European secondary education truly is: given the present range of subjects that can be studied, comprehension is virtually impossible. But a very loose comparison still has validity in this respect, that in America an interest in general education remained at the university (hence it never semantically ceased to be a "college," a place where general education was appropriate). When the graduate school came into being at the end of the nineteenth century, it too began to be circumscribed in mission by the realities of the undergraduate curriculum. As the undergraduate program of studies was affected by developments at the secondary school, so were postgraduate studies affected by the undergraduate curriculum. Each sector above was required to "borrow" time from the sector below, and to this day graduate students in the humanities and social sciences cannot be assumed to have pursued a common program of preparatory studies and are often required to take compensatory courses or general examinations before proceeding on to research proper. In the sciences the difficulty has been addressed by turning the undergraduate curriculum into preparation for graduate school, using the first two years to compensate for the inadequacies at lower levels. But this has merely compounded the problem of general education.

The intensity of debate within American higher education today is a consequence of these historic developments. General education courses are most often a combination of subjects from the humanities and social sciences, usually work that has not been undertaken in the lower schools, while the engineers and scientists within the university adhere to more specialized majors and premajors and are accused of resisting the effort to provide comprehensive sources of general education. Current differences of opinion are also a result of the American conception of a university which made it at one and the same time the home of general, specialized, and professional education. The structural expression of this historical evolution is the division of the university not into "faculties" as in the European mode, but into colleges, each with a separate educational mission, the one most pertinent to this discussion being the college of letters and science, or arts and sciences, the home of general education.

General Education Movements

The general education movements of the twentieth century can be said to be a reaction to the reforms occurring at the end of the preceding century. Essentially, there have been two responses. The first has been a continuation of the late nineteenth-century effort to find a suitable mix of courses, programs, and choices that would provide at one and the same time breadth, specialization, and partial coherence, a balance of pressures and forces. The second represents a radical break in attitude and action. It has sought to establish general education within separate and distinct foundations, sometimes breakaway colleges or affiliated experimental colleges or special programs within existing universities in which older ideas about the importance of breadth and coherence might find new expression and forms, and where a separate "college" faculty could be recruited or distinguished to end the "standing antagonisms" found in the undergraduate/graduate/professional school mix.[7] In this category one finds the college at Columbia in the 1920s and the college at Chicago in the 1930s, but also many other types of institutions such as Shimer College, Rollins, Black Mountain College (a spinoff from Rollins), Hamilton, and the University of California at Santa Cruz. Not all such institutions are solely interested in the restoration of ideas about breadth and coherence. Some, such as Bennington, are more interested in coaxing out the creative imagination than in imparting breadth, although it can be and has been claimed that since creativity is "liberating," it satisfies the requirements of general education. Hamilton is an exponent of "active learning" where undergraduates pursue their natural bent and design their own program of studies, although within broad collegiate frameworks. A number of institutions wish to regain some of the ancient spirit of liberal rather than general education, and some are particularly interested in such untraditional educational notions as "creativity" and personal expression (untraditional because education for individuality is a very late historical intrusion into the undergraduate curriculum, the result of a change in culture generally and a shift toward the older and more self-reliant student).[8]

The second response has had limited success for a number of reasons: failure in the market, changing student interests, the death or departure of leading innovators, or the natural tendency of experiment to run its course, since experiment by definition is short-lived. The first kind of response has dominated American higher education. It is in many respects a remarkable educational adaptation to the variety and values of American life, expressing both strengths and weaknesses, but the absence of a unified approach and the hegemony of the single course continue to provoke criticism.

Little in Common

Theoretically, breadth is not difficult to achieve. The proliferation and subdivision of disciplines are inevitable consequences of the growth of knowledge and have always threatened to divide the curriculum in the absence of institutional or social restraints—the age of students, for example, as has been shown, or the limits imposed by scarce resources. (Specialism is always more expensive than general education, and it was expense that originally "protected" the old college core.) Coherence or integration, bringing the separate parts of learning into closer relationship with one another, has been more difficult, even where a unifying paradigm of knowledge has existed, for paradigms are often at variance with hypotheses and facts.[9] In some periods of history the integrating medium has been religion or philosophy or rhetoric, but none of these is a single discipline with a single method or objective. They have been useful as integrating strategies only insofar as contemporaries agreed on the kind of religion, the kind of philosophy, or the kind of rhetoric that bore the best chance of furthering the ends that drove the curricular means.

Modern culture exists on diversity, flexibility, and individual initiative. We should not therefore expect much agreement about an ideal type called an "educated person." This explains why means dominate ends in debate and so often take the form of a latter-day battle of the books, a dispute between the disciplines as to which is the most (or the least) "useful," or the purest, the highest, or the one best exemplifying "culture." Where all knowledge is equally important, where all have the same claim on resources and values, there can be no supremacy of one over the other. All that can be expected is an approximation of "balance" in parts of the curriculum. But this is not a general education: it is a standoff, an inability to persuade the communities of scholars and scientists, of politicians, publicists, and policy analysts, that one subject or one grouping of subjects should comprise a single core of learning for all undergraduates.

It must not be thought that there existed, until a century ago, a common language for discussing the aims and purposes of general education. This is a mistake often made. Plato did not agree with the sophists, the schools of logic at medieval Paris and Orleans disagreed vehemently. The humanists of the Renaissance fought, as did Christian humanists of the Reformation. Eighteenth-century Englishmen discussed how they would "order" the arts and came up with different rankings, and the battle of the books raged throughout the Enlightenment and right on through the nineteenth century, with traditionalists, reformers, innovators vying with one another for attention and support. The historian can only suggest that where agreement on the means and ends of general education existed, it was within a thin layer of institutions that drew from a fraction of the available youthful cohort.

That thin layer—the college—has been greatly enlarged in the twentieth century. It exists in many versions, and within it there is no longer a single language for discussing any part of the learning process. The curriculum is an impossible accumulation of courses, disciplines, specialties, facts, attitudes, styles, values, and opinions from the past, all of which are attacked or defended as they suit the interests, the ideals, and the prescriptions of many protagonists. Few speak to the same point in the same way or share assumptions. There are advocates of analysis in general education who say that the ability to think and reason are the main objectives. There are also advocates of synthesis, the capacity to join information and methods together.

But there are and have always been many kinds of analytical and synthetic methods, many kinds of logical, philosophical, mathematical, and historical models; and current debates, understandably if not excusably present-minded, do not pay sufficient attention to the educational variety and confusion of the historical record.

General education is achieved—this has been one line of reasoning—through a sampling of the basic modes or methods of modern thinking. The characteristic division is into humanities, social sciences, natural and physical sciences, but this is often only a taxonomic or administrative convenience. An overlap in methods and assumptions, even between professional schools and letters and science departments, is the greater reality. Since the methods and modes of modern categories of thought are perpetually changing, we return to the inevitable conundrum of determining which kind of social science or which version of humanistic learning is absolutely indispensable to the functional well-being of an educated person.

A general education should be based on what educated people throughout history have considered to be (in Matthew Arnold's influential Victorian phrase) the best that has been thought and known. But when asked *his* opinion (for the question of "best" is ancient), Jonathan Swift, that bitter Tory humanist of the reigns of Queen Anne and George I, replied with the most uncompromising attack on modern science and technology that has ever been mounted. Surely no proponent of general education, which must have something to do with the way in which life is lived in the everyday world, is likely to exclude from general education all reference to such transforming forces.

To say that the language arts form the basis of general education since communication lies at the heart of all human relationships (a view that reflects the supremacy that rhetoric once held in the curriculum) is to invite the challenge of the historians and their allies in literature, art history, and philosophy or the social sciences, who retort that an overview of western civilization or contemporary civilization or world civilization is the only effective means for inculcating breadth and coherence. But this, according to a recent and persuasive position, lacks rigor and precision and in its very breadth may offer a weaker form of coherence. The case study as developed in the professional schools of law and business is suggested as more appropriate to the times, since all disciplines are employed in the service of a concrete problem. The general intelligence is a problem-solving intelligence, according to this view, especially under present social and political conditions; but how, comes the reply, does one acquire the requisite disciplines in the first place?

Behind every educational proposal there lies a theory of human nature or a philosophy of learning, a view as to how the mind receives, arranges, and makes use of information; but there is no shared position on either human nature or cognition today. There is no contemporary substitute for the pervasive and influential theory of mental powers or faculty pyschology whose history goes back to antiquity but whose heyday was the nineteenth century. The association between a given subject and a corresponding mental faculty to which it bore a functional relationship justified every old and new subject in the curriculum. No matter how badly or superficially taught, a subject increased the intellectual capacity of the mind. The imagination could be impregnated, the intelligence sharpened, the understanding enlarged, desire excited, the will strengthened, the judgment improved, and so on, depending upon the number of mental operations existing in the brain. In the long run, the phrenological theory of the cortical localization of functions actually undermined the purposes of general education. Being a friend to all books, it was helpless to intervene in the general melee. But for a time it at least supplied ends for the means carried by the curriculum.

General and Liberal Education Compared

Discussions about general education almost instantly elide into discussions about liberal education. The two are often confused for a simple reason. General education, as a reaction to the powerful and successful movement of the nineteenth century to replace the college with the university curriculum, needs the rhetorical support of liberal education. As a modern development, general education does not conjure up venerable traditions of learning or immediately bring to mind the names of paragons and exemplars. It does not fill the imagination with notions of a better or higher life nor bring to mind irresistible theories about human potential. It does not, as does liberal education, address the problem of the human condition. By contrast, liberal education possesses historic associations, meanings, and resonances. It advocates (or appears to advocate) the liberation of the imagination and intelligence and freedom from the servility caused by doctrine, superstition, and narrow authority. It is the grand manner brought into everyday life. General education, therefore, needs liberal education to legitimate itself, to acquire an ancient and honorable pedigree; and so, like a desolate hermit crab, it scuttles along a historical beach in search of a comfortable home.

General education is not synonymous with liberal education. It belongs to our own century, whereas liberal education has a remarkable ancestry, at least as an idea and aspiration. Its history runs parallel to much of that of the history of western civilization, and it exhibits within itself many of the same contradictions and paradoxes, the continuities and discontinuities, that characterize western thought generally. As we would or should expect, there are many variations on the theme of liberal education, but as a historical ideal-type there is a constant. It descends from the sophists of fifth-century Greece to the early modern period, from thence to Georgian England and from there to colonial and republican America, more or less departing at the conclusion of the last century but reappearing from time to time in the twentieth, as in the Progressive Era.[10] That constant is a concern for the whole person, or as we might say, the integrated personality at home in the world and with himself. To be at home in the world and with oneself presupposes a high degree of self-confidence, an absence of crippling self-consciousness, and a disposition to take broad and tolerant views. Such a person—let us use the traditional designation, such a "character"—has been educated for leadership. He (and also she) must be sufficiently levelheaded and flexible to cope with the contradictions and uncertainties of public affairs, to remain self-composed in the face of the unpredictable, and to be—education prepares the leader for this—a good judge of the character of others. How broadly educated must one be in order to be "whole?" How many great books does it take? How much coherence in the curriculum? The answer has always been elusive; but when the ideal of the rounded person is put into the context of different historical periods, one begins to see that breadth and coherence refer to more than intellectual proficiency. Body and feelings are also relevant. Hiding under the draperies of the ideal is even the suggestion that too great an emphasis on method, critical analysis, the sharpening of the mental faculties, unless accompanied by equal attention to the nonintellectual parts of the personality, is likely to produce an unbalanced and confused and hence illiberally educated person.

It is from liberal education that general education takes breadth and coherence as its objects, but liberal education emphasized ends not means. One started with a particular kind of character and worked back to the curriculum, which could be a core or a series of cores. Even the "anarchy" of the present melange of university offerings would not necessarily be inappropriate if something else was also provided, something that fulfilled the requirement of education for the whole or total person.[11]

Ends have in fact been joined to means in general education. These most often take the form of "correctives." Their aim has been to mitigate the effects of some perceived national flaw or personal failing, to avert a catastrophe or to promote a cause. "Correctives" are correlated with periods or problems. A time of heavy immigration produces an emphasis on language skills, communication, and toleration. After a national crisis, such as war, or a period of intense national disagreement, there is a concern with citizenship and public responsibility. Where there is strong international economic rivalry, as at present, an emphasis is placed on encouraging competitiveness, discipline, and technological literacy. Periods of hedonism or narcissism produce calls for greater adherence to religious morality; of relativism, a return to former (imagined?) standards of moral conduct; of individualism or indifference, a concern for self-sacrifice. In periods of fierce competition between individuals, a cry is raised for community, and where faddism and present-mindedness reign, we hear talk of recovering legacies and regaining a sense of continuity.

Thus at one time or another in the twentieth century general education has been offered as an antidote to demagoguery, a way of preventing the spread of communism, a prophylactic against modern relativism, pluralism, amoralism, secularism, bohemianism, and the avant-garde, a means for correcting the inevitable concern for relevance in the curriculum and for counteracting the pervasive and pernicious influence of technology and applied science. One may also find arguments of an entirely different nature linking general education to cost-effectiveness in mass higher education.[12]

Something approaching the characterological ends of liberal education can also be found in the historical literature about general education. These can be summarized as arguments either on behalf of creative individualism and the autonomy of the individual or on behalf of the individual in a "public" role, that is, as the citizen who puts the good of the community above the pleasures of private life. Historically, the latter argument takes us closer to what "character formation" may have produced in practice; but the former, which is related to the revolution in human relationships that occurred two centuries ago, is not likely to yield pride of place.[13]

Ends as correctives are by their very nature short-lived. Society is in continual flux, to quote Heraclitus among others, and no system of general education can be changed as frequently as social and political conditions may require. Furthermore, ends defined as correctives will no more produce a common core of studies than has the battle of the books. In a world filled with controversy and anxiety, there will be as many correctives as there are diagnoses.

Historically, liberal education has not been viewed as a corrective to the problems of society so much as a means of establishing a healthy relationship between the individual and society. To live in the world would have been an eighteenth-century formulation of the general aim, and the question of an appropriate education was therefore phrased in terms of preparation for life. The student of the history of liberal and general education will consequently look beyond the customary debates concerning curriculum, required cores and optional cores, interdisciplinary studies, and alternative colleges and programs to those other institutional mechanisms which, either directly or indirectly, facilitate the integration of the individual with society. Integration is dependent upon the nature of a society; but instead of regarding this as a crude and obvious means of socialization, it is more generous and accurate to see it as the process of forming characters who are at home in the world, insofar as its operations, its value systems, its institutions and culture are not mysterious to them but open to understanding and inquiry. Where there is understanding and inquiry, there can be intelligent choice and freedom of action.

If this is a correct reading of the historical ideals and realities connected to the idea of a liberal education, it thereby follows that amongst the more relevant current discussions about higher education are those which view the campus as a total learning environment. This position is diametrically opposed to the notion of the campus as an ivory tower, isolated from society. The campus may not be a microcosm of the larger world, although in some institutions it is very nearly that, but it is certainly a lively universe of manifold activity. In the past, face-to-face relationships, residential colleges and "houses," compulsory chapel, sports and athletics, student journalism, and clubs in which faculty also participated were the extracurricular or "co-curricular" means by which young persons were to be brought into the world of adult responsibility, cooperation, and self-respect. "Active learning" can be labelled "liberal" in this respect, insofar as initiative and interest are functional to the larger goal of living in the world; but such a conception is distant from the general education format of breadth and coherence through the medium of common cores or a common core.

How the "co-curriculum" functions and how it may be directly joined to the task of general education is now a concern of some faculty, some campus administrations, and many nonacademic professionals and quasi-professionals whose object is the well-being and human development of a class of young people who are, *inter alia*, experiencing the sharp effects of an ethic of competitive individualism and could not possibly see life clearly and see it whole.[14]

A Cautionary Tale

Liberal education historically was expensive education for the privileged. A mass higher education system cannot hope to provide the teaching resources that made possible the more intimate face-to-face tutorial relationships of the older collegiate environment. Nor must we romanticize the success of that environment. Specialism arose because it was necessary to the functioning of modern society, and it was embraced most eagerly by new generations of academics because it provided relief from the tedium of the schoolboy curriculum of time immemorial, which drained curiosity and enterprise from even the most dedicated teacher. Alfred North Whitehead has gone further to maintain that people are naturally specialist, naturally inclined to have a specific interest in life, and it is upon this basis that knowledge grows and develops.[15] The historical record may well bear this out.

It is not specialism *per se*, the division of intellectual labor in the academy, for this has long existed, but the ideal of new knowledge and the possibility of devoting a lifetime of study to discovery that gradually transformed the university. Specialism in relation to original inquiry is a permanent feature of the culture of advanced societies and necessary to their survival. How and in what way it is compatible with general education, both in theory and in practice, and how it may be connected to the larger, more interesting and more ironical complexities associated with the ideal of liberal or general education, are indeed major questions that deserve reflection but excite partisanship.

Passion runs high in debates about undergraduate education because modern society depends upon postsecondary education to maintain itself to a greater degree than in past societies where "knowledge industries" were less critical and pervasive and where a multitude of socializing institutions existed. Current debates will always profit from perspective and proportion, and that is where historical study enters. History is not a story of the possible but a story of the possible under changing circumstances and constraints. General and liberal education have always been subject to the mediating effects of institutions and culture. Hence in practice they are imperfect, the godhead brought to earth. That is not the last word, but it does invite a question. Should one despair because the genteel tradition is at bay? A hasty answer is unwise, but a very good one, at least a very sobering one, exists in Cardinal Newman's pungent comparison of St. Basil and the Emperor Julian. Both studied in the same core curriculum. Both had a general education. Both were liberally educated according to the canons of the day. Both "were fellow-students at the schools of Athens; and one became the Saint and Doctor of the Church, the other her scoffing and relentless foe."[16]

FOOTNOTES

1. Excellent accounts of the history of the curriculum in America appear in George P. Schmidt, *The Liberal Arts College* (New Brunswick, NJ: Rutgers University Press, 1957); Hugh Hawkins, *Between Harvard and America* (New York: Oxford University Press, 1972); George E. Peterson, *The New England College in the Age of the University* (Amherst, MA: Amherst College Press, 1964); and Christopher Jencks and David Riesman, *The Academic Revolution* (New York: Doubleday, 1968).

2. For Scotland, see Richard B. Sher, *Church and University in the Scottish Enlightenment* (Princeton, NJ: Princeton University Press, 1985); Stefan Collini, Donald Winch, and John Burrow, *That Noble Science of Politics* (Cambridge: Cambridge University Press, 1983); and Robert D. Anderson, *Education and Opportunity in Victorian Scotland* (Oxford: Oxford University Press, 1983).

3. Walter J. Ong, "Latin Language Study as a Renaissance Puberty Rite," in Walter J. Ong, *Rhetoric, Romance, and Technology: Studies in the Interaction of Expression and Culture* (Ithaca, NY: Cornell University Press, 1971).

4. For which see Philippe Aries, *Centuries of Childhood* (London: Jonathan Cape, 1962).

5. See Sheldon Rothblatt, "The Notion of an Open Scientific Community in Historical Perspective," in *Science as a Commodity*, ed. Michael Gibbons and Bjorn Wittrock (London: Longman, 1985); John Heilbron, *Elements of Early Modern Physics* (Berkeley and Los Angeles: University of California Press, 1982), chapter 2.

6. See Burton R. Clark, *The School and the University: An International Perspective* (Berkeley and Los Angeles: University of California Press, 1985), especially chapter 11.

7. Sheldon Rothblatt, "Standing Antagonisms: The Relationship of Undergraduate to Graduate Education," in *The Future of State Universities*, ed. Leslie W. Koepplin and David A. Wilson (New Brunswick, NJ: Rutgers University Press, 1985).

8. For experimental colleges, see Gerald Grant and David Riesman, *The Perpetual Dream* (Chicago: University of Chicago Press, 1978), and histories like Martin Duberman, *Black Mountain: An Exploration in Community* (New York: Anchor Press, 1973).

9. Thomas S. Kuhn, *The Structure of Scientific Revolutions*, 2d ed., enl. (Chicago: University of Chicago Press, 1970).

10. See the fascinating remarks of Peterson, *The New England College in the Age of the University*, pp. 201-4.

11. For character formation in liberal education, see Bruce A. Kimball, *Orators and Philosophers: A History of the Idea of Liberal Education* (New York: Teachers College Press,1986), and Sheldon Rothblatt, *Tradition and Change in English Liberal Education: An Essay in History and Culture* (London: Faber and Faber, 1976). For the intellectual dimensions, see Daniel Bell, *The Reforming of General Education* (New York: Columbia University Press, 1966).

12. Ernest L. Boyer and Arthur Levine, *A Quest for Common Learning: The Aims of General Education* (Washington, DC: Carnegie Foundation for the Advancement of Teaching, 1981), particularly Appendix A.

13. For citizenship, see Frank Newman, *Higher Education and the American Resurgence* (Princeton: Carnegie Foundation for the Advancement of Teaching, 1985), chapters 3 and 6. For the co-curriculum, see Ernest L. Boyer, *College: The Undergraduate Experience in America* (New York: Harper and Row, 1987). It should be noted that campuses have become wary of too much involvement in the off-campus or noncurricular lives of undergraduates in an effort to avoid possible liability suits.

14. Arthur Chickering, "The Modern American College: Integrating Liberal Education, Work, and Human Development," in *Preparation for Life? The Paradox of Education in the Late Twentieth Century*, ed. Joan N. Burstyn (Philadelphia: Falmer Press, 1986) relates the wide view of the liberal education ideal to a contemporary setting.

15. Alfred North Whitehead, *The Organization of Thought, Educational and Scientific* (Westport, CT: Greenwood Press, 1974), p. 20.

16. John Henry Newman, *The Idea of a University*, ed. I. T. Kerr (Oxford: Oxford University Press, 1976), p. 181.

CHAPTER III

The Liberal Arts Curriculum and Its Enemies: The Effort to Redefine General Education

HERBERT M. KLIEBARD

Accounts of the rise of the liberal arts as an educational ideal usually begin, quite appropriately, either with the glories of ancient Greece or the revival of learning in Europe which we have come to call the Renaissance. While these time-honored beginnings of a kind of education that is supposed to exalt the human spirit and express many of the central values of western civilization have much to tell us about how that venerable ideal of education came to prominence, they are less illuminating on the question of how it fell into a kind of undeclared disfavor. (Hardly anyone is willing to admit being against a liberal education.) We know little about what the challenges to the liberal arts curriculum were or what accounts for its decline in twentieth-century American schooling. In the case of ancient Athens, the most potent challenger was reputed to be barbarism (which everybody is against) or perhaps Spartan education, and, in the Renaissance, it was probably scholasticism or even that great antagonist to sustained intellectual pursuit, Eros.[1]

The roots of the decline of the liberal arts curriculum are probably more proximate than either ancient Greece or the Renaissance. They are most likely to be found in the great controversies over educational policy that erupted in Victorian England. There is no question that education was then getting public attention. Controversy over educational policy tends to erupt as the perception of significant social change becomes acute, and it was apparent that the changes wrought by the Industrial Revolution in England were profound indeed. Not only were the lives of the working classes massively transformed, but the newly powerful middle class was beginning to flex its muscles.

By common agreement, education in England from at least the middle to late nineteenth century was a mess. The great figures of Victorian intellectual society—Thomas Carlyle, John Ruskin, John Henry Newman, John Stuart Mill, and Matthew Arnold—were aware of its shortcomings and frequently expressed their criticisms in their writings. One of the most potent of the critics of formal education in his time was Charles Dickens. Among other unflattering portraits of schooling in Victorian England, Mr. Gradgrind's address at the opening of his school in *Hard Times* conveyed Dickens's bitter impressions of the prevailing pedagogy of the day:

> Now, what I want is facts. Teach these boys and girls nothing but the facts. Facts alone are wanted in life. Plant nothing else, and root out everything else. You can only form the minds of reasoning animals upon facts; nothing else will ever be of any service to them. This is the principle on which I bring up my own children, and this is the principle on which I bring up these children. Stick to the facts, sir!

When "girl number twenty" (Sissy Jupe), a girl who has grown up with horses, is declared by Mr. Gradgrind to be unable to define a horse, he proceeds in his recitation until he finds one that satisfies him:

> Quadruped. Graminivorous. Forty teeth, namely, twenty-four grinders, four eyeteeth, and twelve incisors. Sheds coat in spring; in marshy countries sheds hoofs too. Hoofs hard, but requiring to be shod with iron. Age known by marks in mouth.

To that response, Mr. Gradgrind remarks triumphantly, "Now, girl number twenty . . . you know what a horse is." With accounts of education like this reaching hundreds of thousands of Dickens's readers, the controversy over the direction that education should follow was reaching beyond an inner circle of intellectuals. To be sure, what Dickens described in *Hard Times* and several other of his novels was anything but what a liberal education was supposed to be, but his criticisms, like those of his contemporaries, opened the way for a serious reexamination of the standard fare of the curriculum of his time.

What Knowledge Is of Most Worth?

Hovering over the brewing controversy as to the course that the curriculum of the Victorian school should take was the pervasive influence of Charles Darwin. While the theory of evolution was popularly conceived primarily as a challenge to the reigning theology of the day, its most lasting impact was in terms of what it said about science itself and what effect the new conceptions of science, as well as science's enormously increased status, would have on what knowledge people thought to be valuable. To a considerable extent, this reexamination had economic roots and is connected to the prominence of commerce and trade in industrial England. Increasingly, for example, critics of English society were observing that England no longer produced enough food for its citizens, and, to maintain its position of power and influence in the world, she needed to achieve preeminence in technology and manufacture. Classical studies, linguistic elegance, and masterpieces of literature as the centerpieces of the liberal arts curriculum were being challenged, and they were being challenged on a number of fronts. Illustrative of the kinds of challenges that were being directed at the traditional liberal arts were the positions of two of the most eminent Victorians who were also influential educational reformers: Herbert Spencer, whose "synthetic philosophy" was perceived to be at least consistent with Darwinism, and "Darwin's bulldog," Thomas Henry Huxley. The impact of their efforts to change the traditional curriculum of the time was ultimately to be felt in the schools of twentieth-century America.

Spencer, of course, is best known in the educational world for his essay, "What Knowledge Is of Most Worth?" (1859), that title having since been appropriated and paraphrased many times, practically taking on the status of being the most central of all the questions that can be raised about the curriculum. His answer to it, like that of many of his forebears as well as his contemporaries, was influenced by his interpretation of the theory of evolution. Spencer's speculative anticipation of Darwinian theory led him to carry forward the principle of natural selection into such areas as the development of knowledge and social relationships. Evolutionary theory, in other words, became not just a way of explaining the development of species in a biological world, but was actually the basis for a cosmic understanding of society, psychology, ethics, and education. Spencer's earlier essay, "On the Genesis of Science" (1854), for example, posited a kind of sympathy between the development of mental concepts within the individual and the evolution of knowledge. His main point was that everyday knowledge could not be distinguished in any significant way from scientific knowledge. The latter was merely the evolutionary extension of the former. Part of the appeal of that doctrine was that it made the lines between aristocratic and ordinary knowledge less distinct. As the study of the world around us, the natural sciences were not as arcane or as exclusionary as ancient languages and classical literature. Nor were they as specialized. "The sciences are as branches of one trunk," he said, "and . . . were at first cultivated simultaneously" with differentiation only occurring later. In fact, science may be said to have a "common root" with language and art as well. Spencer predicted that "whenever established, a correct theory of the historical development of the sciences must have an immense effect upon education."[2]

In that same year (1854), Spencer's "Intellectual Education" turned his theory of the evolution of knowledge into a principle of curriculum: "The genesis of knowledge in the individual must follow the same course as the genesis of knowledge in the race."[3] In general terms, that principle was a rough extrapolation of the commonly held scientific truth of the time that "ontogeny recapitulates phylogeny." The mental development of the individual, in other words, recapitulated the development of human knowledge over the course of history. This is one of the senses in which Spencer can be seen as an advocate of "natural education." According to this view, the course that the curriculum should take is one that follows scientific principles, which, when discovered and followed, lead inevitably to a desirable curriculum. This was an argument not simply in favor of a place for science in the curriculum but for a *scientific curriculum*. Education would proceed along evolutionary lines in the same way that the various plant and animal species, including the human species, proceeded.

Several versions of a scientifically determined curriculum rife in the latter part of the nineteenth century incorporated the idea of a recapitulation of human history within the child, thus setting out not only the sequence but actually the content of the course of study. Like Spencer's version, many of these were, potentially at least, antagonistic to the ideal of the liberal arts. Although the particular subjects that have been proposed as comprising the liberal arts have varied according to time and place, at a fundamental level the liberal arts ideal has always involved the conscious effort to select those elements of the culture that serve to make one fully human. Traditionally, the elements involved are presumed to make one sensitive to beauty, intellectually alive, and humane in outlook. For this liberal arts ideal, the idea of a natural education substituted the notion that education was deterministic in the sense that the search for the good curriculum did not involve casting about for the cultural elements of highest value. Rather, it consisted of *discovering* the laws that the human being followed over the course of development in the same way that Darwin discovered the laws that governed the descent of the human species. Once those natural laws of development were discovered, they could be used to determine the curriculum.

Spencer's "What Knowledge Is of Most Worth?," which first was published as a separate essay in 1859 and then appeared as the initial chapter of his *Education: Intellectual, Moral, and Physical*, offered an even more formidable challenge to the traditional conception of a liberal arts education. In his opening paragraph, Spencer noted with a suggestion of amusement if not condescension that "an Orinoco Indian, though quite regardless of bodily comfort, will yet labor for a fortnight to purchase pigment wherewith to make himself admired" and that an Indian woman would leave her hut unclothed but never unpainted. His point was to illustrate the curious phenomenon that "the idea of ornament predominates over that of use," and he then went on to argue that this principle seemed to hold true "among mental as among bodily acquisitions."[4] In English schools, for example, Latin and Greek, which had no functional value, were the equivalent of the Orinoco Indian's ornamental paint. And ornamental education predominated equally in the education of women: "Dancing, deportment, the piano, singing, drawing—what a large space do these occupy!"[5] "Before there can be a rational *curriculum*," he concluded, "we must settle which things it most concerns us to know," and, "to this end, a measure of the value is the first requisite."[6]

The requisite step in this process, according to Spencer, was to classify in their order of importance the activities that comprise human life. He listed them as follows:

1. Those activities which directly minister to self-preservation;
2. Those activities which, by securing the necessaries of life, indirectly minister to self-preservation;
3. Those activities which have for their end the rearing and discipline of offspring;
4. Those activities which are involved in the maintenance of proper social and political relations;
5. Those miscellaneous activities which make up the leisure part of life, devoted to the gratification of tastes and feelings.[7]

The substitution of these functional criteria for the development of curricula for those that emphasized criteria drawn from some conception of what comprised the great cultural resources of Western culture constituted nothing short of a major revolution in thinking as to how a curriculum should be determined. For one thing, Spencer set up an aim of education (self-preservation) to which education itself would be subordinate. Education, in other words, became an instrument to achieve something that lay beyond it. Specifically, there were categories of activities for which a good education prepared one to perform successfully. Music, poetry, and painting were no longer to be studied as the finest expressions of human aspirations and emotions but in order to "fill up the leisure left by graver occupations."[8] Leisure as an activity, ranking number five and last on Spencer's list of activities, was needed, and the study of certain subjects could help one perform that function successfully. But the task of developing a curriculum was seen in terms of "life as divided into several kinds of activity of successively decreasing importance; the worth of each order of facts as regulating these several kinds of activity, intrinsically, quasi-intrinsically, and conventionally; and their regulative influences estimated as knowledge and discipline."[9]

For Spencer, the subject most suited to the proper preparation for "complete living" was science. Although nature itself provided much of what is needed for self-preservation, deliberate education in the interest of self-preservation was also necessary. Nature could help us ward off such dangers as "want of food, great heat, [and] extreme cold" instinctively,[10] but the absence of "an acquaintance with the fundamental principles of physiology as a means to complete living"[11] led to all sorts of infirmities and chronic disabilities. "Hence, knowledge which subserves direct self-preservation by preventing this loss of health, is of primary importance."[12] Mathematics played a vital role in everything from ordinary carpentry to making a railway. Physics had given us the steam engine and has shown us how to make our smelting furnaces more efficient. Chemistry was vital to the work of the bleachers and dyers. Biology was intricately connected with the production of food. And the "Science of Society"[13] helped us to understand money-markets, to consider intelligently the chances of war, and improve mercantile operations. Science, in short, was the subject *par excellence* for maintaining the vital function of self-preservation in the modern world. According to Spencer, other subjects needed to be examined in similar fashion, in terms of their role in fulfilling the other vital purposes. Thus the absence of attention in the curriculum to the proper raising of children needed to be corrected. Spencer imagined, for example, that a future antiquary surveying the curriculum of the mid-nineteenth century would have concluded that "This must have been the *curriculum* for their celibates."[14] The functions of the citizen must be addressed not by biographies of kings and queens but must be based on what is necessary for the general welfare. As to poetry, that staple of the liberal arts curriculum, Spencer would grant that taste could conceivably be improved through its study, but "it is not to be inferred that such improvement of taste is equivalent in value to an acquaintance with the laws of health."[15] Those subjects that Spencer called "the efflorescence of civilization" (the arts and *belles lettres*, for example) should be subordinated to the knowledge really vital to our civilization. Even the appreciation of the arts required such scientific understanding as the theory of equilibrium and how the effects of nature are produced. Referring to the fate of what we usually call the humanities, he recommended, "*As they occupy the leisure part of life, so should they occupy the leisure part of education.*"[16] Science, in its various forms, was that subject that was associated with the real work of the world, whereas the humanities were associated with mere leisure.

Spencer concluded his revolutionary essay in dramatic and unequivocal terms:

What knowledge is of most worth?—the uniform reply is—Science. This is the verdict on all the counts. For direct self-preservation, or the maintenance of life and health, the all-important knowledge is—Science. For that indirect self-preservation which we call gaining a livelihood, the knowledge of greatest value is—Science. For the due discharge of parental functions, the proper guidance is to be found only in—Science. For that interpretation of national life, past and present, without which the citizen cannot rightly regulate his conduct, the indispensable key is—Science. Alike for the most perfect production and highest enjoyment of art in all its forms, the needful preparation is still—Science. And for the purposes of discipline—intellectual, moral, religious—the most efficient study is, once more—Science.[17]

Spencer's "What Knowledge Is of Most Worth?" turned the traditional conception of the liberal arts curriculum on its head. In the first place, the humanities, to which the liberal arts curriculum had accorded the central place, were relegated in no uncertain terms to a distinctly inferior position. Secondly, both the sequence and the content of the curriculum could be determined scientifically rather than merely representing a judgment as to the most valuable resources of the culture. A "natural education" was one that followed the laws that governed the process. And finally, the purposes of the curriculum could no longer be described in such terms as "liberating the human spirit" or "initiation into the life of the mind," but were to be seen in terms of the curriculum's contribution to the performance of specific and vital activities. In fact, the preservation of life itself became the supreme function of education. In Spencerian terms, education could no longer be seen as an adornment, like the pigment on the Orinoco Indian, but as an instrument necessary for the performance of life-preserving functions like the clothes that shield us from the vicissitudes of weather. The apparent good sense of such a position had an enormous appeal to the rising mercantile and manufacturing class.

The Prophet of Science

Spencer's contemporary, Thomas Henry Huxley, was a considerably more formidable public speaker and a more effective advocate of science than Spencer—and an even greater celebrity in the upper echelons of the Victorian scientific community—but, as an educational reformer, he was far less revolutionary. In a significant sense, however, his interest in educational reform was more abiding and more profound than Spencer's. He was, after all, a working educator for a good part of his life and took a particular interest in the education of the working classes. He had served as a professor of natural history at the Royal School of Mines, an examiner for the Government's Department of Science and Art, a member of the School Board for London and chairman of its influential Scheme of Education Committee, and was the author of several widely praised textbooks in science.

Huxley's best-known expression of his educational ideals is contained in the inaugural address he delivered when he became principal of the South London Workingman's College, an address he called, "A Liberal Education; and Where to Find It." As is implied in the title, Huxley took this occasion to redefine what was meant by a liberal education. Huxley reviewed briefly several of the extant justifications for providing a liberal education. For the politicians, educating the masses was essential because they would one day become masters; the clergy's hopes were built on the idea that education would halt the drift toward infidelity; the "manufacturers and the capitalists" claimed that "ignorance makes bad workmen" and that the market for English goods would suffer as a result. Huxley rejected these positions in favor of the view that "the masses should be educated because they are men and women with unlimited capacities of being, doing, and suffering, and that it is as true now, as ever it was, that the people perish for lack of knowledge."[18] Huxley's emphasis on the intrinsic need to know as the justification for education as opposed to purposes that lie beyond education made his position consistent with the *ideal* of a liberal arts education, although his notion of what the components of that education would be departed significantly from the traditional conceptions.

Huxley scorned the argument that education should be instrumental to some larger good. If the masses in power without an education would be so disastrous, why is it, he asked, that "such ignorance in the governing classes in the past has not been viewed with equal horror?"[19] As to the manufacturers' and the capitalists' position, he asked whether we really want the English educational system "diverted into a process of manufacturing human tools?"[20] Furthermore, Huxley went on, it was not simply the education of the masses that was a matter of concern. To him, it appeared that even the most exclusive of the English schools ought to be made to "supply knowledge" rather than simply performing their traditional function of inculcating "gentlemanly habits, a strong class feeling, and eminent proficiency in cricket."[21] The knowledge that Huxley sought to represent in a modern curriculum, included, to be sure, a strong dose of science, but one that was balanced by other factors:

Education is the instruction of the intellect in the laws of Nature, under which I include not merely things and their forces, but men and their ways; and the fashioning of affections and of the will into an earnest and loving desire to move in harmony with those laws. For me, education means neither more nor less than this.[22]

In Huxley's view, the main thrust of a liberal education could be found in the development of the intellect and not in something that lay beyond it, such as the production of high-quality workers, a course that the rising middle class of the time was advocating. The function of education was something much broader than "a process of manufacturing human tools, wonderfully adroit in the exercise of some technical industry, but good for nothing else."[23]

There is no question that Huxley was a passionate and, as it turned out, effective advocate for the introduction of a much stronger measure of science into the curriculum of his day. There were even times when his passion on the subject led to exaggerated claims for science and something close to a denigration of the traditional humanist curriculum. (Huxley's tendency toward hyperbole and embroidered rhetoric has even been the subject of some study.[24])

Unlike Spencer, however, he was not claiming that one study was actually more valuable than another. His position was that, given the prominence and significance of science in Western civilization, science was getting short shrift in the education of English youth. He was arguing for a redress of an imbalance found in the traditional liberal arts curriculum, not for a new set of criteria by which the worth of subjects would be determined. Opposition to the introduction of the sciences into the standard curriculum of Victorian England, in Huxley's view, came not only from business interests but also from the "Levites in charge of the ark of culture and monopolists of liberal education" who essentially ignored the significance of science in the modern world and its potential role in the liberal education of youth.[25] But despite his eagerness to give a major role to natural sciences in the curriculum, Huxley was not ready to assert unequivocally their superiority to the traditional humanities, or any of the other subjects.

Some indication of Huxley's basic moderation on the issue of redefining the general education of his time may be illustrated through his skirmish with his friend, Matthew Arnold, on educational policy. Arnold, of course, was one of the great defenders of high culture in Victorian society and, as one of Her Majesty's Inspectors of Schools, he was powerfully situated to influence the curriculum. His leadership in the defense of the traditional liberal arts against the onslaught of crass materialism in education was widely recognized. In his *Culture and Anarchy*, Arnold had sought to answer the question of what use is culture by arguing that real culture in its highest form not only "reminds us that the perfection of human nature is sweetness and light," but serves to infuse in us "the passion to make them prevail."[26] Rejecting the idea that culture must be adapted to the condition of the masses in order for them to appreciate it, Arnold argued passionately for what he called the "*social idea*" of culture. Culture, he said,

does not try to teach down to inferior classes; it does not try to win them for this or that sect of its own, with ready-made judgments and watchwords. It seeks to do away with classes; to make the best that has been thought and known in the world current everywhere; to make all men live in an atmosphere of sweetness and light, where they may use ideas, as it uses them itself, freely—nourished and not bound by them."[27]

It was in this sense that the upholders of true culture were "the true apostles of equality."[28]

In his response to Arnold, Huxley did not take issue with Arnold's well-known definition of culture as "the best that has been thought and known in the world." Culture, Huxley agreed, was something quite different from simply learning or a technical skill. But he took issue with the implication that culture was to be equated with the works of classical antiquity and a smattering of the modern classics. "The humanists," he argued, "take their stand upon classical education as the sole avenue of culture" despite the fact that, even in the Renaissance, that period commonly referred to as the "Revival of Letters," there was also a revival of science and learning generally.[29] Insofar as the ancients were concerned, Huxley went on,

> we cannot know all the best thoughts and sayings of the Greeks unless we know what they thought about natural phenomena. We cannot fully apprehend their criticism of life unless we understand the extent to which that criticism was affected by scientific conceptions.[30]

Although he remained a passionate advocate of the sciences, and was even wont to exaggerate the merits of his case on occasion, Huxley's chief concern was that the monopoly on culture that had been traditionally exercised by the humanists had yielded a truncated version of "true culture" as the basis of a liberal education.

Arnold did find it ultimately necessary to reply to Huxley's attack on traditional humanism as the basis for the liberal arts curriculum, but his argument indicated a broader area of agreement with Huxley rather than disagreement on the nature of culture. He objected to the equation of humanism as a fundamental belief with superficial knowledge of *belles lettres*, but he went on to emphasize that "There is . . . really no question between Professor Huxley and me as to whether knowing the great results of modern scientific study of nature is not required as a part of our culture, as well as knowing the products of literature and art."[31] Rather, Arnold parted company with the reformers of the liberal arts when they proposed "to make the training in natural science the main part of education for the great majority of mankind . . . ."[32] The appeal to experience which the humane letters provided was for Arnold of a far more universal appeal than the desire to understand how the universe worked. Implicitly rejecting the approach that Spencer took in "What Knowledge Is of Most Worth?," he proposed instead: "Let us . . ., all of us, avoid indeed as much as possible any invidious comparison between the merits of humane letters, as a means of education, and the merits of the natural sciences."[33] Arnold's commitment to humanistic studies, however, eventually came through. He recalled from one of his own school reports that a young man in an English training college paraphrased the line in *Macbeth*, "Can'st thou not minister to a mind diseased?" as "Can you not wait upon the lunatic?" Arnold confessed in the end that he would rather have someone ignorant about the moon's diameter than someone who was unable to provide a better rendering of Shakespeare's line than that one.[34]

The Curriculum Debate in America

Both Spencer's radical challenge to the way the curriculum was traditionally structured and Huxley's advocacy of a balance in the liberal arts between science and humanities found their advocates in the American context. Both men, after all, had made triumphant tours of the United States. But the political and social climate of the times led Spencer's position to take root and flourish in late nineteenth-century America and to become a burgeoning movement in the twentieth century, strongly influencing the course that the American curriculum would take. Of special appeal to many Americans was Spencer's application of such biological principles as "survival of the fittest" to the conduct of social as well as economic affairs. With such ardent and influential disciples as John Fiske and Edward Livingston Youmans (the founder of *Popular Science Monthly*), Spencer soon became, in Richard Hofstadter's characterization, "the metaphysician of the homemade intellectual, and the prophet of the cracker-barrel agnostic."[35] The idea of a laissez-faire society that was somehow self-regulating made social legislation and economic regulation not only unnecessary but positively dangerous as an unwarranted intrusion on natural law and, therefore, an impediment to true progress. The law of the jungle became an accepted way of perceiving and justifying inequality in terms of wealth and differentiated social functions.

Through the work of such intellectual leaders as William Graham Sumner, one of the founders of American sociology and a professor of political and social science at Yale University, Spencer's social Darwinism achieved wide popularity. Like Spencer, Sumner saw not only the jungle but society generally as governed by the laws of survival. He argued, for example, that the struggle of various interest groups for their share of the fruits of industry should be left "to free contract under the play of natural laws" and that interference would result only in the diminution of the spoils that were left to be divided.[36] The choice, in Sumner's terms, was between "free social forces" on the one hand and "legislative and administrative interference" on the other.[37] Such societal functions as the concentration of wealth, should, according to Sumner, be seen as the product of evolutionary forces. "The concentration of wealth," he said, "is but one feature of a grand step in societal evolution."[38] In an early version of "trickle down" economics, Sumner argued that "No man can acquire a million without helping a million men to increase the little fortunes all the way down through all the social grades."[39] Millionaires were merely the "naturally selected agents of society for certain work" and should be seen as much the product of natural selection as Darwin's evolution of the species.[40]

With Spencer's ideas enjoying such significant acceptance in social and political worlds, it is not surprising that his conception of what knowledge is of most worth should have gained popularity with respect to the American curriculum. Basically, Spencer's conception of a worthwhile curriculum is reflected in three directions that the American curriculum began to take in the latter part of the nineteenth century. First, there was the elevation of the natural sciences to a more prominent role in programs of general education (although that tendency in itself could easily have reflected Huxley's more moderate as well as Spencer's more radical conception of how a curriculum should be constructed). Second, there was the notion that the curriculum was not merely to be a selection of the finest elements of the culture, as Arnold or even Huxley would have seen it, but as a reflection of natural laws governing both the course of human history and the development of the individual. And finally, there was the Spencerian conception of the curriculum as instrumental to some purpose beyond itself. In Spencer's case, that purpose was self-preservation first and foremost, and this made the development of those functions that would achieve that purpose, rather than those elements that would merely add to the stock of high culture, the most desirable as elements in a program of general education.

The new prominence that the natural sciences would enjoy was at least symbolically represented by the elevation of Charles William Eliot, a chemist and an admirer of Spencer's, to the presidency of Harvard in 1869. Although some contemporary interpretations of Eliot's work tend to depict him as a stodgy conservative who used the Committee of Ten report[41] to impose college domination on the high school curriculum, he was in his own time regarded as a radical innovator and representative of the "new education." Eliot was not simply interested in including a measure of science in the American curriculum. He argued for the doctrine of the equivalence of school subjects (a position that was incorporated into the Committee of Ten report). This meant that other subjects would have equal status with the time-honored triumvirate of the classical curriculum, Latin, Greek, and mathematics.

First of all, Eliot sought that status for English language and literature, which had had only a subordinate place in American schools and colleges in the late nineteenth century.[42] Second, he tried to achieve "academic equality" for French and German, arguing that there was no reason for modern languages to be slighted in favor of the classical ones.[43] Third, Eliot saw a larger place for the study of history and the social sciences in the form of political economy (or, as it was sometimes called, public economics).[44] And finally, Eliot sought the inclusion of the natural sciences in what he called "the magic circle of the liberal arts."[45] To some extent, as in the case of modern foreign languages, Eliot's arguments were somewhat utilitarian in character, but, for the most part, he framed his justification for the inclusion of new subjects into the liberal arts curriculum in terms of the doctrine of mental discipline, which had, by the nineteenth century, formed an association, albeit an unnecessary one, with the liberal arts. Eliot argued, for example, that the student of the natural sciences "exercises his powers of observation and judgment [and] acquires the precious habit of observing appearances, transformations and processes of nature."[46] Yet, despite his attachment to mental discipline, Eliot's overall position can be seen mainly as an effort to open up the concept of the liberal arts to a new array of significant elements of the culture, including science.

The success of the effort to redefine the liberal arts is difficult to gauge in terms of school practice. During the period between 1871 and 1875, the Bureau of Education collected figures only on the three types of general curricula then in vogue—English, classical, and modern languages. The English curriculum actually was the most popular with enrollments roughly double that of the other two, but curriculum data on individual subjects are incomplete since only Latin, Greek, French, German, and English were tabulated in the period between 1876 and 1885-86. It was not until 1887-88 that data became available for mathematics, physics, chemistry, and other sciences.[47] Although the data are incomplete, they indicate a rather spotty performance on the part of the natural sciences. In 1890, for example, enrollments in physics as a percentage of total enrollments in grades nine through twelve was reported as 22.8 with a drop to 19.0 in 1900 and a further decline in 1910 to 14.6. By 1949 (the height of the "life adjustment" era), the percentage of enrollments in physics had declined sharply to 5.4, and that figure included not only advanced physics, but applied physics, fundamentals of electricity, radio and electronics, and fundamentals of machines. Although the initially reported percentages in such subjects as chemistry, geology, astronomy, and earth science were not nearly as high to begin with, they experienced similar declines in percentages of high school enrollments. The first figure reported for physical geography in 1900 was a healthy 23.4 percent, but by 1934, this had dropped to a minuscule 1.6 percent.

The reconstruction of the liberal arts through the inclusion of the so-called "moderns" into the American school curriculum as advocated by reformers such as Eliot apparently met with marked success in one sense, but only restricted success in another. Indeed, the sciences, for example, began to enjoy roughly equal status with the classical subjects with about 54 percent of secondary school students enrolled in any science course by the 1948-49 academic year, although it is noteworthy that that figure is somewhat below the 59 percent registered by the combination of business courses in the same year. (Of some significance also is the fact that in 1949, 72 percent of the total science enrollments were in general science and biology.) Likewise, modern foreign languages not only began to attain academic respectability, but eventually surpassed the classical languages in terms of enrollments. That success is tempered, however, by the fact that only 22 percent of students were enrolled in any kind of foreign language study in 1949.[48] This means, of course, that while the traditional liberal arts curriculum had indeed undergone something of a transformation during the first part of the twentieth century, the "modernized" form of the liberal arts was reaching only a select segment of the school population. (If anything, this tendency toward curriculum differentiation, by design or default, has become accelerated in the 1980s with the "shopping mall" becoming the most pervasive model of high school studies.[49]) In effect, there is no program of general education in the United States (defined as liberal arts or anything else); there is only a potpourri of hundreds of subjects from which students make sometimes considered and sometimes haphazard choices as to what subjects they will "buy." The laissez-faire doctrine advocated by Spencer and later by Sumner in social and economic relationships has somehow taken a firm hold in the curriculum of American schools.

Spencer's other vision of a curriculum governed by scientific principles also met with mixed success. The early leader in the American drive to create a program of studies governed by natural law was G. Stanley Hall. Like Spencer, Hall sought to extend evolutionary theory to mental life, even aspiring to become the "Darwin of the mind." As the acknowledged leader of the child-study movement in the late nineteenth century and founder of such influential journals as the *American Journal of Psychology* and *Pedagogical Seminary*, Hall attracted thousands of followers to his idea of an educational system controlled by scientific principles. Insofar as the curriculum was concerned, Hall, like Spencer, subscribed to the position that in their development individuals recapitulated the historical stages through which the human race had passed, and this principle guided many of his pronouncements as to how the course of study should be reformed. "The principle that the child and the early history of the human race are each keys to unlock the nature of the other," Hall affirmed, "applies to almost everything in feeling, will, and intellect. To understand either the child or the race we must constantly refer to the other."[50]

Based on the conclusions of his studies of the child in relation to the race, Hall became suspicious of the effort to develop the intellect particularly in the early years of schooling. Health became for him the all-controlling factor in directing educational policy, and he feared that early intellectual training might be detrimental to the health of children and even adolescents. Since natural laws were to govern the education of children, Hall felt that the safest course was to "strive first of all to keep out of nature's way."[51] As such, education according to nature began to take on an almost antiintellectual character and the development of the intellect began to lose its traditionally central place in educational debates. Although the specific doctrine that the developmental stages through which the child passed somehow recapitulated historical epochs began to lose its credibility, the more general idea that a science of education could redirect the purposes of education continued to have wide appeal and thus served to undermine to some extent the central role that the traditional liberal arts assigned to freeing the intellect.

The Triumph of a Spencerian Alternative
to Liberal Studies

In addition to the predominant emphasis on science and the idea of a curriculum controlled by natural laws, the third implication of Spencer's educational reform was that the curriculum could be finely tuned to the *functions* that needed to be performed in order to survive in the modern world. This implication was revolutionary in its potential impact on the liberal arts ideal and it was substantially, although not altogether, realized as an alternative to the liberal arts as the foundation of general education. Like the other two reforms, this one was linked to science at least in the sense that it was alleged to be consistent with Darwinian theory as applied to society and, by extension, to education. Unlike the other two, however, its success was more visible and more enduring. Even though the victory of a curriculum reform that proposed to substitute the efficient performance of social functions for the ideal of a curriculum that embodied the main intellectual resources of our culture was anything but complete, that reform nevertheless stands today as a most potent enemy of the liberal arts.

Although the reconstruction of the modern American curriculum along directly functional lines was one of the principal motivations of educational reform in the twentieth century, its significance can probably best be illustrated through the work of one of its major exponents, David Snedden. Born in a tiny cabin and educated in a one-room schoolhouse in California in the late nineteenth century, Snedden eventually completed a classical course at St. Vincent's College in Los Angeles. As a young schoolteacher, he undertook to study the complete works of Spencer in his spare time; this experience led him to reject the standard curriculum of his time in favor of one that was directly tied to self-preservation.[52] To Snedden, this meant that a truly functional education could be derived scientifically from the analysis of human activity and translated into a socially efficient curriculum that, in effect, repudiated completely the ornamental trappings of the education that Spencer so much deplored. Later, as state commissioner of education in Massachusetts and a professor of educational sociology at Teachers College, Columbia University, he was in a position to reach a large and receptive audience for his ideas.

Although Snedden is sometimes particularly identified with vocational education, his influence was far more pervasive. In fact, he saw himself primarily as someone who was redefining general education in the twentieth century. Human functioning, according to Snedden, could be roughly classified into two major categories: production and consumption. Vocational education derived its legitimacy from its role in creating efficient producers, and liberal education would constitute that part of education that aimed at making human beings effective consumers or users. "The liberally educated man," he said, "utilizes the products and services of many producers; but because of his education he uses them well, both in the individual and social sense."[53] Together, vocational education for the producer and liberal education for the consumer would create the fully functioning human being. In this sense, liberal education would be as functional and as vital to human survival as vocational education.

Within a few years, Snedden's protege, Clarence Darwin Kingsley, translated that conception of general education into the famous seven aims of the Cardinal Principles report (1918).[54] Consciously or unconsciously, the seven "aims" of that report— health, command of fundamental processes, vocation, worthy use of leisure, worthy home membership, citizenship, and ethical character— followed in rough outline the conclusions of the effort of Spencer of more than a half century before to base the curriculum on categories of vital life activities (with the possible exception of the second of the aims). Kingsley stopped short, however, of actually recommending the abandonment of the traditional subjects of the curriculum; instead, the report recommended that those subjects be reorganized so that each might achieve at least one of those indispensable life functions. In other words, those subjects were no longer included in the curriculum because they represented the major intellectual resources of our culture; they now became *instruments* by which future adults would acquire the skills to function efficiently in their daily lives. So far had the idea of a directly functional education progressed by 1918, when the Cardinal Principles report was published, that its recommendations were considered by some educational reformers to be unduly moderate. By that time scientific curriculum makers such as Franklin Bobbitt and W. W. Charters, as well as Snedden, were calling for the substitution of functional categories for the subjects themselves. Snedden, in fact, declared Kingsley's report to be "almost hopelessly academic."[55]

In other words, the concept of general education was being fundamentally redefined by American educational leaders in the first quarter of the twentieth century. All education was to be specific and directed toward specific purposes. Even vocational education had very limited generality. Snedden declared in 1924, for example,

Two . . . delusions yet persist in much of our unanalyzed educational theory. One is that somehow there can be some general education that is valuable for any and all vocations. The other, a much more modern one, is that vocations or even a vocation can be so taught as to produce large amounts of culture or of civism.[56]

Even in the realm of vocational education, Snedden argued, we make the mistake of trying to prepare general farmers instead of poultry growers. He was critical, for example, of John Dewey's failure to articulate a program of vocational education suited to modern social needs. "The modern world," he said, "divides and again subdivides its vocations," and a modern educational system will reflect that great specificity. The same could be said of civic education, cultural education, moral education, and "educations in the uses of foreign languages." Each required its own specific form of preparation. "Only educational mystics or obscurantists or, shall we say, 'fools' can say otherwise," Snedden insisted.[57] Not only were there thousands of different kinds of education, "every distinguishable species of education and, of each species, each distinguishable degree is or should be designed 'to meet a need' " with each need to be met controlled by "foreseen ends."[58]

As if such specificity were not enough, Snedden argued further that each education had to be designed particularly to fit the characteristics of the person to be educated (what he liked to call the "educand"). A truly scientific education could not be designed until the curriculum was adapted to the traits of those who would be educated, particularly to the social functions that they would one day perform as adults. Since people performed different functions according to such attributes as gender, class, and occupation, the skills to perform those functions had to be anticipated and ultimately incorporated into a supremely differentiated curriculum. Under these conditions, the idea of a general education was, practically speaking, a self-contradiction.

To be sure, Snedden's vision of a minutely differentiated curriculum was never completely realized, but the general idea of different educations for different population groups, variously defined, has taken firm root in modern American education.[59] Moreover, the idea persists that education should be designed with very specific purposes in mind. (Hence, the continued emphasis on stating educational objectives in highly specific terms.) It is clear that despite the call to create a common curriculum endorsed by such influential contemporary groups as the Carnegie Foundation,[60] diversity and particularity reign supreme in terms of school practice.

It would be an obvious oversimplification to say that Snedden's curriculum ideology merely prevailed over the idea that an education should be common to all regardless of future destination. It is more likely that an educational ideology controlled by specific but differentiated social and individual purposes was more congenial to an industrial society itself highly specialized and differentiated. Snedden was probably articulating (albeit in an extreme form) basic twentieth-century values. And one should not overlook the very real obstacles that school officials would face in declaring one form of education to be suitable for all, a policy that would fly in the face of such sacred American values as autonomy and choice.

Conclusion

The idea of a liberal education as a basis for general education in American schools is alive—but barely. The incorporation of science and other "moderns" into a conception of the liberal arts was not, in itself, sufficient to maintain its place in general education. Even the "new" liberal arts competed rather unsuccessfully with a conception of a curriculum that was seen as directly tied to the real business of life. While the liberal arts curriculum maintained its status as an ideal suited to a social (or at least an intellectual) elite who had the leisure to pursue it, a general education tied to efficient performance of life's tasks predominated for the many. The ancient dichotomy between labor and leisure with its implications for strong class divisions was thus maintained. Secondly, the internal reconstruction of the elements of a liberal education proceeded only haphazardly. For liberal education to be successful in an era of mass public education, not simply the addition or substitution of subjects, but a massive reconstruction of what we mean by the arts, literature, history, political economy, and even science had to be accomplished. The liberal arts curriculum, after all, had its origins in the belief that it was an education only for that aristocratic few who had the leisure it required. What had to be created was a path which the masses could also follow to the kind of intellectual liberation that modern advocates of a liberal education such as Arnold and Huxley foresaw.

In place of such a reconstruction, educational leaders such as Snedden advocated a differentiated curriculum designed to fit people specifically for the tasks they needed to perform. Specificity is the great enemy of a liberal education. As Charles Bailey recently expressed it, "The first justification for engaging people in liberal general education . . . is that its very rejection of *specific* utility, and its espousal of intrinsically worthwhile ends, provides the maximum and most general utility."[61] In rejecting specificity, then, the liberal arts does not reject utility; it seeks a broader and grander utility than is represented by the specific and the immediate. It is a utility that lies, broadly speaking, in the development of rationality and the freedom that rationality provides to discover *why* I should believe and act as I do. Moreover, the espousal of intrinsically worthwhile ends should not be equated with education that has no purpose. Ends that are intrinsic to knowing literature, history, and science are ends that can be reasonably associated with their study. They are not external to them. Spencer's convictions to the contrary, knowing Newton's second law of thermodynamics is no more necessary for self-preservation than a knowledge of Homer's *Iliad*. Science is a vital element in a liberal education, not because we as individuals survive through our knowledge of it, but because it is an extension of our need to know about the natural world. It is on principles such as these that a modern conception of the liberal arts, and a general education based on the liberal arts, may be rebuilt.

FOOTNOTES

1. See, for example, Ayers Bagley, *Study and Love: Aristotle's Fall* (Minneapolis, MN: Society of Professors of Education, 1986).

2. Herbert Spencer, "On the Genesis of Science," in *Essays on Education* (New York: E. P. Dutton, 1910), p. 296.

3. Herbert Spencer, *Education: Intellectual, Moral and Physical* (New York: D. Appleton and Co., 1860), p. 117.

4. Ibid., pp. 1-2.

5. Ibid., p. 4.

6. Ibid., p. 11.

7. Ibid., pp. 13-14.

8. Ibid., p. 15.

9. Ibid., pp. 19-20.

10. Ibid., p. 22.

11. Ibid., p. 23.

12. Ibid., p. 25.

13. Ibid., p. 36.

14. Ibid., p. 40.

15. Ibid., p. 62.

16. Ibid., p. 63.

17. Ibid., pp. 84-85.

18. Thomas Henry Huxley, "A Liberal Education; and Where to Find It," in *Science and Education: Essays* (New York: D. Appleton and Co., 1896), p. 77.

19. Ibid., p. 78.

20. Ibid., p. 70.

21. Ibid.

22. Ibid., p. 83.

23. Ibid., p. 79.

24. See, for example, Charles S. Blinderman, "Semantic Aspects of T. H. Huxley's Literary Style," *Journal of Communication* 12 (1962): 171-178; Walter E. Houghton, "The Rhetoric of T. H. Huxley," *University of Toronto Quarterly* 18 (1949): 159-175.

25. Thomas Henry Huxley, "Science and Culture," in *Science and Education* (New York: D. Appleton and Co., 1899), p. 137.

26. Matthew Arnold, *Culture and Anarchy* (Cambridge: Cambridge University Press, 1960; [1869]), p. 69.

27. Ibid., p. 70.

28. Ibid.

29. Huxley, "Science and Culture," p. 149.

30. Ibid., p. 152.

31. Matthew Arnold, "Literature and Science," in *Discourses in America* (London: Macmillan and Co., 1885), pp. 94-95.

32. Ibid., p. 99.

33. Ibid., p. 125.

34. Ibid., p. 127.

35. Richard Hofstadter, *Social Darwinism in American Thought* (Boston: Beacon Press, 1944, 1955), p. 32.

36. William Graham Sumner, "State Interference," in *Social Darwinism*, ed. Stow Persons (Englewood Cliffs, NJ: Prentice-Hall, 1963), pp. 105-106.

37. Ibid., p. 109.

38. William Graham Sumner, "The Concentration of Wealth: Its Economic Justification" in *Social Darwinism*, ed. Persons, p. 151.

39. Ibid., p. 156.

40. Ibid., p. 157.

41. National Education Association, *Report of the Committee on Secondary School Studies* (Washington, DC: Government Printing Office, 1893).

42. Charles William Eliot, "What Is a Liberal Education?" in *Educational Reform* (New York: Century Company, 1898), pp. 97-101.

43. Ibid., pp. 101-104.

44. Ibid., pp. 104-109.

45. Ibid., p. 110.

46. Ibid.

47. John Francis Latimer, *What's Happened to Our High Schools?* (Washington, DC: Public Affairs Press, 1958), pp. 12-15.

48. Ibid., pp. 21-57.

49. Arthur G. Powell, Eleanor Farrar, and David K. Cohen, *The Shopping Mall High School: Winners and Losers in the Educational Marketplace* (Boston: Houghton Mifflin, 1985).

50. G. Stanley Hall, "The Natural Activities of Children as Determining the Industries in Early Education, II," in National Education Association, *Journal of Proceedings and Addresses* 43 (1904): 443.

51. G. Stanley Hall, "The Ideal School as Based on Child Study," in National Education Association, *Journal of Proceedings and Addresses* 40 (1901): 475.

52. Walter H. Drost, *David Snedden and Education for Social Efficiency* (Madison, Wis.: University of Wisconsin Press, 1967), p. 5.

53. David Snedden, "The Practical Arts in Liberal Education," *Educational Review* 43 (1912): 379.

54. National Education Association, *Cardinal Principles of Secondary Education: A Report of the Commission on the Reorganization of Secondary Education* (Washington, DC: Government Printing Office, 1918).

55. David Snedden, "Cardinal Principles of Secondary Education," *School and Society* 9 (1919): 522.

56. David Snedden, "The Relation of General to Vocational Education," in National Education Association, *Journal of Proceedings and Addresses* 62 (1924): 1003-1004.

57. David Snedden, "Progress Towards Sociologically Based Civic Education," *Journal of Educational Sociology* 3 (1929): 483.

58. Ibid., p. 485-486.

59. See, for example, Jeannie Oakes, *Keeping Track: How Secondary Schools Structure Inequality* (New Haven, CT: Yale University Press, 1985).

60. See, for example, Ernest Boyer, *High School: A Report of the Carnegie Foundation for the Advancement of Teaching* (New York: Harper and Row, 1983).

61. Charles Bailey, *Beyond the Present and Particular: A Theory of Liberal Education* (London: Routledge and Kegan Paul, 1984), p. 35.

CHAPTER IV

The Fate of Knowledge

HAZARD ADAMS

> Where is the wisdom we have lost in knowledge?
> Where is the knowledge we have lost in information?
>
> T. S. ELIOT
> "The Rock"

The subject assigned, education and knowledge, is so vast that I trust the reader will allow me at the outset to venture some broad historical generalizations. I begin by inquiring into what people in western society over time have thought knowledge, or at least important knowledge, to be about. My presumption will be that education has always been regarded, in part, as the transmission of important knowledge. But the notion of what knowledge is important has changed over the ages. I speak broadly when I divide the history of attitudes toward knowledge in the West into three great phases, each of which implies different objects and aims for education, and in the third of which these objects and aims remain a matter of sometimes bitter debate, advocation, resistance, and indecision. The three ages I shall call, respectively, the age of the knowledge of Being, the age of the knowledge of knowing (epistemology), and the age of the hegemony of language. I shall then proceed to a discussion of what the word "knowledge" has meant. This will be followed by an inquiry into how the word has been used in some recent well-publicized reports on education. Finally, I shall offer some brief suggestions toward a redefinition of "knowledge" and the establishment of certain kinds of academic courses.

A History of Knowledge

It was Plato, of course, who invented a hierarchy of imitations leading at the top to pure Being or the Idea, which is regarded as the ultimate object of knowledge. In *Cratylus*, he summarizes, using the example of a circle: "We have then, first a name, second, a description, third, an image, and fourth, a knowledge of the object."[1] But beyond these, we are reminded, there is a fifth, which is the Idea itself. Names and descriptions are verbal and have the arbitrary relation to the object that characterizes language. The image is phenomenal and temporary like a model worked on a lathe. What Plato calls "knowledge of the object" is "one thing more that is found not in sounds nor in shapes of bodies, but in minds."[2] This differs from the preceding three, but falls short of the real circle, which can be known fully only by proceeding up the whole hierarchy, leaving behind all but what reason reveals as the truth, not the phenomenal particular but the essential Idea, for which particulars merely stand in either an arbitrary or an imitative relation. Thus true knowledge is of that "essence which is eternal, and is not wandering between the two poles of generation and decay."[3] Rising above language, image, and opinion, Platonic knowledge would reside in mathematics and geometry as the avenue to the pure Idea and as the model of the proper process:

. . . that which the reason itself lays hold of by the power of dialectic, treating its assumptions not as absolute beginnings but literally as hypotheses, underpinnings, footings, and springboards so to speak, to enable it to rise to that which requires no assumption and is the starting point of all, and after attaining to that again taking hold of the first dependencies from it, so to proceed downward to the conclusion, making no use whatever of any object of sense but only of pure ideas moving on through ideas to ideas and ending with ideas.[4]

The Socrates of *Republic* admonishes the young to study mathematics and reminds us of the ancient and continuing quarrel between philosophy and poetry.[5] Whether Being is lodged in the Idea or in teleological nature, as in Aristotle, the means to its apprehension is reason, and reason is identified by Plato with number. Language must, if it is to aspire to anything like truth, seek the condition of number, which in turn leads to the Idea or *logos*, the principle by which the world of flux and appearance is activated and ordered.

For Plato, any education not leading to Being by rational means is false, and probably dangerous to the order of the state, which requires the governorship of reason. For centuries following Plato, the aim of knowledge was this *logos* or later, in medieval theology, God. In Plato, it is the state, maintained by the wisdom of an elite educated in reason, that stands for *logos*. In medieval theology, it is the Church. Both ideally control education.

The age of the knowledge of knowing (or epistemology) arises with the development of modern science. In this age, knowing itself becomes an object of knowledge, whether the method is rationalism or empiricism. Otherwise knowing is aimed at phenomenal nature, and soon the human being becomes a part of that nature. If in the age of the knowledge of Being the fundamental opposition is that of appearance and Being, with Being privileged, in the age of epistemology the opposition exists entirely in the realm of what Plato called appearances. It is that of the perceiving subject and perceived object, with the object privileged. After this division is established and knowing declared to be based on it, true knowledge becomes knowledge of the object without the subject's interference. The object replaces *logos* as the residence of what Being there is. But this truth, rather than remaining located in external matter, tends to become idealized in the language of mathematical structures.

It is of importance that the privileging of the object nevertheless presents a scenario in which one begins with the subject looking outward toward the object. Coleridge, following Schelling, tried to show that given the distinction of subject and object some form of idealization was inevitable. Whether this is so or not, it is clear enough that in the age of epistemology knowledge was hewn in two, producing what William Blake called a "cloven fiction"—subjective experience divided from objective knowledge. The latter was that which was amenable to verification (later falsification). The former, because connected to individual experience, could not be declared to have the universality necessary to qualify it for privilege. This occurred even though the fiction had centered all knowing on human acts and a secularized natural Being. The old concerns for Being enunciated in their particular ways by Plato and by the medieval theologians remained, of course, but they lost ground after a long struggle in the universities to what was first called "natural philosophy" and finally "natural science." In this process the dominant model for learning ceased to be language—in practice, Latin and Greek—and number was regarded as the avenue to the material world. The dominant science was physics, but the methods of experiment and systematic investigation generated new disciplines, each attempting to capture for its own prestige the valuable verbal currency "objective knowledge."

In these disciplines, the problem of the subject remained a vexation. Could the subject's presence ever be eliminated as an influence on data? To what extent could social events and human behavior be mathematicized? Could there be such a thing as a science of the subject? A subjective science? The tendency of each such science, in order to capture the power that comes with the ownership of "knowledge," was to try to objectify the subject or to create the concept of a body of knowledge that constituted the subject (or in this case "object"). In the humanities this resulted in the establishment of a literary canon or established object to be known. Knowing took the form of establishing texts according to developed methods, of remembering them, and of interpreting them according to methods secularized from those of theology in the age of the knowledge of Being. Generally the early history of the social sciences was characterized by an effort to establish behavioral objectivity by means of number and experiment. All of these developments were efforts to capture "knowledge" according to the new rules of the game, which were grounded in the subject/object fiction.

Even as the age of epistemology reached its apotheosis it would have been possible to notice two things. First, there remained the vestiges of the age of the knowledge of Being. If we look, for example, at the writings of Dr. Johnson or the *Discourses* of Sir Joshua Reynolds in the late eighteenth century, we notice that the idea of what the artist presents is a curious mixture of empiricist and Platonic notions: the artist seeks that central or original form from which all other forms are deviations. Yet the artist seeks also that generality which contains the common characteristics of all the instances of the type.[6]

Second, the epistemological age flowers only to provide the seed for its successor, the age of the hegemony of language. The notion of the passivity of the subject as a recipient of sense data capable of making nothing new of this material except rearrangements of it generated its opposite, the notion of the activity of the subject in forming the object, as in Kant's concept of the categorical understanding or Coleridge's later definitions of primary and secondary imagination. Kant did not offer a theory acknowledging language's role in such a process, and Coleridge's writings are full of ambiguity about language; but writers of a neo-Kantian bent from von Humboldt to Cassirer eventually offer a theory. Knowledge came to be seen as something *produced* rather than discovered—and produced in a variety of symbolic forms, of which the most fundamental is language itself. Number is regarded as a refinement of language in the direction of abstraction from any referent. Artistic forms are regarded as languages that abstract toward the fictive particular.

At the same time, the development of phenomenology marks an effort to replace the isolation of the subject's consciousness from objects by declaring for intersubjectivity and transcendental consciousness, but comes to have to cope with the presence of language. It tries to establish language as a mediation where the distinction subject/object disappears; but its very retention of the term "subjectivity" tends to condemn it to the distinction it opposes.

The early stages of the hegemony of language are characterized by a wrenching of the term "reality" away from the object as the privileged holder of truth passively apprehended in sense experience or copied in linguistic or mathematical formulas. The shift is to the active *constitution* of the object in symbolic forms, which constitutions blur and often erase the distinction between the object and knowledge of it. This bundle of object and knowledge is called by some a fiction with none of the connotation of untruth but all of the connotation of making that is implicit in the word's etymology. If there is an object beyond this symbolic form, one cannot know it anymore than one can know the Kantian thing-in-itself, which always remains hidden behind the understanding's operations.

There is a sense that in this new age not just Being and God are reduced to objects of faith or to words trapped in the system of language, but so is the material world itself displaced into the operations of symbolic fictions to be judged for their elegance and coherence rather than their adequacy of correspondence to a Being only constitutable in their forms in the first place. The model for all forms of knowing becomes language.

But this linguistic humanism, as one might call it, with man as the creator and manipulator of his languages, was soon seen to have another and darker side. Heidegger's often echoed observation that language speaks man, that man lives in language, reveals it. Though language can be treated in the way Cassirer did, as a liberation from the nearly mute condition of the other animals, it can also be regarded as a limitation that separates man from Being. Heidegger himself tried to relocate Being so that it could be available to human consciousness. This was attempted by striving not to recapture the word "knowledge" but to substitute the term "consciousness" itself as the privileged term, while at the same time denigrating the age of epistemology as the ominous mastery of technology over the object. Consciousness was always, according to Husserl, the consciousness of *something*. Yet language had to be the mediator of this something, and so the whole problem of subject/object seemed to repeat itself.

Further, the idea of the knowing subject or of subject-oriented knowing seemed in some views to be a product of political forces that had given rise to or came concurrently with the hegemony of the *laissez-faire* individual and with it economic tyranny. Perhaps, it was thought, it would be better if the concept of Man identified at least historically with this robber-baron figure (the new form of feudal lord) were to disappear. Therefore, the hegemony of language over Man, in the sense in which epistemological man was taken to exist, was welcomed in some quarters as politically good, that is to say, a liberation from the old idea of the isolated subject in an endless struggle to cope with or subdue and master the world around him in the form of the other object or "it." Human beings were seen as products deeply woven into cultural structures, which were themselves treated on the model of linguistic systems.

This meant that language itself was now the concern of knowledge as well as constituting the shape of knowing, the structure from which everything emerged and to which everything returned, like Being in the old Platonism. The model of language became the container of a variety of disciplines. But there were different models of the model. One of the most influential of these was that offered by structural linguistics usually associated with the theories of Ferdinand de Saussure. This model can be seen to have operated somewhere in all of the human sciences in recent times—anthropology, economics, politics, psychoanalysis, and literary criticism, among others. But even where structuralism did not rule, language in some sense became the center, as in ordinary-language philosophy and one of its outgrowths, speech-act theory. In a different way, language became the central term in the new discipline of computer science. Books entitled *The Prison House of Language* and *The Rule of Metaphor* appeared. Eighteenth-century theorists of language like G. B. Vico were revived.

Language, no longer a copy or arbitrary allegory of the real and no longer an emanation of Man, became now the ruler of men, the shaper of its own linguistic real. No longer beyond language, as Plato averred, Being (now merely being) is, if anywhere, lodged in the structure of language itself.

Changes in thinking about the natural sciences have been equally profound, and although the model that has driven these changes has not been the structuralist one of language, it is fair to say that a concept of symbolic fictions or makings has been central. The idea of empiricism as the foundation of science has been largely dismissed.

The whole realm of the philosophy of science has become a battleground since the notion has been put forward that science and its processes are governed to some considerable extent by the social and institutional fabric in which the work is carried on and the nature of that work is constituted. From Michael Polanyi's concept of "tacit knowledge" to Gerald Holton's "public science," the role of the scientist has been hemmed in and structured according to laws that have little to do with the old idea of the autonomous subject investigating an object. Even the idea of progress, so closely identified in many minds with that subject, and gradual development, in which the process of verification and of falsification is the rule, have been modified in some quarters by the concept of relatively sudden shifts of paradigms, as expounded in the work of Thomas Kuhn. The idea of discontinuity, fissures, gaps (that is to say, differences) has dominated the revolutionary writings of Michel Foucault about the human sciences.

This notion of differences is itself at the center of the structuralist model as put forth by de Saussure. Foucault's method is to treat all things on the analogy of differential systems, or, more accurately, to study relations rather than things, on the ground that things are products of relations rather than the other way around. Gone is the synthetic activity of the subject. Present is the "proliferation of discontinuities."

The intellectual activity known as deconstruction seeks to extend structuralism to its logical and possibly absurd conclusions. At the same time, while still linguistic in its model it may well signal the passing of the apotheosis of the hegemony of language. It has its counterparts in the previous ages: the Greek skeptics and, in another aspect, the Sophists; the Berkeleyan reduction by extension of Locke's empiricism. It plays in language, from which Jacques Derrida, its leading exponent, claims we cannot escape:

From this language it is necessary for us to try to free ourselves. Not actually to *try* to free ourselves from it, for that is impossible without forgetting our historical condition. But to imagine [*rever*] it. Not actually to *free* ourselves from it, which would be senseless and would deprive us of the light of sense. But to resist it as far as possible.[7]

This fine honing of the problem of the age of the hegemony of language has not yet been surpassed, at least insofar as the problem is treated in terms of a particular sort of differential linguistics.

Where education has not tacitly or deliberately and openly resisted the age of the hegemony of language, it has for the most part failed to enter it. To the extent that this is so, it has been a reactionary force.

If this short history has had anything to it, it would appear that "knowledge" in the sense of "knowing that," as scholars of education say, is unstable in meaning because "that" is given different significances and values in the different ages I have named. In each succeeding age there has been a struggle to bring education, whether powered by church or state, to recognize the new significances.

Knowledge: The Word

Another way to constitute a history of "knowledge" is to study how "knowledge" has been employed over time. I am no expert on the history of the word, and so I shall steal as much as I can from the *Oxford English Dictionary*. The earliest meanings of "knowledge" in English seem to have been acknowledgement, confession, legal and other forms of cognizance, judicial investigation, notice, and recognition. Later uses had to do with the fact of knowing a thing or a person, familiarity gained by experience, personal acquaintance, sexual intimacy, acquaintance with a fact or matter, a state of being aware or informed, consciousness (of anything), intellectual acquaintance with a perception of fact or truth, clear and certain mutual apprehension, and the fact or state or condition of understanding. These last would include Locke's concept of knowledge: ". . . nothing but the perception of the connexion and agreement or disagreement and repugnancy of any of our ideas." (By "idea" Locke meant something like a mind-dependent representation of external objects.) In addition to these, "knowledge" has meant acquaintance with a branch of learning, a language, or the like; theoretical or practical understanding of an art, science, or industry; the skill to *do* something; the fact or condition of having been instructed or of having information acquired by study of research; acquaintance with ascertained truths, facts, or principles; information acquired by study; learning; erudition; the sum of what is known; a branch of learning; and, last, a sign or mark by which anything is known, recognized, or distinguished—a token. But this last is said to be obsolete, in the sense in which it was used in 1523 in the following sentence: "At theyr departyng they thought to make a knowledge that they had been there; for they set the subbarbes afyre." This old meaning, it may turn out, still has a certain relevance in that it makes knowledge inhabit a symbol or a token, and thus involves something rife with *meaning*.

Now, generally speaking, what A. D. Woozley says in his introduction to epistemology has been fairly common usage among philosophers. There are facts, propositions, and sentences:

Required to use some name for the object of a man's belief, philosophers commonly use the word "proposition": what I believe is a proposition, and my belief is true if the proposition corresponds to the facts, false if it does not. Again, a proposition is normally distinguished from a sentence by saying that a sentence is a form of words combined according to the grammatical and syntactical rules of the language to which the sentence belongs, while a proposition is not a form of words at all, but is what the sentence means.[8]

This statement raises more problems than it solves. What is the status of the proposition? Where can we find it, or how can we constitute it? If we cannot locate it, does that mean we cannot have knowledge, since the proposition seems to be conflated with meaning and knowledge seems to be the meaning of the facts? But is it not fair to say that meaning is itself linguistic and does not merely appear in sentences but comes *as* sentences (to continue to use Woozley's terms)? Further, the meaning of these sentences will come as sentences, and so on and on. And do not the facts come as sentences or other symbols, which remain facts when verified or unless falsified (according to Popper) by their failure to exist in accord with other sentences or symbols and/or (according to Kuhn) made obsolete by a shift in the prevailing paradigm? If this is so, it appears that the obsolete meaning of "knowledge" as a sign or mark may not be quite obsolete after all and may actually take precedence over some of those more common usages recited by the *Oxford English Dictionary*.

Of course, some will say that to discuss education in connection only with knowledge is foolish because it is tacitly to assume too narrow a concept of education or too narrow a concept of knowledge, excluding consciousness *of*, acquaintance, and recognition—terms that might apply, for example, to training in connoisseurship in the fine arts, and even to what Polanyi calls "tacit knowledge." Indeed, these terms and their connection to the privileged term "knowledge" have been fought over, the aim frequently having been to identify appreciation with knowledge or to define it as a form of knowledge, as if to succeed in doing so would establish the discipline involved higher up on the hierarchy of educational subjects. The association of knowledge with the natural sciences in the age of epistemology also had the result of causing other disciplines both to seek to steal the term or to adopt so-called experimental or empirical methods (or unconscious parodies of them like Zola's experimental novel or Taine's history). Another strategy was to fly to the apparent opposite, eschewing the equation knowledge/objectivity and claiming for subjectivity a different (sometimes occult) kind of knowledge, or accepting solipsism, as in the famous conclusion to *The Renaissance* of Walter Pater, or establishing intersubjectivity, as in some versions of phenomenology.[9] Such tendencies appear today in, for example, reader-response literary criticism, though it ranges all the way from a rigid empiricism to attempts to establish an objective ground or subjective universality in a reading community.

Debates in the arena of general education have been riddled with confusions about the current meanings of "knowledge" and the degree to which they overlap terms like "appreciation" and "wisdom."

Knowledge and General Education

The educational profession has been bombarded over the last few years with panel and commission reports on what is wrong with education in the United States, what should be done about curriculum, how best to prepare teachers, and so forth. The term "knowledge" plays in these reports in ways that may throw some light on fundamental current attitudes and reveal to what extent thinking in high places has adequately engaged itself with the problems posed by the age of the hegemony of language. *Involvement in Learning: Realizing the Potential of Higher Education* divides educational aims into providing knowledge, capacities, and skills.[10] Two statements illustrate the fate of "knowledge" in this widely circulated report. First, "capacities and skills are the truly enduring effects of higher education." The skills specifically mentioned are those of writing and speaking, critical thinking and analysis, synthesizing, imagining, and creating. (The report does not tell us what the difference between a skill and an ability or a capacity is.) The report claims not to underestimate the importance of the "content or raw material of [a] discipline," but it does not go on to say what such content should be. Whether "knowledge" is involved in any of this, beyond apprehension of "content" or "raw material of a discipline," is uncertain. It appears that "knowledge" refers to ownership of some substance.

Second, "we were not charged to define 'the knowledge most worth having,' and it would be inappropriate for us to do so." It is interesting that the phrase "knowledge most worth having" is in quotation marks, as if it referred to a fiction or unreal entity. The responsibility for declaring what *is* most worth knowing is said to be that of the individual academic institution. A wedge is driven between the concepts of knowing *how* (though "knowing" is not used principally in this sense in the report) and knowing *about* or *that*. The former seems to be the province of blue ribbon panels, the latter of institutions; but there is little doubt that the panel thinks rules about the former are more important than constituting the latter. Further, one might notice that the panel itself could be imagined as representative of yet a larger institution, for it seeks to speak in the best interests of the nation.

In other words, skills, capacities, and abilities are containers in this report for a content (the objects) of knowledge never specified except insofar as they are declared tacitly to be things properly to be sought, pursued, or owned. Institutional faculties should indicate what knowledge, skills, and capabilities are expected of students and should assess their and their students' success in providing and gaining these things. Presumably the institution would develop some means of accountability, and all of this is declared possible because there already is much knowledge about "conditions under which student learning and growth can be maximized and about the methods and benchmarks by which these changes can be measured." But something is missing from this formula, and the reason is the separation of knowledge from skills and so forth, as if one of these things were the broth and the other the pot. What happens if the institutional decisions about the objects of knowledge are inadequate? (The question, of course, is "inadequate to what?") Will all the skills in the world then be of any value? And vice versa? Can a report that does not speak of the *what* of knowledge be more than a series of encouraging (or discouraging) shouts? Is the problem deeper than this? Does the division lead to hollow pieties? Do these pieties mask, however innocently, a position heavily laden with the ideology of classical liberalism as it became established in the age of epistemology? Is it inadequate in a new age?

The Carnegie Task Force report *A Nation Prepared: Teachers for the 21st Century* is forthright about its vision of the aims of education.[11] They are aims designed to further the goals of the state in its economic competition with foreign governments. It is these aims and that of "binding . . . citizens together in a commonweal" that dictate the need to provide access to a "shared cultural and intellectual tradition." The problem here is the tacit notion that the traditions of the culture are a fixed content and adequate to a dynamically changing population. This gives the metaphor of "binding" with all its good intentions a sinister side.

At first glance, the program proposed does not seem to place much importance on the word "knowledge." The term appears very late. The following paragraph does not contain it, but rather emphasizes the need for a new burst of American know-how treated in terms of "skills," "feeling for," and "ability":

The skills needed now are not routine. Our economy will be increasingly dependent on people who have a good intuitive grasp of the ways in which all kinds of physical and social systems work. They must possess a feeling for mathematical concepts and the ways in which they can be applied to difficult problems, an ability to see patterns of meaning where others see only confusion: a cultivated creativity that leads them to new problems, new products, and new services before their competitors get to them; and, in many cases, the ability to work with other people in complex organizational environments where work groups must decide for themselves how to get the job done.[12]

The following sentence does introduce "knowing," with more than one sense implied: "They [citizens] will not come to the workplace knowing all they need to know, but knowing how to figure out what they need to know, where to get it, and how to make meaning out of it." One sense here is knowing *how* or skills; another is that of ownership or appropriation of an object or substance. A third, which we have not seen before, involves the introduction of "meaning" in connection with knowledge. This is complicated by a metaphoric description of knowledge as Protean in form, for the report refers to the need to learn all the time as the knowledge required to do work "twists and turns with new challenges and the progress of science and technology." It is difficult to sort out all of this and get at what is implicit. On the one hand, knowledge is a sort of commodity; on the other, it is synonymous with a skill. Finally, it fades away in both of these senses to be replaced by created meaning. Perhaps one could say that in addition to the split between knowledge *that* or *about* and skills, there is another split, every bit as specious, between knowledge and meaning. Meaning seems here to be something that knowledge is submitted to. Further, this report declares there is nothing static about knowledge, though perhaps the report intends to

say that there is nothing static about what needs to be known. But
perhaps what the report should have acknowledged was that, like a
proposition, knowledge has no existence except as meaning and that
we cannot conceive of meaning in any form but that of words or
symbolic systems and that it is this meaning that is Protean, for in
definition it gives way to other words and so on, and that meaning is
itself an endless building or process.

Before our eyes the received concept of knowledge *that* or *about* on
which these reports are tacitly based seems to unravel. But before we
consider this, it is worthwhile to examine a third report, that written
by William J. Bennett, then chairman of the National Endowment for
the Humanities, now secretary of the department of education. The
title of the report is *To Reclaim a Legacy* and is concerned with higher
education and the humanities.[13] In this report, the word "knowledge"
is employed eight times, and the word "know" five. The former is
preceded in its various appearances by "fundamental," "rudimentary," "essential," "explicit body of," and "certain essential areas of."
All of these employments are honorific. In addition, the term
"knowledge" is treated as a possession or something it is desirable to
possess. The word is employed pejoratively when it is followed by
"seen as relative." The verbal form is used when reference is made
honorifically to knowing "a common culture rooted in civilization's
lasting vision," to knowing "what is worth knowing," and to
knowing "what is important in our heritage that all educated persons
know." At first, Bennett does not appear to take the nationalistic line
of the Carnegie report. He claims for his community western culture
or civilization, though he seems to regard it as having been a progress
toward American political and judicial institutions.

Like the authors of *Involvement in Learning*, Bennett declares that
it is up to academic institutions to decide what knowledge is most
worth having, but one suspects that the principles he puts forward
tend to narrow the definition of such knowledge. The agenda is clear;
as the title of the report implies, Bennett's aim is to turn the clock back
to a time when supposedly the heritage *was* claimed. The educational
establishment has somehow lost touch with truth and morality. This
happened when, first, knowledge came to be seen as relative in
importance, relative especially to consumer interests, second, the
desired ends of education changed from "knowledge" to "inquiry,"
from (in other words) contents to skills, and, third, college curricula
became based on doubt about the possibility of reaching a consensus
about the most significant thoughts, thinkers, and so forth.

The program implicit here harkens back to Plato's approach in *Republic* and *Laws*. Education begins to look like an initiation ceremony into a tribal structure. It involves establishment of membership in a culture, and this membership is at one point tellingly described with the word "shareholders." The program looks to the past for all of its values, and fixed institutions are apparently to be protected. The specific knowledges called for are unexceptionable. We have heard of them before: knowledge of the origins and development of western civilization, basic chronology, careful reading of literary masterworks, understanding of the most significant debates in the history of philosophy, proficiency in a foreign language, study of a nonwestern culture, and study of the history of science and technology. It is a content-based curriculum that is being advised, in contrast to the Carnegie report's skill-based approach. The former seems to be looking to a fixed wise past or at least a teleological accumulation of wisdom. The latter seems to look to the future, though it is hardly Promethean.

Richard Ohmann has recently pointed to a problem that he sees in Bennett's approach: ". . . [B]odies of knowledge and the people (professionals) who mediate them work through institutions designed to serve in part the self-interest of the practitioners and . . . these institutions and practices must respond in part to dominant groups and powerful forces in the society at large."[14] I would put this somewhat differently and emphasize the power of institutions themselves to dominate groups and interests, to develop a life of their own that dominant groups and powerful interests have difficulty controlling. When institutions and the language of the tribe cease to be put in a position where questioning of them is possible, the very values that both Bennett and the Carnegie report seem to profess become more uncertain of preservation.

General Education and Knowledge

Is not the splitting of knowledge between skills and content the problem that makes all of these reports seem so arid? This causes me to return to the curious archaic meaning of "knowledge" that the *Oxford English Dictionary* adds to more familiar usages: "A sign or mark by which anything is known, recognized, or distinguished; a token." This definition is not going to be wholly satisfactory, but with a little work we may be able by its means to heal partly the "cloven fiction" of a split between content and skill. Let the token be language or symbolic system. Rather than language being something that points beyond itself, let it be a structure that takes in unformed masses of whatever is out there and shapes this material into its own form, giving it that form. Let us notice again that the language and symbolic system are always in movement. Language is finite, as a dictionary is finite, but the process of definition leads ever onward from word to word. If in a process of defining we discover ourselves returning to the word with which we began, we are unhappy and label our thinking "circular."

Knowledge is implicated in this process. Regarded as a substance or content it is something never arrived at and always sought. This leads to a sometimes bitter skepticism. But if we identify it with process itself, we treat it neither as a content nor as a skill but as the contrary to this opposition. Bennett would have us, like the pathetic Urizen in Blake's *Four Zoas*, declare what the knowledge worth having is—in the sense of content. This knowledge would not be of the Platonic idea that can never be spoken but the idea which when spoken looks like the embodiment of an idol. We can name that idol "authoritarianism." We shall have the choice of joining, that is, knuckling under, though this option is described in terms of being a "shareholder," or of falling into what the Carnegie report calls a "permanent underclass." There may not be so much difference between these states as some would like to think.

General education, unfortunately so named because it too easily suggests that what we now call the "smorgasbord" approach (I regret this, because true smorgasbords have a definite character) is tossed back and forth by curriculum makers between the two poles of negations, one set of which is content/skills and another practical (professional)/everything else. General education must face the question of how to define knowledge anew in a contrary fashion. It must acknowledge that there is no such thing as the simple, direct gift of nontheoretical knowledge, free of perplexing questions. What we so often think free of theoretical implications is always laden with assumptions. It is frequently the product of what Althusser has called "state apparatuses."

Is it ever possible to escape this situation and develop a position "outside" and free from which to determine truth? Or is one, like Urizen, always already surrounded? Yes, one is, if one thinks of knowledge as only content or only skill or some apparently happy combination of the two. If one could consider knowledge as a process, then it would be possible always to be in it and keep going, and both a past and a future would come into view. It would be a future of questioning and a past consistently queried and reformulated. This would not be the meaning of knowledge merely for intellectuals; it would be practical, for it avoids what Blake called "fixities and definites," which when lodged in people's minds make it impossible to meet the economic competition the Carnegie report worries about or to renew for creative purposes the texts of the past (on which Bennett wishes to center humanities study) in ways not already prescribed by those who interpreted them for another time and place.

Somehow general education must be built to emphasize knowledge as process. A program that attempts this might begin by fashioning courses of study that:

1. Inquire into the underlying rationale of a particular discipline, and into its history and development.

2. Make possible an inquiry into the relationship between a particular discipline and the culture at large, including other disciplines and in some cases the local community.

3. Raise questions that are approached in different ways by different disciplines, and lead to study of the implications of those differences and of points of contact between the disciplines.

In each of these cases, the process includes and emphasizes or at least gets to inquiring into why we proceed as we do. There is wariness of the fixed law. Very puzzling questions are likely to appear from time to time in the process, but in a context where embarrassment is less likely to suppress their discussion: What is the authority behind the rule or way of proceeding? How did the situation come about? Why does the discipline have the boundaries it has?

Many people fear this kind of process. I regard it as necessary to the alleged aim of both Carnegie and Bennett, though it is contrary in means and attitude to both. It is based on an ethic that refuses to accept tyranny, particularly intellectual tyranny. As Yeats remarked, an "intellectual hatred" is the worst of all kinds. In any case, I believe that until the sort of process I suggest is seriously attempted, general education, which should be called liberating education, will be subject to the negations that have been my concern here.

A panel of deans of colleges of education has recently complained that " most Americans think nothing of requiring teachers to carry out a late 20th-century assignment while locked into a mid-19th century job description."[15] It is worse even than this. The intellectual world-picture on which so much general education is based remains that of the age of epistemology with a residue from the age of Being. General education must acknowledge the existence of the age of the hegemony of language, preferably before it, too, passes into something else, as it is soon likely to do. Perhaps, then, students, who may sense change better than others, will discover their general education courses more pertinent to knowledge and will not regard them merely as things to "get out of the way."

FOOTNOTES

1. Plato, *Cratylus*, 342.b.

2. Ibid., 324.c.

3. Plato *Republic* VI, 485.a-b.

4. Ibid., VII, 511.b-c.

5. Ibid., X, 607.b.

6. See Hazard Adams, "Revisiting Reynolds's *Discourses* and Blake's Annotations," in *Blake in His Time*, ed. Robert N. Essick and Donald Pearce (Bloomington, IN: Indiana University Press, 1978), pp. 128-44.

7. Jacques Derrida, *L'Ecriture et la Difference* (Paris: Seuil, 1967). (My translation).

8. Anthony D. Woozley, *Theory of Knowledge* (London: Hutchinson, 1949), p. 29.

9. Some of the sad history of this is told in Hazard Adams, *Philosophy of the Literary Symbolic* (Tallahassee: Florida State University Press, 1983).

10. U.S. National Institute of Education, Study Group on the Conditions of Excellence in American Higher Education, *Involvement in Learning: Realizing the Potential of American Higher Education* (Washington, DC: U.S. Government Printing Office, 1984).

11. Carnegie Forum on Education and the Economy, Task Force on Teaching as a Profession, *A Nation Prepared: Teachers for the 21st Century* (Hyattsville, MD: Carnegie Forum on Education and the Economy, 1986).

12. Ibid., p. 20.

13. William J. Bennett, *To Reclaim a Legacy: Report on the Humanities in Higher Education* (Washington, DC: National Endowment for the Humanities, 1984).

14. Richard Ohmann, "English in America, Ten Years Later (with an aside on dechairing the Department)," *ADE Bulletin* 89 (Winter 1985): 12. This essay strongly criticizes Bennett's *To Reclaim a Legacy.*

15. *Tomorrow's Teachers: A Report of the Holmes Group* (East Lansing, MI: Holmes Group, 1986).

CHAPTER V

Knowledge, Power, and a General Curriculum

THOMAS S. POPKEWITZ

Debate about a common curriculum involves not only fundamental assumptions about the purposes of schooling, but, as significantly, issues about the relation of individuals to society. Curriculum presupposes philosophical assumptions about human "nature," political assumptions about the relation of people to their institutions, and cultural assumptions about the central values and patterns that should give direction to our social affairs. The complex and profound problem of curriculum can be expressed as a conflict between the hope we place in schooling and what happens as people seek to create, sustain, and renew the conditions of their world.[1] The history of curriculum is one in which theories are never realized in the manner they are intended. There are always unintended, unanticipated, and unwilled consequences as theories are put into social practice.

This essay focuses upon the tensions around the issues of general education and the common curriculum by considering the relation of knowledge to power. It recognizes that there are general and seemingly transcendent values about democracy and reason that we wish to maintain in schooling. But, however noble our hopes, curriculum is a socially constructed practice and is politically bound. The major strands of twentieth century analytic philosophy, sociology of knowledge, cultural studies, and discourse analysis make us aware of the boundaries to our existence, the ambiguity of knowledge, and the fundamental relationship of social practices with knowledge. At all times, our language and social practices are precarious and limited. What are defined as our possibilities are also our prisons as we engage in the tasks of constructing a curriculum.

Three interrelated themes of the contradiction between hope and happening in curriculum are given focus in this essay.

1. The problem of a general curriculum involves a prior question about how it is possible to think about general knowledge and a curriculum for all. As we approach this problem historically, we can understand how issues of reflection and analytic discourse are tied to

changes in the social patterns by which power is exercised. There are historical conditions that underlie the manner in which we pose questions about a schooling for everyone and a knowledge that is democratic. There is nothing "natural" or inevitable about our thinking about the world, our sciences of human affairs, the forms taken in our literature, or our definitions of selves as having personality or individuality.

Once we confront the broad question about the structure that gives a form to our thought, we can consider the relation of knowledge to power in the construction of schooling. The discourses of pedagogy can be viewed as socially created "texts" that define possible relationships between people and their institutions. The second and third sections of this essay will focus upon the assumptions and implications of these texts.

2. The public rhetoric of school knowledge focuses upon certain formal categories such as science and mathematics, or such general educational purposes as reflection, critical thought, or problem solving. But the construction of a subject matter gives these words a particular form and direction. What is that form and direction? How do the formulations of a subject matter of science, art, or literature tie knowledge and power into a dynamic relation?

3. We can also think of the everyday world of schooling as a lived text. The forms of speech and the practices of teaching are not common to all but contain multiple layers of meaning and interpretation. In back of the rituals of a common institution are social differentiations: What knowledge is to be transmitted to whom? Different cultural and social messages about personal competence in classroom interactions have implications for the issue of curriculum.

The paradoxes of knowledge create paradoxes for the curriculum designer or researcher. To pose the possibility of a general curriculum is to assume a transcendence of knowledge that has a universal potential for achieving a better society; yet to propose one form of knowledge as dominant is to structure out other possibilities, and this process is never neutral and never without social implications. The contradictions of curriculum are those of our occupational roles. Knowledge is always located in a social and material world.

While this essay can only highlight some tendencies that shed light on these limitations of a general or common schooling, its purpose is also didactic. Our three themes about knowledge and power relations pose central questions about our humanity and the purposes of our institutions. The intent is not to take away from the struggle of forming an adequate institution, but to pose the problem as one of irony, basic contradictions, and dilemmas.

What Historical Conditions Underlie Questions about a Schooling for Everyone?

To understand our talk about curriculum, we must first consider our discourse as a historical and social construction. The manner in which we speak, the forms through which we construct our social affairs, and the categories that express intent about schools are not natural, universal, or inevitable. The socially constructed quality of our world is hard to illuminate because we are continually confronted with what seem to be objective facts of our existence. Our dispositions toward schooling, childhood, and rationality are so pervasive that it is extremely difficult to think of these conceptions as inventions of the last three hundred years. But they developed as a part of a humanism that coincides with the rise of a bourgeoisie, the development of nation-states, and a secularization that followed the Protestant Reformation. The promise of the new humanist discourse was to make people more responsible and enlightened about their social conditions; but that new discourse also involved new power relations as everyday language and social practices encompassed new relationships in society and culture. It is the tension between human agency and social control that forms a contradictory link in our contemporary discourse about social institutions and pedagogy.

The work of Michel Foucault, a social philosopher and historian of ideas, provides a way to think about the problem of knowledge that underlies a general curriculum.[2] Foucault has sought to understand how social practices produce a discourse about individuals and society. Our signs, gestures, routines, and behaviors, Foucault argues, contain rules about what is to be considered normal, reasonable, and legitimate. The discourse of our everyday world sets the conditions by which events are interpreted and "self" is located in a dynamic world. From Foucault's work we can identify prior assumptions and social interests that make it possible to entertain the questions posed in this volume, but at the same time understand the issues of power that underlie the discourse.

FROM REPRESENTATION TO AN ANALYTIC WORLD OF SELF-REFLECTION AND INDIVIDUALITY

The possibility of a mass schooling that makes knowledge

accessible to all is an outgrowth of the fundamental shift in social consciousness that occurred in Western Europe between the seventeenth century and the nineteenth century. Prior to this period, the Classical Age involved a direct relation between the word and the thing that it represented. Existence could not be called into question, since language was not about interpretation but offered a nexus of representation and being. The locus of creation was God, with people providing the clarification of His work. In art, theology, and literature, the word was taken as literal. Precise canons guided church painting to present the teaching of the Bible and the image of God. Thought was to construct a universal method of analysis which would yield certainty by perfectly ordering the representations and signs that mirror the order of the world.

The role of human beings in constructing representations and things could not be made problematic. To think was to clarify the order of the world and to provide an artificial description of the already existing order. Concepts were thought to contain the same essential elements as the objects themselves, and human thought would identify and classify those given elements of the world.

This view of thinking as representation was replaced as people became objects of their own scrutiny. From Kant on, an analytic orientation emerged to show how representation is possible through an analysis of language, social practice, and history. Foucault argues that the attempt to treat facts as existing within contextual boundaries and the further attempt to establish the condition of the possibility of all facts were entirely new notions in the eighteenth century. "The modern themes of an individual who lives, speaks, and works in accordance with the laws of an economics, a philosophy, and a biology, but who also, by a sort of internal torsion and overlapping, has acquired the right, through the interplay of those very laws, to know them, and to subject them to total clarification—all these themes so familiar to us today and linked to the existence of the human sciences were excluded by classical thought."[3]

The shift to a consciousness which makes problematic the world of nature, human institutions, and self has implications for social practices. Science became possible. A theological conception of salvation was secularized and the focus became people's work on earth. Ideologies of democratic states appeared as individuality was made into a political doctrine. Human cognition was the theme of the Enlightenment and undergirds the emergent belief in a mass schooling.

But to speak of the change in social consciousness as such is to accept a progressive view of humanity, defining modernity as a logical outcome of a search for enlightenment and a millennium. Foucault reminds us that the consciousness of modernity contains no notion of progress. The new discourses were related to social practice and issues of power. It is this part of a social history that needs to be accounted for in considering issues of a pedagogy.

KNOWLEDGE AS A TECHNOLOGY OF POWER

The new knowledge about society and "self" was also a technology by which power was articulated. Control by overt force was replaced by a power exercised through control over the patterns of communications. The battle of domination was no longer simply the relationship of rulers and ruled, dominators and dominated. Fixed in the rituals of the new social practices and the detailed procedures of civil law that imposed rights and obligations were fundamental issues of power. While claiming to temper and prevent the violence that would supposedly exist without their civilizing constraints, the new rules and obligations created finer differentiations of everyday behavior by objectively separating and ranking individuals.[4]

While Foucault focuses upon specific institutions such as prisons, madhouses, and hospitals, his concern is with the language of reform and the institutions in which the details of everyday life and individual biography are made potentially definable. Statistics of social affairs and psychologies of personal life made private problems into public problems of administrative scrutiny and control. There were penalties of time (lateness, absences), of activity (inattention, lack of enthusiasm), of behavior (disobedience), of speech (idle conversation, rudeness), of the body (correct attitudes, irregular gestures, lack of cleanliness), of sexuality (impurity, indecency). One needs only to consider the current educational language concerning students who are "at risk" to see the implications of these forms of control. Through a combination of hierarchical observations and normalizing judgments, all individuals become a potential category of observation and social administration. The most intimate behaviors and thoughts of individuals are made into objects that can be manipulated.

The human sciences emerge in this historical context as an element of institutional control.[5] The sciences were first situated in particular places, such as prisons and hospitals, in which new and more refined and operationalized discourses and practices were needed. The discourse of human science was later incorporated into the state as its power became more centralized and expansive. The administrative apparatus of government needed knowledge that was concrete, specific, and measurable in order to operate effectively. The gathering of information on the state's environment, its population, resources, and problems involved the development of a whole array of empirical methods. The new empiricism was planning, organizing, and monitoring social activities. History, geography, climatology, demography became crucial elements in a new complex of power and knowledge. The development of British empiricism was to assist in the administration of an empire; American sociology, economics, and political science were to provide expert advice to policymakers. Through the specification of the most detailed aspects of everyday behavior, it was believed that almost anything could be regulated.

The individual emerges in this context as an object of political and scientific concern. Power becomes invisible through rationalizations that make people into individuals who have visible attributes, qualities, and behaviors. Individualization shifts from identifying those at the top (such as in burial rituals and tomb art) to an individualization that focuses upon people at the bottom who can be surveyed, observed, and controlled. Individual biographies are seen as containing discrete characteristics that were open to scrutiny and manipulation. The child, patient, criminal are to be known in infinite detail. As Foucault suggests, the dossier replaces the epic.

Human needs were no longer conceived of as ends in themselves or as subjects of a philosophic discourse which sought to discover their theological origins or essential nature. The new type of rationality paid no attention to goals but to means that assumed the goals of the existing system. According to Foucault, state administrators expressed the issue of reform of human welfare and state intervention in terms of biological issues such as reproduction, disease, work, or education. Human needs were seen as instrumental and empirical, as the means to increase the state's and a civil elite's power.

The shift in social discourse was an element in fundamental changes of social practices. A deep restructuring of social sensibility and economic relations was taking place between the seventeenth and nineteenth centuries. While humanist discourse spoke about equality, fraternity, and liberty following the American and French Revolutions, a tighter discipline in manufacturing workshops, regimenting of vagabonds, increased police surveillance of every member of society produced at the same time a set of relations different from those expressed in the humanist philosophies. The rationality associated with Machiavelli becomes part of a discourse about social welfare, upbringing, education, and economy.

The development of mass education occurs within these dual conditions of an individuality as an acting subject and the technologies of administering and disciplining individuality. The patterns of school conduct not only were to make knowledge available. The sociologies of organization and psychologies of learning were conceived as problems of social control.[6] Methods of social administration were invented to order the thoughts, attitudes, emotions, and practices by which people were to think about their 'selves' and their participation in the world. As with the eighteenth-century humanist, the public rhetoric of schooling affirmed the noble myths of the age while the specific technologies of organizing teaching and learning reflected a merging of power with knowledge.

How can we summarize the preceding discussion about knowledge? First, the categories of knowledge found in schooling presupposed a fundamental shift in social consciousness and practice. Science, literature, philosophy, among others, were made possible by new conditions which made reflection and analytic thought possible. Second, the conditions represented not only new possibilities for considering human lives. Analytic knowledge also introduced technologies of control as the most minute and personal instances of social life were placed under scrutiny. Third, the human disciplines were central in the transformation in the manner by which power was exercised. The individual became a focus of administration and internalization of a new identity regulated by psychology. The problem of knowledge as a technology of power is a central political motif of contemporary discourse and social practice.

School Subject Matter: A Discourse of Power

In the previous section, the problem of knowledge was posed by locating issues of power in the shift in the nature of "cognition" between the classical era and modernity. That shift, it was argued, was related to changes in social practices, in the economy, and the formation of the modern state. A dual edge existed in these developments. The discourse that enabled people to make their worlds objects of scrutiny also imposed new forms of coercion and domination. That dual quality was captured in the concept of individuality. My intention in the previous discussion was to raise the issue of how we think of curriculum as a problem of knowledge. I now want to consider the relation of power and knowledge more directly by focusing upon the selection of a school text. The discussion is followed by a consideration of the reading of the school text through the patterns of social conduct in schooling.

THE PROBLEMATIC QUALITY OF WHAT IS BROUGHT INTO SCHOOLING

I begin with what might seem obvious and noncontroversial. Schools are places that deal with knowledge. By knowledge, I refer not only to the facts or contents that become part of the curriculum. Underlying the words and practices of curriculum are dispositions that have the potential to fashion and shape our consciousness. In fundamental ways, the practice of curriculum is mired in the problem of modernity. Words like "science," "social studies," and "literature" are part of a larger discourse in which people have sought to be reflective and analytic about their social conditions.

The forms of knowledge chosen in schooling have implications for issues of power and control. From Foucault, we understand that the structure that disciplines modern thought is not only about self-reflection and critical analysis. The rationalities of our social affairs are also technologies to direct, order, and control the formation of our subjectivities.

To consider the struggle of knowledge, we can focus upon the various occupations from which we select the content of schooling. From physics, chemistry, biology, and social sciences come concepts, generalizations, and methods of inquiry to consider the patterns of life. Literature, visual media, and the arts give reference to forms of expression and ways of appreciating culture and society. In general, the knowledge of curriculum is considered nonproblematic as discourse: educators assume the problem is to select the "right" order of concepts and generalizations and then develop appropriate strategies through instructional design and management systems.[7]

When we examine these fields of inquiry away from their curriculum definitions, we understand them as maintaining the central analytic tenets of knowledge posed by modernity; yet, at the same time there is conflict about the purpose, character, and limitations of knowledge. The conflict has reference to the underlying rules of order and patterns that define knowledge. While I want to explore this conflict as raising profound issues about the selection of school subject matter, I also want to argue that our contemporary conception of the knowledge of schooling has a different set of dynamics and social imperatives than those found in the practices of science, literature, and art. The imperatives of schooling are not to produce scientific knowledge or art but to present a codified knowledge that addresses problems of upbringing and labor.

SCIENCE AS STRUGGLES ABOUT THE INTERPRETATION

The distinction between the analytic perspectives of science and those of schooling can be illustrated in mathematics. We often think of mathematics as the most abstract and, in certain senses, the most philosophical of the sciences. It is also the field in which educators tend to think there is the greatest consensus about what should be taught in schools. Two recent debates, however, illustrate the difficulties of forming a consensus—and the issue of power as a text is created which can be brought into schools.

One debate in mathematics relates to questions of causation. An approach to scientific modeling assumes that precise predictability can be achieved through gathering and analyzing sufficient information. This view has been challenged by a discovery that simple deterministic systems with only a few elements can generate random behavior. The movement of water downstream, the flight of a baseball, or the movement of billiard balls illustrate seemingly random movements. Mathematical work has illustrated, however, that the randomness has an underlying geometric form, and therefore an order. The focus upon this paradox of randomness and order is called Chaos.

Mathematics implies new and fundamental limits on the ability to make predictions. Chaos brings a new challenge to the view that a system can be understood by breaking it down and studying each piece. In social science as well as physical sciences, a belief that one should study the constitutive elements of a system has dominated. This reductionism is no longer warranted. "Chaos demonstrates . . . that a system can have complicated behavior that emerges as a consequence of simple, nonlinear interaction of only a few components."[8] The process of verifying a physical theory, it is argued, becomes a delicate operation that relies on statistical and geometric properties rather than detailed prediction.

A second source of debate focuses upon the study of discrete mathematics. Until recently, calculus was *the* mathematics of science and technology. It was convenient and accurate to deal with matters of physical systems as if they had properties of continuous functions, thus making calculus the standard way of modeling physical laws. With the development of computers and the discipline of computer science, the world of applied mathematics has refocused upon discrete mathematics. Digital computers are discrete machines which function as though there is a specific set of points on the line rather than a continuous set of points. Instead of using differential equations, the digital machines have made it possible to find approximations of physical problems through the use of arithmetic. The growth of discrete mathematics is reflected in undergraduate education and in the production of textbooks.[9] Between 1983 and 1985, at least a dozen discrete texts were published and a larger number is expected in the next few years.

The conflict about the "nature" of the world is not only contained in mathematics; it is a condition of modern analytic thought. In biology, for example, there is no disagreement about whether evolution occurred. There is, however, "bloody warfare on the question of how it occurred."[10] The concept of power in political science has different nuances of meanings when one moves among paradigms within the field. C. Wright Mills, for example, drawing upon European sociology of knowledge, asked the question of "who rules" and found that there was an interlocking elite.[11] Robert Dahl, posed the same question from a behavioral tradition and located the multiple interest groups having the power to make policy.[12] Dahl concluded that no one group rules but society is pluralistic.

The illustrations raise at least three important considerations for our current deliberations about a general curriculum. First, the fields of sciences involve continual debate about the "nature" of the field, and by implication, how people should define, interpret, and challenge our understanding of the world around us. Second, science involves epistemic drift in which cognitive and methodological foci are strongly influenced by external as well as internal assessments of relevance.[13] Industrial, military, and government agendas are elements in the production of knowledge and organization of science. Third, what is brought into school as science or mathematics responds to competing social interests. The choice of discrete mathematics and calculus, for example, may have more to do with their functional character in the world of business and technology than any "pure" concern about the pursuit of knowledge. But what is given emphasis in curriculum is not straightforward: at points knowledge may be narrow and utilitarian in value. In other instances, such as in post-Sputnik science, the emphasis has been academic and elite-related. In either instance, curriculum responds to social values and dispositions in existing economic and political structures.

The issue of different assumptions and paths to understanding could be "just" an academic concern if it were not for the interpretation of the sciences and arts in the design of curriculum. The subject matter is recast into a form thought appropriate for schools. The social and political as well as cognitive issues that guide biology, psychology, or art are redefined as questions of children's thinking, stages of development, and issues of management. The redefinitions, I will argue in the following section, introduce technologies of control.

<h3 style="text-align:center">DECONTEXTUALIZATION OF SOCIAL EXPERIENCE
AS THE SCHOOL CURRICULUM</h3>

At one layer of analysis, we can indicate that our models of curriculum and teaching often fail to recognize that our discourses are dynamic in construction, multiple in interest, and value-laden. But the curriculum issue is not only one of representing conflict in the selection of content. Pedagogies substitute a discourse about knowledge production in science and the arts with a structure that relates to technologies of control and power. This occurs through a process by which curriculum decontextualizes the informal everyday experiences and communications found in other institutional contexts and refocuses these experiences as abstractions related to the conditions of schooling.[14]

We can illustrate the issue of decontextualization by contrasting the meaning of a commonsense language that talks about a child as "bad" or "not reading" into a discourse which speaks of a socially maladjusted, dyslexic, or a learning-disabled child. Commonsense language involves highly textured words that have little theoretical potency in relating particular behaviors to essential and long-term characteristics of an individual's success or failure. When the commonsense language is recast into a seemingly neutral, scientific discourse which contains hierarchical ordering, observation, and monitoring, the problem of the individual becomes institutional and subject to invisible patterns of control.

The procedures and performances of science, art, and literature are decontextualized in a similar manner as they enter the school. School subjects are seen as having logical consistency and psychological properties. The social dynamics of science or art are made into abstract, logical relations. The discipline-centered curriculum movement, for example, defined concepts as having fixed parameters for children to internalize.[15] It was assumed that concepts like evolution or political decision making are ideas that have a singular definition. Concepts and generalizations are to be mastered; the process of science is a series of steps, such as forming hypotheses or collecting data. Literature is defined as reading, comprehension, and decoding skills.

Social values are carried into teaching and teacher education through a complex pattern of institutional arrangements that relate power and knowledge. A shift in purpose and function between science and curriculum occurs as the concepts of science and art are crystallized in a manner that makes existing arrangements seem natural and inevitable. Consensus and stability are emphasized. Practice is made to seem devoid of human involvement and intent.

PEDAGOGY AS AN EXPRESSION OF SOCIAL INTEREST

In discussing the decontextualization of experience, we saw the curriculum focus as continually, if not explicitly, placing value upon an individual's ability to manipulate symbols. This type of activity, which we can call *mental work*, is not neutral. The value of mental work is related to the socialization patterns associated with professional segments of society.[16] Verbal facility, a tentative attitude toward knowledge, and interpersonal skills are paramount for the socialization of these strata. The "new" science and mathematics curriculum reforms of the 1960s and the contemporary concern with computer "literacy" illustrate this bias. The formal emphasis is upon a tentativeness of ideas and development of interpersonal skills. But curriculum reforms, publicly proclaimed to provide students with ways of thinking that could challenge their world by providing greater understanding, may in fact serve as part of the processes of social production for the professional expert in contemporary society. The resulting instruction may serve only a few.

The significance of the school text has implications not only for the knowledge given status but to the occupational structures legitimated by the knowledge. School textbooks make institutional arrangements and occupational divisions seem inevitable by positing information as "scientific." The definition of human work in social studies textbooks, for example, is formed around the division of labor found in industry.[17] The conception of labor is viewed as "natural" because it furthers the accumulation of capital. The view of labor and capital are made authoritative because the knowledge provided is thought to be produced scientifically by economists. The manner in which academic knowledge is positioned in school texts as certain functions to establish the professional expert as the modern arbiter of truth and salvation.

The emphasis on mental work has a double edge. It deemphasizes or gives a negative connotation to a polytechnical education. The latter focuses upon both mental and manual labor as social practices. Soviet educators, for example, define human labor as the mediating element between consciousness and the world. A leading Soviet pedagogical researcher, P. R. Atutov, described polytechnical education as "not only directed toward learning about the surrounding world but toward transforming one's surrounding."[18] While American debate about vocational education in the early 1900s had similar concerns to those expressed in polytechnical education, the curriculum debate was narrowed by the 1920s to economic or trade issues.

The emphasis on mental activities obscures the productive elements of manual labor and the ways in which professional (mental) work involves productive elements. As argued earlier, schooling maintains a conception of science, social science, or art as having formal logical or psychological properties. What is obscured are the ways in which concepts, generalizations, literature, or paintings are products of working communities and individual labor, located in particular social structures which sustain values and dispositions for interpreting our social affairs.

The reconceptualization of experience as a social bias can be seen in the histories of school subjects.[19] Social studies, biology, art, reading, among others, had little to do with classical notions of enlightenment and education. The function of the subjects was to respond to issues of industrialization, immigration, and socialization produced by the social transformation of the turn of the century. Mass schooling was to bring civility to those who came from foreign lands, primarily those of eastern and southern Europe. Students would learn to work in an urban environment and ameliorate their immediate surroundings by adopting the values of the democratic, corporate, and Protestant nation. Schooling was also seen as an instrument of progress. As part of the Enlightenment, human control over nature and moral excellence were thought to occur through development of the intellect.

The dominant concepts of "intellect," however, were infused with *particular* notions of civility, ethos of politeness, and norms of labor. School biology, art education, social studies, and early education, for example, were to provide moral values to those who did not have the appropriate ones. Biology was to teach children about hygiene and, in the 1930s, temperance with respect to alcohol and tobacco. The picture study movement from the late 1890s to the early 1920s was to illustrate good and moral character and God's handiwork in earthly practices. Schooling was also to prepare for an emerging middle class who would have a semileadership role in society. Some working classes and immigrant groups were taught art appreciation and certain aesthetic sensitivities. Strands of biology and mathematics focused upon a content necessary for college entrance.

The conflicting assumptions and social values in the worlds in which school subjects were invented are lost in contemporary schooling. Discourse about curriculum takes subjects as givens, considering neither the social interests which formed school categories nor the contradictions between the practices of curriculum construction and more general statements about school purposes.

PSYCHOLOGY AS A TECHNOLOGY OF SOCIAL CONTROL

Central to this decontextualization is the reliance on psychology. Psychology transforms the social imperative of schooling into problems that seem personal and concerned with issues of efficiency. This occurs through assumptions that science is concerned with functional questions and a view of individuals that has no reference to social conditions or history.

If we consider the relation of psychology and pedagogy historically, the problem of power can be further illuminated. The practices of psychology were created for purposes other than the understanding and transmission of mathematics, science, and the arts.[20] The history of American educational psychology involved the development of an academic discipline concerned with the successful adjustment of the individual to the environment. Psychology was to help mitigate the crisis of religion as late nineteenth-century theology confronted evolutionary theory. The development of psychology was also to disseminate and advance a practical knowledge in an emerging industrial nation. The practical concerns of psychology gave focus to a discourse about schooling which was functional in nature, objective in methods, and which transformed the moral, ethical, and cultural issues of knowledge into problems of individual differences.

Psychology was conceived not as a science but as a "professional tool" for school administrators.[21] It could provide a way to monitor and control the work of teachers and students. Edward L. Thorndike and G. Stanley Hall, among others, argued that the tasks of teaching and learning could be given to exact measurement, that such measurement was beyond the capacity of ordinary teachers, and that the formation of curriculum should be left in the hands of psychologists. These psychologists believed that they could act as an evolutionary elite who had sufficient knowledge and disinterest to bring about a better world through promoting institutional change.[22] Educational sciences need to be considered in this context. They make the technique of control and power invisible by focusing upon the visible qualities of individuals that can be administered through an examination of the most minute behaviors and innermost feelings.

The changing art curriculum during and following World War II illustrates this phenomenon.[23] The changes followed a more general shift in social thought. Fascism and democracy were seen as problems of psychology and therapy; a good society involved a mental health which schooling was to promote. In this context, art curricula focused upon particular definitions of freedom, autonomy, independence, and personal feeling that teachers were to monitor and direct in certain ways. The therapeutic orientation of the curriculum, however, concealed a potentially powerful form of social control. Children were defined as patients to be guided toward a functional relationship to existing social relations. Consensus, harmony, and adjustment rather than critique were central to mental health. The notion of a democratic individual shifted attention from concrete practices to attitudes and characteristics that produced a conception of individuality that was antidemocratic and illiberal.

To summarize, the selection of a school subject involves a transformation of human experience into a particular text that crystallizes institutional life and establishes power relations through the manner in which knowledge is codified. The formal structure of school subjects obscures the way in which social values are maintained and control exercised. The problem of seeking a general curriculum, from this perspective, is not only to identify what knowledge is worthwhile, but also to consider the nature of the discourse in which that question is initially posed.

Schooling as Different Social Texts:
Inequities of Classrooms

As the organization of school knowledge establishes a legitimacy to a social order, daily patterns introduce rules of the game which maintain and challenge that social order. The world of schooling contains the social differentiations found in the larger society. Social groupings, such as those of class, gender, religion, ethnicity, and race, interrelate to influence what is deemed normal, self-evident, and possible in schooling. The differentiated experiences are made nonproblematic in schooling, while at the same time establishing superior and inferior ontological status to different linguistic structures and perceptions. Social knowledge is made to seem universal and the processes of differentiation are seen as objective through such mechanisms as testing. The social processes of classroom interaction also mute the discourse of power as inequities are made to seem normal and failure is made to appear as personal.

The focus on the organization of everyday life enables us to consider the mundane transactions of schooling as "carriers" of linguistic conventions, dispositions, values, and experiences that involve issues of knowledge and power. The particular social knowledge of schooling not only gives status and priority to certain ways of organizing and interpreting our social worlds. The practices of schooling have an identity-bestowing quality that makes legitimate (or not) particular ways of defining oneself as a social participant. The sense of "self" achieved in schooling has implications for other institutions in which we participate. The processes of selection, emphasis, and omission in the social affairs of schooling help to merge objective structures with our subjectivities in producing conceptions of possibilities. The problem of a general, liberal curriculum, then, must confront the question of whose sense of social relevance is to be made plausible and reasonable through the everyday experiences of schooling.

DAY-TO-DAY SCHOOL LIFE AS CONTAINING DIFFERENT CURRICULA

A consideration of this second layer of knowledge requires that we focus upon schooling as containing different social forms. The ways in which ideas, social values, and control are considered are not the same for all students. Some students are taught that mathematics involves a personal playfulness with numbers, and that science has a tentativeness and skepticism toward the phenomena of the world.[24] For others, mathematics is a maze of facts, and science is a body of predefined tasks and facts. In these latter schools, the problem of teaching becomes mastery of the objects of knowledge; teacher's work is to order tests and provide practice to produce mastery learning. Instruction is concerned with certainty; the pedagogical task is "direct instruction." Another form of schooling organizes classes into fifty-minute subject-matter periods but there is little actual teaching of content. Rather than sustained attention to the teaching of reading skills or the learning of science content, the social interactions in classrooms stress that children lack appropriate moral values as a result of their improper upbringing and community disorganization.

These different expectations and demands are not based on objective achievements of children but are related to social criteria which define the possibilities of children in schools. The everyday transactions of schooling contain informal assessments about children's work that are based upon their social identities. The way that children speak about events in their homes influences teachers' judgments about intelligence and group placements—and can have substantial implications for further learning.[25] Taking standardized tests involves social negotiation in which social cues are provided in the test-taking situation to influence outcomes.[26] The cultural differences, however, are not uniform and automatic but operate "probabilistically in specific situations, becoming implicated in the production of children's failure . . . ."[27]

SOCIAL PRIORITIES IN EVERYDAY SCHOOLING

Certain dynamics that influence the differentiation of knowledge can be identified from social and cultural analyses of school conduct, such as class, race, religion, gender, and professional practices.[28] The way in which these elements influence classroom organization differs at any historical moment. The discussion here seeks, first, to recognize the need to give them priority in considering school curriculum, and, second, to recast further the question of a general curriculum as one of questions about knowledge and power.

While our commonsense understanding tends to see social class as important to schooling, the history of American thought has made class analysis a technical issue of social stratification or narrowed the terrain of debate to problems of social mobility.[29] One can locate a shift in debate between 1880 and 1920 from issues of class and religion to a concern about access to schools, identifying and fostering merit, and developing standardized procedures of assessment. The technologizing of debate was related to the professionalization of schooling in which more and more issues of schooling were defined as administrative problems. This technologizing of school discourse was furthered by "scientific" research which made class or race a constant rather than exploring the relational interactions of class with other dynamics of schooling.

But whatever the public rhetoric, examinations of schooling illustrate that class is a major issue of differentiation. Willis, for example, describes how English working-class boys confronted the structure of schooling in a manner that inverted manual skills over mental work, and in the process, celebrated patriarchy.[30] While working-class boys had a choice, those who valued manual labor tended to diffuse their resistance to political hegemony through a recreating of a patriarchal occupational culture. An exploration of the relation of curriculum, pedagogy, and pupil evaluation practices in five American schools illustrates the central relation to class differentiation.[31] Practices in working-class children's schools appropriated a mechanical and routine work; middle-class schools encouraged a bureaucratic relation to capital; children in affluent professional schools acquired linguistic, artistic, and scientific skills suitable for the professional middle class; and the school of the executive elite gave children the grammatical and mathematical vocabularies and rules that were suitable to the control of production.

Issues of class often interrelate with those of race. While nonwhite students are often given equal access to school subjects, the social processes contain expectations and demands that accept low academic achievement.[32] The social distinctions occur in the classroom in ways that are not consciously determined, but made plausible through a technical language of efficiency and administration. Studies of Native American classrooms, for example, illustrate that children are often in conflict with the forms of social etiquette and discourse found in schools. The indirectness of social control and the reluctance to make oneself conspicuous by displaying superior knowledge to others is in contrast to the discourse practices of schools.[33] Differences in speech patterns are not consciously maintained but are a subtle background assumption which places value on the social relationship. In a different study of Native American schools controlled by white school districts, the discourse of reform assumed that problems of equality and culture were procedurally defined. The focus on administrative issues, however, carried assumptions about community "pathology" and the function of schooling as a morally uplifting institution.[34]

The history of American schools also illustrates a central role of religion. American schools were built upon Protestant values of the eastern seaboard to the extent that a rival Catholic system developed to prevent the encroachment of values of church beliefs about upbringing.[35] The Protestant underpinnings of schools were recognized by the immigrants from Eastern and Southern Europe as their children sought to reconcile certain cosmopolitan values of American culture with their religious and cultural traditions.[36] The outcome was an accommodation with American Protestant and bourgeois notions of civility rather than an outright adoption.

Less obvious is the manner in which Protestant values about progress, change, and individuality have been incorporated into our conceptions of learning and models of reform.[37] Curriculum maintains a millennial outlook that is derived from the Protestant Reformation. A secular notion of salvation and perfection emphasizes a growing confidence in the power of people over their environment and ultimately their destiny. The reconceptualization of theology was a part of an emerging power of a bourgeoisie and a deepening liberalism in political thought. These theological notions underlie the faith in schooling and science that guides pedagogy.

The issue of gender poses a different issue of knowledge that interrelates with class, race, ethnicity, and religion. In subtle and nonsubtle ways, the organization of classrooms focuses upon distinctions between what boys and girls do. At a deeper level, the classroom maintains patriarchal relations that constitute a primary element in social formation in contemporary societies.[38] The same process of decontextualizing and recontextualizing discussed earlier occurs as gender relations reinforce the probability of occupational destiny and divisions in the organization of production.

The issue of gender, however, is not only one of learning by students but also of the social organization of teaching.[39] The transformation of teaching to a profession produced distinctions in autonomy between men and women, differences in salary and occupational advancement, and a rationalization of teaching that minimized teachers' control over their work. While the movement of women into teaching did provide an avenue of social mobility for women excluded from most occupations in the early 1800s, the organization of teachers was transformed by 1900 into technical and bureaucratic forms that deflected attention away from social issues.

In other words, what is posed as legitimate knowledge raises profound questions about what is valued as curriculum knowledge and whose knowledge it is. Feminist literature has argued that women's organization of social experience contains elements that are in contradiction to patriarchal knowledge but are important in a construction of a just and humane world.[40] Different ways of organizing social relations for learning can be found in the Jewish yeshiva in the European shtetl and in the Islamic madrasa.[41] Each tradition contained images of knowledge, community, and social relations different from those found in centers of learning in Euro-American societies. These examples do not exhaust the possibilities of the relation of social affairs to what is considered reasonable and rational, but point to the complexities of our assignment of reason and knowledge in a general curriculum. *To select self-consciously is at the same time to recognize a social location and value to that choice.*

WORK CULTURE AND PROFESSIONAL IDEOLOGIES

While our discussion has focused upon social affairs as introducing a differentiation in sensibilities and awareness, external social influences do not come into schooling without debate and conflict. The occupational life of teachers is a dynamic element in defining how a general curriculum is realized. Occupational ideologies and teacher cultures interrelate with social, cultural, and economic factors as a discipline of schooling is constructed.

The occupational culture of teachers can be viewed as involving "frame factors" by which teachers learn to be competent members of a social situation, including attributes of status, skill in mastering routine practical problems, and a shared view of the situation which makes members' actions predictable and regular.[42] The work of teachers, for example, tends to be based upon consideration of power and crowded conditions, in which intellectual concerns take a secondary position to issues of management and social control.[43] One can consider much of the current focus on teacher reasoning and teacher education as a way to produce greater cultural competence in the everyday working of schools rather than a concern with the social or intellectual quality of schooling.

Teaching is a response to an environment which involves the contradictory character of schooling. The school charter is to create homogeneity, yet provide for differentiation, to produce a meritocratic society, yet contribute to labor selection. It is to offer a contribution to upbringing that makes students socially responsible and personally autonomous. The contradictory demands produce coping strategies, such as recitation and direct teaching, and steering lessons toward some modal point regardless of whether children have understood the information being taught.

Teacher coping strategies are also formed in relation to administrative structures of control.[44] In one study, teachers were seen as trivializing course content and producing student disengagement from significant interaction as administrative rules and actions worked against teachers exploring their content knowledge. In a magnet school situation, an opposite reaction occurred as teachers developed a collective sense of mission. Teachers were able to sustain a more elaborate instructional program.

The issues of knowledge and power take on particular forms in each of the previously discussed transactions of everyday life in schooling. The practices are not necessarily formed as analytical judgments about what is worthwhile but as a response to issues located in conditions of social differentiation. In certain ways, the systems of thought, value, belief, and experience of schooling are implicated in larger issues of the constructions of a consciousness in a differentiated society. Children learn an identity in schooling and a manner to effect that identity in their social world. Class, race, gender, religion, and professional ideologies, it is argued, interrelated in the social organization of schooling in ways that establish systems of relevance that make individuals objects of control and manipulation.

Conclusions

A search for a common or general curriculum contains paradoxes and contradictions. On one hand, belief in a common curriculum resonates with our most cherished beliefs about the role of school in a just and equal society. But the problem of reform as a search for a "general curriculum" embeds us in a discourse that assumes there is something general and universal; that there is an appropriate formula or recipe by which to consider knowledge and social practice. Attention can be deflected from the formation of schooling as struggles among different social interests and the relation of knowledge and power. Debates about a common school and a general curriculum at the turn of the century did focus upon political issues related to social class and race. The moral and political commitment is narrowed in the current reforms when problems of knowledge are made into issues of effective selection.

This essay has focused upon the ways in which the form and content of contemporary schooling interrelate as a discipline of control and power. While the public rhetoric of schooling focuses upon the humanistic intent of education, the actual technologies of reform may serve to discipline the person and make that person an object of control. Standardization or defining a common core of curriculum may legitimate a view of a common school, ignoring how knowledge, competence, and achievement are derived from social criteria and have a strong relation to social determinants.

The issue of knowledge has been considered not as information but in a broad sense as that of the formation of consciousness. In pursuing the broader issue, I sought to illustrate a variety of questions that interrelate epistemology, ontology, and power with the organization of school experiences. I have also suggested that the discourse and social practices of pedagogy tend to function more as technologies of power than as that of enlightenment. The structural argument, however, does not preclude people reacting with detachment or revolt to the dominating forms of schooling. It does suggest, though, that the creation of agency is difficult.

This leads me to a final point. I realize that while posing the problem of a general curriculum in such a manner, I have not offered a solution to the humane quest that underlies mass schooling. At best, this essay can orient practices by considering the limitations of knowledge, and, in the process, making fragile the causality of history. Karl Mannheim best expressed this view of change when he spoke of people who believe they are free of social restraint as those who are most dominated. Possibility and choices in our institutional lives are contained in our poking holes in causality; and considering with humility the complexity of our socially constructed world.[45]

FOOTNOTES

1. The contradiction between the intent and practices of educational policy and social dreams is drawn in an essay by Ulf P. Lundgren, *Between Hope and Happening* (Geelong, Australia: Deakin University Press, 1983).

2. See, for example, Michel Foucault, *The Order of Things: An Archaeology of the Human Sciences* (New York: Vintage Books, 1973); idem, *Discipline and Punishment: The Birth of the Prison*, tr. A. Sheridan (New York: Vintage Books, 1979).

3. Foucault, *The Order of Things*, p. 312.

4. See Hubert L. Dreyfus and Paul Rabinow, *Michel Foucault: Beyond Structuralism and Hermeneutics*, 2d ed. (Chicago: University of Chicago Press, 1983), p. 20.

5. Thomas L. Haskell, *The Emergence of Professional Social Science: The American Social Science Association and the Nineteenth-Century Crisis of Authority* (Urbana, IL: University of Illinois Press, 1977); Philip Abrams, ed., *The Origins of British Sociology, 1834-1914* (Chicago: University of Chicago Press, 1968); Edward T. Silva and Sheila A. Slaughter, *Serving Power: The Making of the Academic Social Science Expert* (Westport, CT: Greenwood Press, 1984).

6. Barry M. Franklin, *Building the American Community: The School Curriculum and the Search for Social Control* (Philadelphia, PA: Falmer Press, 1986); Thomas S. Popkewitz, "Professionalization of Knowledge and Policy Legitimation: Social Science during the Formative Years of Schooling" (Paper presented at a symposium on

Professionalization, Swedish Colloquium of Advanced Study in Social Science, Uppsala, Sweden, May 1986); Tomas Englund, *Curriculum as a Political Problem: Changing Educational Conceptions, with Special Reference to Citizenship Education*, Uppsala Studies in Education 25 (Lund: Student Litteratur, 1986).

7. There is and has been debate about the meaning of curriculum. See Herbert M. Kliebard, *The Struggle for the American Curriculum*. (London: Routledge and Kegan Paul, 1986), and Franklin, *Building the American Community*. However, curriculum as management has come to dominate the administrative organization of schools.

8. James P. Crutchfield et al., "Chaos," *Scientific American* 255 (December 1986): 46-57.

9. Anthony Ralston, "Discrete Mathematics: The New Mathematics of Science," *American Scientist* 74 (November-December 1986): 611-618.

10. Richard Lewontin, "Darwin's Revolution," *New York Review of Books* 30 (June 16, 1983): 21-26. See also, idem, "The Corpse in the Elevator," *New York Review of Books* 29 (January 20, 1983): 34-37.

11. C. Wright Mills, *The Power Elite* (New York: Oxford University Press, 1956).

12. Robert A. Dahl, *Who Governs? Democracy and Power in an American City* (New Haven, CT: Yale University Press, 1961).

13. Aant Elzinga, "Research, Bureaucracy, and the Drift of Epistemic Criteria," in *The University System: The Public Policies of the Home of Scientists*, ed. Björn Wittrock and Aant Elzinga (Stockholm: Almqvist and Wiksell International, 1985), pp. 191-220.

14. Basil B. Bernstein, "Aspects of the Relation between Education and Production," in Basil B. Bernstein, *Class, Codes, and Control*, vol. 3, *Towards a Theory of Educational Transmissions*, 2d ed. (London: Routledge and Kegan Paul, 1977).

15. Michael W. Apple, "Community, Knowledge, and the Structure of the Disciplines," *Educational Forum* 37 (November 1972): 75-82; Thomas S. Popkewitz, "Latent Values of the Discipline-Centered Curriculum," *Theory and Research in Social Education* 5 (April 1977): 41-60. See also, idem, "Methods of Teacher Education and Cultural Codes," in *Preservice and In-service Education of Science Teachers*, ed. Pinchas Tamir (Rehovot, Israel: Ballaban Press, 1983).

16. Bernstein, *Class, Codes, and Control*; Alvin W. Gouldner, *The Future of the Intellectual and the Rise of the New Class* (New York: Seabury Press, 1979).

17. Popkewitz, "Latent Values of the Discipline-Centered Curriculum."

18. P. R. Atutov, "The Polytechnical Principle in Teaching Basic Science," in *Studying Teaching and Learning: Trends in Soviet and American Research*, ed. B. Robert Tabachnick, Thomas S. Popkewitz, and Beatrice B. Szekely (New York: Praeger Press, 1981). While the theoretical intent is noble, the actual function in Soviet schools may be to legitimate modern economic production, and thus be similar to the consequences of American vocational education.

19. Thomas S. Popkewitz, ed., *The Formation of School Subjects: The Struggle to Form an American Institution* (New York and London: Falmer Press, 1987).

20. John M. O'Donnell, *The Origins of Behaviorism: American Psychology, 1876-1920* (New York: New York University Press, 1985); Donald S. Napoli, *Architects of Adjustment: The History of the Psychological Profession in the United States* (Port Washington, NY: Kennikat Press, 1981).

21. Arthur Powell, *The Uncertain Profession: Harvard and the Search for Educational Authority* (Cambridge, MA: Harvard University Press, 1980).

22. Napoli, *Architects of Adjustment*; O'Donnell, *Origins of Behaviorism*.

23. Kerry Freedman, "Art Education and Changing Political Agendas: An Analysis of Curriculum Concerns of the 1940s and 1950s," *Studies in Art Education*, in press.

24. These different social contexts are discussed in Thomas S. Popkewitz, ed., *Change and Stability in Schooling: The Dual Quality of Educational Reform* (Geelong, Australia: Deakin University Press, 1983).

25. Elizabeth G. Cohen, "Design and Redesign of the Desegregated School: Problems of Status, Power, and Conflict," in *School Desegregation: Past, Present, and Future*, ed. Walter G. Stephan and Joe R. Feagin (New York: Plenum Press, 1980).

26. Aaron V. Cicourel et al., *Language Use and School Performance* (New York: Academic Press, 1974).

27. Frederick D. Erickson and Gary J. Bekker, "On Anthropology," in *Contributions of the Social Sciences to Educational Policy and Practice: 1965-1985*, ed. Jane Hannaway and Marlaine Lockheed (Berkeley, CA: McCutchan Publishing Corp., 1986), p. 174.

28. See, for example, Roger Dale, Geoff Eland, Ross Ferguson, and Madeleine MacDonald, eds., *Politics, Patriarchy, and Practice* (London: Falmer Press, 1981); Paul Willis, *Learning to Labor: How Working Class Kids Get Working Class Jobs* (Farnborough: Saxon House, 1977): Philip A. Cusick, *The Egalitarian Ideal and the American High School* (New York: Longman, 1983); Robert W. Connell, D. J. Ashenden, S. Kessler, G. W. Dowsett, *Making the Difference: Schools, Families, and Social Divisions* (Boston, MA: George Allen and Unwin, 1982).

29. See Ira Katznelson and Margaret Weir, *Schooling for All: Class, Race, and the Decline of the American Idea* (New York: Basic Books, 1986).

30. Willis, *Learning to Labor*.

31. Jean Anyon, "Social Class and the Hidden Curriculum of Work," *Journal of Education* 162 (Winter 1980): 67-92.

32. Carl A. Grant and Christine E. Sleeter, *After the School Bell Rings* (London and New York: Falmer Press, 1986).

33. Susan U. Phillips, *The Invisible Culture: Communications in Classrooms and Community on the Warm Springs Indian Reservation* (New York: Longman, 1982).

34. Thomas S. Popkewitz, "Reform as Political Discourse: A Case Study," *School Review* 84 (November 1976): 43-69.

35. For an excellent study of the interrelation of religious values of the denominational groups and the production of knowledge, see Peter McLaren's discussion of Catholic schools in Toronto in *Schooling as a Ritual Performance* (Boston: Routledge and Kegan Paul, 1986).

36. See Terry A. Cooney, *The Rise of the New York Intellectuals: Partisan Review and Its Circle* (Madison, WI: University of Wisconsin Press, 1986); Howard Brick, *Daniel Bell and the Decline of Intellectual Radicalism* (Madison, WI: University of Wisconsin Press, 1986).

37. See Thomas S. Popkewitz and Allan Pitman, "The Idea of Progress and the Legitimation of State Agendas: American Proposals for School Reform," *Curriculum and Teaching* 1, nos. 1, 2 (1986): 11-24.

38. Madeleine MacDonald, "Schooling and the Reproduction of Class and Gender Relations," in *Politics, Patriarchy, and Practice,* ed. Dale et al. See also, Kerreen M. Reiger, *The Disenchantment of the Home: Modernizing the Australian Family 1880-1940* (Melbourne: Oxford University Press, 1985); Mark Poster, *Critical Theory of the Family* (London: Pluto Press, 1978).

39. Michael W. Apple, "Gendered Teaching, Gendered Labor," and M. Ginsburg, "Reproduction, Contradiction and Conceptions of Professionalization: The Case of Preservice Teachers," in *Critical Studies in Teacher Education: Its Folklore, Theory, and Practice,* ed. Thomas S. Popkewitz (New York and London: Falmer Press, 1987). See

also Paul H. Mattingly, *The Classless Profession: American Schoolmen in the Nineteenth Century* (New York: New York University Press, 1975).

40. Carol Gilligan, *In a Different Voice: Psychological Theory and Women's Development* (Cambridge, MA: Harvard University Press, 1982).

41. Tomas Gerholm, "The Ethos of Higher Education Systems: A View from Anthropology," in *Disciplinary Perspectives on Higher Education and Research*, Report 37 (Stockholm: Group for the Study of Higher Education and Research Policy, University of Stockholm, 1987).

42. See Ulf P. Lundgren, *Model Analysis of Pedagogical Processes*, 2d ed. (Lund: CWK/Gleerup, 1981); Gunnar Handal and S. Vaage, "The Occupational Culture and Working Knowledge of Teachers" (Paper presented at the ISATT Conference, Leuven, 1986).

43. Philip W. Jackson, *Life in Classrooms* (New York: Holt, Rinehart and Winston, 1968).

44. See Linda M. McNeil, *Contradictions of Control: School Structure and School Knowledge* (New York: Routledge and Kegan Paul, 1986); idem, "Exit, Voice, and Community: Magnet Teachers' Responses to Standardization" (Paper given at the Annual Meeting of the American Educational Research Association, San Francisco, April 1986).

45. Karl Mannheim, *Ideology and Utopia: An Introduction to the Sociology of Knowledge* (New York: Harcourt, Brace, 1936).

Section Three
CULTURAL LITERACY AND
THE CURRICULUM

CHAPTER VI

The Place of the Human-Made World
in General Education

WILLIAM M. PLATER

Despite its title, this chapter considers the impact of the computer on general education because at this late date in the twentieth century computers have become both the dominant metaphor and the culminating symbol of the human-made. With apologies to those whose sensitivities are offended by the term "the computer," we easily grant these machines an individual, even personal, identity (as some specific computer that I may use at my desk) while preserving for them an abstract quality as well (as something like "the text" we consider in examining the impact of writing on knowledge). However, "the computer" implies nothing less in this essay than the current end product of the human-made world: physical and spectral. Its place in our discussion on general education may thus approach the ultimate function of the object as noun suggested by Jonathan Swift's playful discovery of a "universal language" in 1726.[1]

Given the economic (even cultural and national) stakes involved, we can ill afford to underestimate the impact of the technological imagination that permeates every facet of American life—an impact as great as that of the literacy revolution which Plato takes up in *The Republic*. In a particularly compelling reading of this still useful text, Eric Havelock has shown that Plato was assessing the fundamental changes literacy introduced into the relationship of the knower with the known, into the displacement of knowledge by information, into the reification of skills into techniques, and into the primacy of expectations and values in the uses of general education.[2]

There are many ways of relating Plato's concerns with those of our own generation. One is suggested by Abraham Moles who, nearly a quarter of a century ago, reflected on the philosophical importance of information theory—an area of inquiry clearly relevant to education, technology, and literacy. Scientific theories are useful to philosophy because from them universal concepts can be drawn. Information theory, Moles concludes, seems

to impose its point of view in a definitive way, making acceptable the picture of the universe given by the individual's perception with all its uncertainties; it concretely returns man to the material world. In this picture, man becomes the very condition of knowledge of the world, instead of becoming asymptotically eliminated as in the science of the nineteenth century—the science which saw in an immense thermodynamics, conceived by an omniscient being, the ultimate description of the universe.[3]

Enhanced by information theory, the computer—epitome of the human-made world—reorders our knowledge of ourselves by creating a system capable of the most complex manipulation of symbols imaginable.

If your imagination lags, as mine sometimes does, consider with the help of a ten-year-old the world George Lucas created in his *Star Wars* movie trilogy. Here, imagination takes form through special effects produced with the aid of a supercomputer, which in turn may become even more communicative (powerful) because of the role fantasy has played in conceiving a strategic defense initiative. Or consider the implications of computers being programmed to play chess with such sophistication that individual machines (for example, HITECH or CRAY BLITZ) have identifiable styles and even earn status as champion players along with their human counterparts. The chess-playing computers have begun to raise fundamental questions about distinctions between human and artificial intelligence, and it is likely that our understanding of those elements which are uniquely human will increasingly be defined by the criterion of stating what computers cannot do.[4]

Within the limits of our current understanding, there seem to be two significant reference points: Plato's announcement of a new order of knowing and the contemporary physicist's pronouncement that we cannot know anything for certain. In between—where most of us are—we may recall that great theories help us rediscover banal, though at times useful, facts and that old truths are set aside for new paradigms.

In his book on "the human use of human beings," Norbert Wiener said that "society can only be understood through a study of the messages and the communication facilities which belong to it." The purpose of cybernetics, as established by Wiener, is to develop the language and techniques for understanding communication, and by this Wiener meant the complete range of the most complex symbol system imaginable. He specified that "the process of receiving and of using information is the process of our adjusting to the contingencies of the outer environment, and of our living effectively within that environment."[5] By such a standard, education succeeds or fails to the degree that it meets the needs of the process of adjusting to a contingent world.

Wiener and Moles force us to consider the place of the human-made world in education, and thus in every other realm of human endeavor. The purposeful manipulation of symbols is now the essence of the human-made world, and the computer has altered forever our ability to process symbols. A teacher who works with students using computers but who is not familiar with at least some significant aspects of information theory should be considered—in this age—unprepared if not foolish.

Imagining Technology

Since Athens of the fourth century b.c. (and arguably earlier), the concept of general education—as a generative and prescriptive form of liberal education—has won a consistently secure place in the self-conscious, deliberate act of placing humankind in some knowable relationship to the discovered world of experience, both scientific and abstract. The centuries have been unusually kind to general education as a worthy goal, perhaps because it has been increasingly nonthreatening and is now almost to the point of boredom, despite the efforts of William Bennett, Alan Bloom, and others to resuscitate an interest in what appears to be an almost moribund, if benign, concept. Regardless, general education is still somehow *perceived* as important for economic survival and a mediated existence, perhaps principally because it has few nonpartisan critics.

The content of general education has evolved to reflect an expanding experiential domain, just as the ends of education have been changed from time to time to secure some presumed better world for posterity. However, the limits of general education, or its failures, as some would argue, have typically been political as well as historical and, consequently, known if not accepted. The contrast of the coherence of a perhaps elitist value system of general education with the heterogeneity of the student population that entered secondary schools and universities after World War II is but one example of an inherent limitation. Abruptly, the subjects of general education were found to be unequal to the expectations of students. This view of history is consistent with information theory, which postulates that history, as a function of information, may be totally recoverable. Not surprisingly, general education has been associated more and more with the process of revealing discoverable, though not necessarily human, truth. The ascendancy of science is but one manifestation of this phenomenon.

As a social process, general education teaches discovery by drawing upon the examples and the certainty of the past, which itself has been ordered and sorted so that especially significant examples can be preserved. Darwin's method can be taught. General education is thus both process and content and, by showing connection with the past while permitting incremental and evolutionary change, it has been an instrument of social stability. Knowledge is advanced, but only as an extension of the known. The paradigm shifts which Thomas Kuhn has described are not even special cases in education because nothing is lost even if it is changed. The old paradigm might be needed again.

Knowledge is self-limiting and cannot exceed the bounds of the way in which it is itself represented. Hence the importance of symbol systems and the relevance of information theory. Walter Ong has shown, more eloquently than others, that language itself sets the limits of the knowable. As he says in *Interfaces of the Word*, "Since writing came into existence, the evolution of the word and the evolution of consciousness have been intimately tied in with technologies and technological developments."[6]

With the accelerating accumulation of created rather than discovered knowledge, the special and temporal uses of general education change and make the familiar form, which seems to remain constant, subtly more potent in the short run. The human-created world, most conveniently thought of as technology itself, changes in surprising ways without a necessary relationship to eternal verities or incremental school learning.

With an ascendancy of technology, the purposes and means of education take precedence over content without ever displacing it. In his description of the knowledge machine (the first "computer") encountered by Gulliver in the Academy of Lagado, Jonathan Swift satirically relates how, in order to overcome the inconvenience of both language and knowledge, the professor would combine random, machine-generated fragments of meaning into "a complete body of all arts and sciences." His machine would thus eliminate the need for general education by removing its function of preserving what is known and discovering what is unknown by generating the knowable: "Every one knows how laborious the usual method is of attaining to arts and sciences; whereas by his contrivance the most ignorant person at a reasonable charge, and with a little bodily labor, may write books in philosophy, poetry, politics, law, mathematics, and theology, without the least assistance from genius or study."[7] Of the other inventions in the academy of speculative knowledge, only the invention of a "universal language," whereby people express themselves with "things" rather than words, might have more appeal for a Swiftian technocrat. Software for computer-assisted design and graphics permit us to communicate using objects which have no other physical reference beyond imagination and the computer's screen.

Before a knowledge machine could be satirized to its full effect, however, the idea of human-made knowledge—and a Newtonian clockwork universe—had to be assimilated into the processes of general education. Thus the persisting interest of Gulliver's tale. But long before the implications of Newtonian physics had made an impression, Europe had already been forced to come to terms with an early analog to Swift's machine, namely the printing press.

In addition to Gulliver, Swift gave us *The Battle of the Books* in 1704, which pits the ancient writers against the modern and ridicules the lengths to which educators can go in advancing their theories; it is still a useful reminder. And, of course, Laurence Sterne was well aware of the technology of the book when he finished *Tristram Shandy* in 1767. What irony is yet possible in the reader's relation to the virtual text of the cathode ray tube, especially if the reader can also be the writer?

Politics of Technology

There are many other colorful and similarly Swiftian illustrations of the human-made world's intrusion into the content and process of general education. Eric Havelock has said that in Plato's lament about poetry as a monopoly on training in citizenship—a fair definition of a principal aim of general education today—Plato is describing a "total technology of the preserved word.''[8] In contrasting written knowledge with the oral tradition of Homer (and others), Plato explained what is surely the chief characteristic of the human-made world: the separation of the knower from what is known, and thus the distinction of the subject (that is, the self) from the object which can be analyzed and evaluated. It is this distinction which so delighted Sterne in his toying with the reader's discomfort in being confronted with the separation from the text.

Plato favored rationalism and logic, the scientific method, the classification of experience, and the proper arrangement of cause and effect. Better than anyone else, he defined the place of the human-made world in general education. Of course, he also advanced a rationale for separating secondary and university levels of education. How many college catalogs still echo, without irony, the goals for general education which Plato set down so long ago.

If, as regards formal learning, we accept technology as a fair approximation of the "human-made," it is interesting to note that, according to the *Oxford English Dictionary*, the word "technology" was first used early in the seventeenth century to describe a systematic discourse on the arts and the terminology of the subject in particular. "Techne" is Greek for "art," as opposed to science, although both are systematic, analytic studies—one of the human-made and the other of the natural. Indeed, "techne" also is the Greek word for "skill." Although the "technology of grammar" would have been readily understood by Swift, rhetoricians have begun to rediscover technologies of grammar only very recently. In the mid-nineteeth century, "technology" came to stand for the practical arts and scientific or systematic study.

Accordingly, we can substitute "technique" for "skills" when discussing general education, because it refers expressly to the *manner of execution* of formal learning as distinct from the mastery of general concepts or principles. We find in the *Oxford English Dictionary* that Coleridge was one of the earliest users of this term when he spoke of "illogical phrases, which hold so distinguished a place in the *technique* of ordinary poetry.''

With such a putative tradition of technology's role in education, why the alarm over computers, on the one hand, and the headlong rush to embrace them, on the other? We seem to have absorbed completely the technology of printing—and all that Marshall McLuhan implied by his Gutenberg Galaxy—as a self-reflexive aspect of general education. And we seem to have made peace, uncomfortably perhaps, with the electronic media of telephone, television, and radio. Just as humankind was never called upon to study printing when coming to terms with the book, we are not likely to be expected to know "computing" when learning to use databases.

The point, of course, is that technology has been an essential component of general education since young men (and too much later, women) were educated for citizenship. Plato's position might even imply that without technology, which differentiates subject from object and thus makes rational analysis possible, there could be no general education. One reason the topic of "place" is so important in considering technology in general education is that every major advance in technology has been a major advance in the democratization of knowledge, that is, a much broader dissemination of what is known among a much larger community.

However, the dissemination process has itself been a dependent variable of education, especially of general education. Frequently, the learning process has been determined by the communication technology. Written language required literacy. Texts required libraries. Television required monitors (and, we are slowly learning, much more).

In all cases, the technology of communication and learning has been a means of access to knowledge. Learning has not changed with technological innovations as much as it has accreted: discourse supplemented by text extended by telecommunications. The contemporary classroom is a nearly complete diorama of the history of technology in education. When the computer is added, ironically including a system called PLATO (perhaps the first truly effective computer-assisted program of instruction, developed at the University of Illinois in the 1970s), the result is more than the sum of its parts.[9] The knower is not only separated from the known, but what is known—or can be known—becomes a function of the technology itself rather than an externally verifiable truth or the knowledge of the individual knower. Information becomes constant, and knowledge variable, in a literal sense.

If we recall that one of the traditional goals of general education—and perhaps its most noble—is citizenship, or some similar responsibility to the communal, rather than individual, use of learning, then the importance of understanding the function of technology, and specifically the computer, becomes critical. Access is not solely a matter of technique. Not only is literacy a prerequisite, but so is the book or the computer. Because knowledge is a variable, dependent on the act of using information, the computer makes the potential for abuses in learning greater than anything encountered thus far.

Consider, for example, information which exists only in an ephemeral state as a virtual text. As Swift so cleverly showed, technology increases the trivialization of knowledge by making it possible to substitute nonsense for discovered truth. But the goal for the general educational system is to make learning the means for knowing the difference.

Broken Necks

In the journey from Plato toward PLATO, few have captured the ambivalent place of the modern sensibility as well as Henry Adams or, except Sterne, taken as much pleasure in their own discomfort. Reflecting at the turn of the century on his own education, Adams looked into the face of technology with a (studied) naiveté that is no longer possible. We might feel a certain nostalgia when reading of Adams's trip to the Great Exposition of Paris in 1900, where he discovered that the dynamo, the engine of electricity, was "the symbol of infinity." Contemplating the computer some might even empathize with Adams's figurative collapse in the hall of engines, where he found himself lying "with his figurative neck broken by the sudden irruption of forces totally new."[10]

Electricity, of course, made the contemporary world possible and Adams's broken-neck paralysis is not unlike what many educators experience today as they look down the gallery of computers at large exhibition centers all over the country. Adams's preoccupation with the dynamo is helpful because it shows, in one sense, that he was wrong about the symbol. Generators have become as invisible as the electricity they generate, and we no longer pause to think about the motors which run our clocks, refrigerators, or compact disk players. Invisible but not infinite, not yet. We may be as self-conscious as Adams was about the dynamo, but in a decade or two, the computer *will* be as invisible as the dynamo. The forces, however, will be even more overwhelming than Adams imagined, especially if we think of information as the analog to electricity.

Always an educator, of himself and others, Adams concluded his self-reflexive education by postulating "the law of acceleration" that has become so familiar to us as we try to account for the rapidity of change in our own lifetimes. Adams predicted that the corresponding "style of education promised to be violently coercive."[11] If we recall that the forces are imperceptible and yet coercive, we have a fair prediction of the role and practice of general education in the United States today. It is largely a mode of education almost totally determined by technology rather than by discovered knowledge or truth, whether natural or divine. No wonder that educators are concerned about the role of television and computers in the curriculum. Far more than delivery systems, these media have the potential of becoming the content, or "technique," of general education.

We know no more about the twenty-first century than Adams did about the twentieth, even if he was, in his own way, probably right: ". . . every American who lived to the year 2000 would know how to control unlimited power. He would think in complexities unimaginable to an earlier mind."[12] Like Adams, we sense the relationship of knowledge to power, and like him we recognize a technology of relation.

It is into this highly self-conscious tradition that we must place the computer age and the converging electronic technologies predicted by Adams in his concept of a supersensual world. Although there are many vantage points from which we could look into the new gallery of wonders, three are especially important in education: information processing and symbolic computing; xerography and reproducible forms; telecommunications and other devices that accelerate temporal consciousness. These three together suffice for purposes of assessing the place of the human-made world in general education. Each requires a slightly different reckoning, but it is their convergence which is likely to determine the general education we will use on the American of 2000. And they converge in technique.

Technique

Elsewhere in this yearbook, there are several definitions of general education, all more or less right. But general education has one specific purpose, whose conditions were laid down by Plato when he wrestled with the first historically (that is, recorded) significant change in technology. The introduction of writing into education differentiated the components we still hold together under a rubric of general education. Because of Socrates' commitment to a technique, and a technology, which could be realized in a written form, Plato forever tied education to the social problems of the city-state and to the methodologies of separation (of theory from practice, or vice versa).

It took technology to create what we now regard as disciplines and, more recently, specializations. And it is through such sequencing, as Adams would call it, that we find ourselves at the brink of a new era.

In looking for corroborating evidence, we turn to the professions, the specialized users of knowledge, for a status report on the role of general education in society. Late in 1985, the engineering profession released a self-study titled *Engineering Education and Practice in the United States: Foundations of Our Techno-Economic Future*. The report indicates that general education is one key to the techno-economic future—which may be the *only* future—and appropriately, it recommends that "the curriculum must be expanded to include greater exposure to a variety of nontechnical subjects (humanities, economics, sociology) as well as work orientational skills and knowledge."[13] Two other of the twenty-three recommendations touch on general education in a similarly oblique fashion. And we wonder, what is a nontechnical subject?

Similarly, the American Association of Colleges of Nursing describes the essentials of education for nurses in late 1986. Even though the report reflects a much greater recognition of the fundamental role of liberal, or general, education than the parallel report on engineering, it too gives priority to technique. Nurses are to acquire an ability to "write, read, and speak English clearly and effectively in order to acquire knowledge, convey and discuss ideas, evaluate information, and think critically."[14] Seemingly, general education is the means to still higher ends. Similar reports from other associations repeat the essential sentiment.

As we sort out the subtleties of difference among knowledge, skills, and values, we must analyze the cultural ends of general education according to alternative systems of belief. Yet all of these analyses must inevitably return to the issues of technology and technique, the same issues that concerned Plato and his successors. The human-made world both generates the need for general education and prescribes its ends as a function of literacy—itself now a trendy topic of discussion.

There is a need for general education because the technologies of communication have their generative as well as prescriptive grammars. As both ends and means, general education is subtle and sufficient. Without the technologies there would be no perceived need for a common core of knowledge and the implementing skills because community and knowledge would be codeterminant. Technology makes it possible to expand both community and knowledge, which in turn permits the development of new technologies. The general education curriculum presumes mastery of a significant portion of the body of texts (knowledge) and skills, but skill (or technique) is the actual social end of education. It is, once again, the technology of relation.

Consequently, the fact that there is little agreement on the iteration of a common core of knowledge does not seriously affect our practice of general education because the skills are not content-determined. If anything, technique determines content. In its explicit linking of skills with a "techno-economic" future, *Engineering Education and Practice* is thus highly illustrative of the definition, practice, and purpose of general education: "Among the most important [advantages in promoting general education] is an improved facility for communication, both written and oral. In an era in which communicating information has become a major component of virtually all professional work, the possession of good communication skills is increasingly important for engineers."[15] And all other professionals, we might add.

General education is the foundation of professional education precisely because of these skills and not because of any aspiring engineer's or accountant's need for information about western civilization. We do not even have to agree on an iteration of the skills which comprise general education because literacy, in both the cultural and verbal senses, and communications are the irreducible minima of technology. This fact was at the heart of Plato's announcing the change in education, and it has been present at each major technical change in media ever since. But a new uncertainty is creeping into our formulations, and "information" invariably is added to—if it does not replace—"knowledge" as a code word for the content of general education.

While it is difficult to make pronouncements about the ultimate significance of events as they are unfolding—unless we are a Plato or Darwin or Henry Adams—there can be little doubt that this is an auspicious time. One consequence of the current revolution will surely be a further democratization of knowledge, similar to that which followed the widespread use of writing, printing, and telecommunications. Although television and related media have freed literacy from a dependency on reading, the massive effort to use television to emphasize the importance of literacy, especially among adults, also shows that reading has not yet been displaced.

The community of shared knowledge is expanded and diversified in sometimes surprising ways. The fact that visual information can be conveyed more efficiently—and effectively—than print will in time have its own impact when related technologies converge with television into a sensorium worthy of the complexities and power Adams imagined for his descendants in the year 2000. One of his inheritors, Thomas Pynchon, one of the most enigmatic and interesting novelists of the United States, explains through his fiction what it means to live in such an age. As he disappears from *Gravity's Rainbow*, the leading man, Tyrone Slothrop, thinks "M-maybe *it exists*. Maybe there *is* a Machine to take us away, take us completely, suck us out through the electrodes out of the skull 'n' into the Machine and live there forever . . . in a clean, honest, purified Electroworld."[16] It is interesting that we do not have to be concrete in feeling the palpable effects or the inevitability of the convergence. Expectation creates its own probable end.

But as technologies have the capacity to make information more widely available, access is more narrowly controlled: a paradox of the democratization of knowledge. Television reaches into virtually every home in the United States, but very few individuals have access to the transmission of information. Printing presses and writing in any form have posed similar dilemmas in the past. But the greater the capacity for democratization, the tighter the control; the more powerful or sophisticated the technology, the more distanced it seems to be from the user.

Once again, computers pose a special dilemma for social policy because control is a formal requirement of any software program, and thus a matter of intent. Even the seemingly democratic and participatory networking systems available to computer users are dependent on control as well as intent. If we accept as probable the emergence of self-programming computers through an aptly named "artificial" intelligence, then something equivalent to a value system will be required to make control decisions. The distance between knower and known thus itself becomes artificial, and a matter of probabilities.

In separating the knower from the known, writing inherently linked technology with control. In its written form, poetry inherently is purposefully limited communication. When the audience and the experience of knowledge were united in the performance of poetry, control and access were not recognizable issues. In widening the gulf between knower and known, the computer makes the issue of access and control paramount—and gives an unexpected meaning to Adams's prediction of a violently coercive style of learning for the late twentieth century.

At its root, this issue stems from the *representation* of knowledge. The abstract symbol system of writing ensured a stability for the representation of knowledge during the transition from an oral to a written society. But the computer changes the potential of the symbol system, and therein lies the revolutionary nature of the computer: for representation, for information, for knowledge, for democratization, for education.

The Familiar Technologies

In *The Universal Machine*, Pamela McCorduck assesses the importance and magnitude of change that computers are having on society and tries to solve the problem of the misnomer "computer." In her view, "universal machine" is a more fitting term to describe the instrument of the revolution now underway. It is a term Henry Adams would have recognized and appreciated, though Swift would probably have thought of it as a device for his "universal language." As is appropriate of irony, he would have been right—in a sense. She draws, of course, on Alan Turing's earlier concept of a universal computing machine in selecting her own name.[17] Even if McCorduck's term does not stick, it is a more accurate moniker for the technology unfolding around us.

Drawing on a concept advanced by Alan Newell and Herbert Simon, McCorduck makes the point that the computer is a *processor* of symbols and that it "has permitted an explanation, at a rather basic and scientific level, of what symbols are. The explanation goes beyond metaphor to theory, which is to say, it makes a scientific proposition about nature, empirically derived (and susceptible to empirical testing), that accounts for phenomena that would otherwise be inexplicable."[18] Simon and Newell's idea of a physical symbol system is as close as we could hope to come in describing an analog to Plato's world. Their description of the "universal machine" goes to the heart of any assessment of general education because computing is, finally, merely a form of symbolic behavior, and the explanation makes clear why computers are far more than mathematical instruments. New theories rediscover useful truths.

As a physical symbol system, the computer empowers other technologies, such as television or xerography. The photocopier has a role to play in our understanding of the status of general education not because of its physical capabilities, remarkable as they may be, but because of its redefining the individual's relationship with text-based knowledge. Until xerography, expertise depended on an individual's physical linkage with the subject of expertise, which usually meant the objects on library shelves. Now it is possible for an expert to photocopy whatever is needed to establish expertise and transport it, giving rise to the modern system of distributed research expertise (aided, of course, by the telephone, jet air travel, and, most recently, computer databases). Thus in the United States most of the major definitive textual editions of the works of major authors are completed at places where the original documents are not. The works of Charles Peirce, for example, are being edited at Indiana University-Purdue University at Indianapolis, though his papers are in vaults at Harvard and elsewhere.

Using a computer and laser printer, an individual can publish a text for a small or large group (without there ever being an original). The point is essentially social, not technological, because of the cost and control factors. Printing made large numbers of texts available at a comparatively low cost, enabling a democratization of knowledge and an enlargement of community. In the Gutenberg Galaxy, cost and scarcity controlled the process and extent of printing, effectively prescribing a common core of knowledge by standardization on specific texts and accepted truths. There has always been the potential of choice, but it has been limited by cost and by time. Now, however, an individual teacher can publish his or her own text by creating one or by modifying an existing text to reflect preconception or to incorporate changes and new discoveries. In either case, the traditional authority of an established canon is eroded if not destroyed. Education, even knowledge, can be shaped by expectation.

In its relationship to the knower, xerography has an antecedent in Homeric poetry—and the preliterate world so objectionable to Plato—in that learning took place by a technique of oral copying. Indeed, the highest virtue of learning in the preliterate world was copying since the only way to preserve and perpetuate learning was by memorizing and repeating the learned text. Copies also preserve the virtual texts of our Electroworld, as anyone would concede whose thoughts have been sucked forever into the lost regions of "the Machine" where the signpost "disk read error" is a reminder of what is there but cannot be seen, or read.

What meaning can a common core have when texts are virtual instead of perpetual? The text exists only as it is experienced, a phenomenon not unlike mimesis in poetry. Like the photocopier, the computer will thus help make the virtual text the norm in both its physical existence and its constantly changing condition. The power of publishing is transferred not only to the individual, but to almost *any* individual; cost can no longer serve as the control mechanism (instead of social policy, as it still is in most other countries) when photocopying is one of the cheapest social services available.

The 1976 copyright act recognizes this fact in its exacting restrictions, and it anticipates the inevitable charge-per-use economy of the twenty-first century. As photocopying is microprocessor-controlled and the copies are made from a virtual text instead of an original (even if the virtual text, the new "master," is a digitalized copy of a unique image), the cost of maintaining and using information can be shifted from the community to the individual, thus reordering the traditional concept of community-subsidized access to knowledge.

A significant portion of known information will be available on a per-item-cost through individual access—but at a real cost. The trade-off between access to more information and reduced access because of cost should be, and likely will be, a matter of conscious, deliberate social policy. In his last two years as president, Ronald Reagan proposed the elimination of a $132 million federal subsidy for library operating costs as a part of a general move toward privatization of public services.

In an article published in 1986, Herbert and Anita Schiller (economist and author of *Information and the Crisis Economy* and reference bibliographer at the University of California-San Diego, respectively) look at the subject of the library as emporium and suggest that the economic survival of libraries may well depend on fee-for-service operations. Technology, of course, makes it possible to bypass the library altogether, thus changing in a fundamental way the function of the library: "Accompanying the new electronic techniques is a new set of social arrangements. These, in conjunction with the pressure exerted by private interests and the current conservative fiscal policies, will introduce the mechanics of the marketplace into what has traditionally been an institution dedicated to circulating knowledge as a public good."[19] Predictably, the results are hardly responsive to the felt needs of academicians.

Already subscription databases and customer-defined information searches are economically viable both as a library subsidy service and as a for-profit private enterprise. It is unlikely that social function of the library will undergo a clear change at one precise time; the change will be gradual and influenced by changes in equipment, facilities, and software with consumer demand driving the services. Just as grocery stores charge for products using a universal bar code at the checkout station, libraries have the capability of charging for books on a per-use basis.

Despite the enormous implications of the information distribution systems made possible by the new technologies, the consequences for general education are greatest in redefining the relationship of knower to known. Television has similarly redefined the traditional relationship, although the content (even of serious documentaries or news programs) is so trivial that the real impact is still difficult to assess. But Howard Gardner and his colleagues have established, among other findings, that television has an impact among children in differentiating levels of reality and in retaining of information among children. Television tends to be "more of a self-contained experience" than book reading in that viewers have more difficulty in relating television events to external experiences, including temporal and spatial relationships.[20] As a more immediate and visually complex experience than reading, television viewing also tends to be less enduring (unless it is reinforced by repetition). It shares the limitation of preliterate technologies and societies. There are thus implications for general education in what is learned and how it is learned as society is conditioned to expect information in blocks of time with a minimum of causality or temporal contextuality—a tendency reinforced by much contemporary music where juxtaposition of information and reflected levels of reality depart radically from earlier musical forms, which tended to relate experience, causality, and real time.

We now read texts with our expectations conditioned at least in part by the temporal consciousness of electronic media. While Melville or Cooper may well belong in the common canon, both the rationale for their being there and the mode of presenting them has changed in the past forty years. They cannot be read as they were written since both authors relied on verbal description to involve the reader in the action by creating a sense of place. Hawthorne, however, seems almost to have anticipated the economy of television; his condensed emblematic language strikes a responsive, if not conditioned, chord, without painting verbal pictures of place and time. Hawthorne has also been rediscovered by theorists as a source to be mined for ready examples of reader-defined textuality and abstract meaning.

As with photocopying, television is empowered by its combination with the computer and a communication network through the telephone system. Experience thus far is perhaps trivial, but already the integrated use of these technologies for banking, merchandising, and other interactive economic transactions is predicting a new mode of our relating to social and economic services. The status of individuals within the social system will inevitably change. Learning as a democratic institution is, at root, an economic activity since an educated work force is mandatory; an educated citizenry has become a fringe benefit.

The new technologies will make possible new modes of teaching and learning, modes which inherently will make it easy for learners to acquire the skills they need to use the technologies effectively. The implications of this are staggering when we assume that our world has actually changed since the Greek Enlightenment, beyond the mere addition of technology. As Thomas Pynchon says in his novels, it is no accident that the formulas for entropy in information theory and physics look very much alike.

Whether considered in its liberal arts or its core curriculum guise, general education has also changed: as a body of knowledge, an orchestration of skills, and a system of values. As Jacques Ellul observed:

Ends and means can no longer be separated—they are interdependent, defined by each other—but it is always technique which supplies the means, whose power and thrust dominate the entire field of contemporary thought and life. Thus, if we want to assess accurately the problem of ethics today and guide the direction of research in ethics, it must be in the context of this growth of power and this universe of means. Here we must take our stand and not, as many are currently prone to do, in a universe of hypothetical ends.[21]

What, then, are the implications of "the universal machine" for general education? If we use Plato's attack on poetry and the oral sensibility as a cultural analog, we should first be aware of the magnitude of the change already under way without necessarily looking for exact parallels. Writing introduced communication and human interaction based on a physical symbol system. The system was well known and in use, principally for economic purposes, perhaps three centuries before Plato wrote *The Republic*. It takes a while for changes of the magnitude we are considering here to be fully recognized or known, which at the moment may be more evident in the potential of television than of computing.

As the knower was separated from the known in Plato's time because the text could exist independently from the experience of it, the universal machine makes possible another kind of separation in which the relationship between knower and known is relative. Because of such properties as speed, large capacity for storing information, exact and unforgiving recall, virtual texts and images, and potential for self-generation of new information (if not knowledge—artificial intelligence in computers is, after all, only a matter of time and there are expert, or intelligent, software systems capable of generating case-specific information), computers represent a wholly new way of experiencing knowledge. The experience of Plato should be illustrative.

In his curriculum, Plato sought to institutionalize scientific relationships and causality. As Eric Havelock has noted in discussing Plato's concept of the known, the philosopher uses the visible and invisible worlds to describe the known as a world, or system, in which abstractions and experience are related through integrating and interconnecting relationships: "So it is here, as he advances the notion of the known as a sum total of knowledge, that he is drawn also to stress that nonvisual and nonimagist condition, which dissolves the vividness of the story into a language which is wholly abstract."[22] A central thrust of Plato's innovation was to specify the nature of the relationship between knower and known with the objective of reducing uncertainty or relativism; this may be the principal function of the theory of the Forms.

On the other hand, the universal machine changes the relationship of knower and known by establishing a referential system which must be relativistic and uncertain. The specification of the relationship becomes as important as the known itself. Accordingly, when applied to general education, the development of the human-made world means that technique, or skill, emerges as the dominant element, taking precedence over knowledge and values. Because skills are so critical to any systematic use of knowledge (that is, the practice of a profession), the place of general education in the curriculum is assured—although technique is not necessarily bound by the content of the core curriculum or the values of a liberal arts education.

In essence, the universal machine introduces probability rather than certainty (of a discovered truth, whether natural or divine) as the mode of analysis, precisely because of its capacity as a physical symbol system. Knowledge must be a function of probability if the symbol system is open rather than closed—not unlike the state of learning implied by the uncertainty principle of quantum physics. The more we know about position the less we know about momentum, and vice versa. The act of observing affects the outcome of any precise knowledge we can have about a particle or about a fact. In specifying general education, the more certain we are about technique the less we are concerned with content.

In trying to explain the implications of the uncertainty principle in physics, Sir Arthur Eddington offered in the 1930s a classic explanation which works well for our purposes. He suggested that what we know or learn from experiments (or our experience of knowledge) is affected by our expectations. If an artist says that the literal shape of a human face is hidden in a block of marble and then proceeds to reveal it with hammer and chisel, the artist's own relationship—expectation—with the process of creating (or knowing) has found what is there. Another artist could find a wholly different shape in the same stone. What is found is a matter of probability rather than certainty.[23]

The most important consequence of the new technology—aside from emphasizing skills in a specific common core of knowledge—lies in recognizing that the biases or expectations of the observer, or knower, will play a more explicit, even determining, role in the learning process. Computers make it possible for a text to remain the same while constantly changing.

The implications of applying the uncertainty principle to the learning system have been explored by Thomas Pynchon, who has used print technology as his medium—and communications as his subject—in *The Crying of Lot 49*. It is a novel well worth rereading two decades after it was composed because, as readers who have experienced the technological changes Pynchon anticipated, we are now better able to understand the implications of the subject matter. The appropriately named heroine, Oedipa Mass, searches for a truth but discovers that her act of observing always interferes with any certainty at all.[24] The text, or common core of consensual knowledge, is changing, and relative to the seeker; the text is everywhere and it can be accessed at any point with an infinite set of alternative relationships. Significantly, it is *relationships* which can link all of the knowable world—what Plato thought of as the known—into a single physical symbol system. It is technique that Oedipa can master instead of truth or a system of all that is known.

The universal machine places its emphasis on the *relation* of individual to individual (or person to machine), not on an abstract core of knowledge or values. As Jacques Ellul has astutely observed, the educational premium lies with the communication and organizational skills so highly valued by professional training programs—the consumers of general education.

FOOTNOTES

1. Jonathan Swift, *Gulliver's Travels* (Cambridge: Riverside Press, 1960), pp. 150-1.

2. In recent years, Eric Havelock's 1963 *Preface to Plato* (Cambridge: Belknap Press, 1963) has become particularly useful in supporting such a reading of *The Republic*.

3. Abraham Moles, *Information Theory and Aesthetic Perception* (Urbana, IL: University of Illinois Press, 1968), p. 209.

4. Brad Leithauser, "A Reporter at Large: The Space of One Breath," *New Yorker*, 9 March 1987, pp. 41-73.

5. Norbert Wiener, *The Human Use of Human Beings* (New York: Avon Books, 1967), p. 25.

6. Walter Ong, *Interfaces of the Word: Studies in the Evolution of Consciousness and Culture* (Ithaca, NY: Cornell University Press, 1977), p. 42.

7. Swift, *Gulliver's Travels*, p. 148.

8. Havelock, *Preface to Plato*, p. 44.

9. PLATO is the acronym for Programmed Logic for Automatic Teaching Operation.

10. Henry Adams, *The Education of Henry Adams* (Boston: Houghton Mifflin Co., 1974), p. 382.

11. Ibid., p. 498.

12. Ibid., pp. 496-97.

13. National Research Council, *Engineering Education and Practice in the United States: Foundation of Our Techno-Economic Future* (Washington, DC: National Academy Press, 1985), p. 12.

14. American Association of Colleges of Nursing, *Essentials of College and University Education for Professional Nursing* (Washington, DC: American Association of Colleges of Nursing, 1986), p. 4.

15. National Research Council, *Engineering Education and Practice in the United States*, p. 69.

16. Thomas Pynchon, *Gravity's Rainbow* (New York: Viking Press, 1973), p. 699.

17. There are many interesting accounts of Alan Turing and his idea of a universal machine. Two books which treat Turing from different perspectives are: Andrew Hodges, *Alan Turing: The Enigma* (New York: Simon and Schuster, 1983) and Douglas Hofstadter and Daniel C. Dennett, *The Mind's I: Fantasies and Reflections on Self and Soul* (New York: Basic Books, 1981).

18. Pamela McCorduck, *The Universal Machine: Confessions of a Technological Optimist* (New York: McGraw-Hill, 1985), p. 76.

19. Anita R. Schiller and Herbert I. Schiller, "Commercializing Information: The Library as Emporium," *Nation*, 4 October 1986, p. 308.

20. Howard Gardner, *Art, Mind, and Brain: A Cognitive Approach to Creativity* (New York: Basic Books, 1982), p. 239.

21. Jacques Ellul, "The Power of Technique and the Ethics of Non-Power," in *The Myths of Information: Technology and Postindustrial Culture*, ed. Kathleen Woodward (Madison, WI: Coda Press, 1980).

22. Havelock, *Preface to Plato*, p. 229.

23. There are many different versions of Eddington's analogy. I have drawn on the account in John Gribbin's, *In Search of Schrödinger's Cat: Quantum Physics and Reality* (New York: Bantam Books, 1984).

24. Thomas Pynchon, *The Crying of Lot 49* (New York: Bantam Books, 1967).

CHAPTER VII

The Technological Society and the Concept of General Education

WILLIAM A. REID

The curriculum of schooling is a selection of forms and contents sustained by arguments connecting it to sources of justification found in social, cultural, political, economic, and religious conditions. When the newly independent states of the United States framed laws, they wrote that public education was needed for the preservation of democracy and the ideals of the Revolution. Curricula were devised and defended on the basis that they contributed to these goals. Such justificatory connections have, however, proven contradictory and paradoxical.[1] For example, it is claimed that democracy is fostered by common experience leading to social cohesion and patriotic commitment. At the same time, it is equally held that democracy requires nurturance of individuality to produce a nation of freethinking people who can, as Jefferson put it, "be enabled to know ambition under all its shapes, and prompt to exert their natural powers to defeat its purposes."[2] And even if this paradox could be resolved, a problem would still exist about how curriculum activities relate to outcomes of this sort. We have no firm evidence that flexible, interactive curricula produce independence of thought, plausible as that inference may seem. Indeed, Margaret Wolfenstein points out that the nonconformist French, ever ready to take to the barricades, experience one of the most rigid, transmission-type curriculums in the Western world.[3] We must conclude, therefore, that although arguments founded on the nature and development of society may be very effective in marshalling political and economic resources to sustain the curriculum of schooling, this does not mean that they are logically provable or defensible. *The work they do is rhetorical: they are persuasive rather than conclusive.*

This is the point we need to hold in mind as we approach curriculum questions arising·from our latest revolution, the one produced by modern technology, especially from those elements of it

115

that affect the gathering, storing, transmission, and analysis of information. Since this revolution is termed "technological," it provides the expectation that it can be understood on a scientific basis, thus permitting logical rather than merely persuasive links to be made to desirable forms of curriculum. I will argue here that this is not the case; that, in fact, as we examine the responses of various nations to the "technological revolution," we find differences that are to be explained in terms of the broader social context within which countries understand their past inheritance, their present status, and their future ambitions, as well as in terms of their traditional curriculum structures. Reasoned discussion about the future development of the curriculum of schooling, then, demands that we become self-conscious about this broader context and avoid the assumption that arguments based on appeals to technological advance can be simply "logical" or "obvious."

"General education" will enter these discussions as both "form" and "premise." Certain kinds of education, especially those offered in the lower secondary school, are typically described as "general" and arguments are mounted about why this should be the case.[4] On the other hand, "general education" is, in another guise, a formative idea in which are embedded notions of how people should relate to the societies in which they live and, as such, is a source of justification for curricular practice. In this respect, as in others, it parallels the concept of liberal education which also figures in curriculum discussion as both form and premise. As Sheldon Rothblatt points out,[5] it is of the essence of a liberal education that its forms are never settled since there lies at the core of the idea a debate about the part education should play in connecting the individual to society—with the implication that the character of liberal education is essentially determined by the set of issues around which that debate takes place.[6] For the case of general education (to which liberal education is related[7]), I would assert that four fundamental and related issues can be distinguished:

1. What kind of general mapping of knowledge should form the basis of the curriculum of schools?

2. At what point, and for whom, can contact with this map be considered to be complete?

3. What kind of a total human character should define the purpose of the curriculum process?

4. What balance should be struck between private and public goals in the transaction of the curriculum?

Let me comment briefly on each of these issues before considering how understanding of them may be affected by the advent of the "technological society." The key word in the first of them is "general." We are not here concerned with mappings of particular disciplines, arts, or practices (though this too may become an issue as goals of general education are pursued). The issue is how, for pedagogical purposes, do we understand the *total* map of knowledge and knowledge production? To state this question is not to claim that all programs which declare themselves to be devoted to goals of general education are guided by sophisticated epistemological models (indeed, a widely voiced criticism of much that passes for general education in American high schools is that it is informed by only the crudest of models or by no model at all), but simply to say that the mapping model will always be an issue.

Of course, any model with even a pretension to completeness or sophistication will produce curricula which are problematic in two ways: Will there be students for whom they are inaccessible? And how do we know when contact with them is sufficient? This is our second issue. The experience of the curriculum is seen as intrinsically desirable, but some will inevitably fail to engage with it and, just as inevitably, demands of occupations or specializations will at some point claim the time which could be devoted to general education. So how do we determine who should experience it and for how long? This question is rendered the more important because the curriculum of general education deals with knowledge as means as well as knowledge as end. This is to say that the content of the curriculum is important not just for its instrumental benefits (though these benefits will supply arguments for choosing the content) but because people who have had contact with it will, we anticipate, develop a particular kind of character that will be expressed not just in terms of traits, values, or attitudes desirable for the individual, but also in terms of civic virtues and participation. Here our third and fourth issues are conjoined. But again we note that general education does not inevitably produce virtuous individuals or virtuous citizens, nor does it necessarily have a clear idea of what such persons would be like. However, this issue too is one for debate wherever schools entertain provision of a curriculum of general education as part of their mission.

The Technological Society

As we search for justification for the present and future curricula of schools, we are confronted with the contention that the technological society is not only quantitatively but also qualitatively different from other kinds of society: that, although it may have been true in the past that the connection to be made between social context and curricular forms was unclear, a new situation has arisen wherein definable technical features of society have clear implications for the introduction to, or removal from, the curriculum of specific kinds of learning. First, it is suggested, modern technology is unique in that it is all pervasive; none of our activities, private or public, individual or collective, official or unofficial, can escape influence or regulation from some application of computers. Second, the claim is made that modern technology is unlike all previous technologies, which were founded on the production and application of energy, in that its strength lies in the generation and processing of information. Third, and perhaps most crucial, it is emphasized that technological advance is no longer functioning simply to extend human capacities: it is replacing them. How we use the nature of the "technological society" as a source of arguments for pursuing or not pursuing general education, or for seeing it as needing major or minor reappraisal, will depend on our reaction to this claim of qualitative difference. In all these ways technology is held to be an overriding source of curricular justification. Crudely, I will classify two contrasting kinds of response to this as stemming from "logistic" or "problematic" perspectives.[8]

The logistic perspective wants to see the world in terms of well-defined categories yielding measurable inputs to social decision making. It believes that solutions are found in extensions of knowledge of facts through the work of subject specialists or technical experts. Such aspirations have surfaced in the past only to run into trouble. Nineteenth-century utilitarians were ultimately thwarted by Hegelian philosophers and Bagehotian public policymakers who raised the imperatives of tradition above the calculus of current wants and resources.[9] But the computer age raises new possibilities for an "end of ideology" in favor of logistic determination of policy and planning, or, at the very least, it refurbishes logistic arguments as justifications for politically determined initiatives in controlling and directing public institutions such as schooling. And these become the more persuasive if the advent of an information-rich technology and the replacement of human decision makers and workers by machines can be represented as marking a break with the old society in which arguments for what should be taught in schools were fundamentally rhetorical. Progressively, it is claimed, we will be able to make better and better decisions on such issues as this as technical advance equips us with more information and improved information processing. Therefore logistic connections can and should be made between technological development and educational contents and forms. The job of the schools will be to produce skilled and specialized workers, as defined by the roles that machines create; to ensure that the workforce is "flexible" to allow for continuing technical advance, and to foster a favorable attitude toward technology which is seen as the guarantee of social ease and economic prosperity.

The problematic perspective, on the other hand, embraces a historically rooted rather than future-oriented conception of how society works. It does not see the possibility of an "end of ideology" through technical, political, or any other means and regards adaptation to change as something in which the whole society should play a part and not simply political leaders or professional experts. Whatever is new takes its place as part of the problem to be deliberated on. It has no claim to stand outside it. Thus, the problematic perspective denies discontinuity and places the impact of modern technologies within a continuing process of social evolution. It poses questions about how, where, and to what degree technology should be applied in human affairs. Pervasiveness is seen as having problematic rather than logistic implications. Must we take technology to be a reflection of rational, instrumental needs? Might it not, for example, be evidence of the rising power of new "defining technology" (a symbolic rather than rational term which we will shortly examine in more detail)?[10] Within such a perspective, changes in the way information is stored and processed are inseparable from wider political and cultural issues, and calls for more and more specialized expertise raise the problem of how the curriculum should act to provide initiation into common experience and civic responsibility just as much as the problem of how it can be planned to deliver instrumental skills. Thus, depending on the perspective adopted, the "facts" of the technological society can be made to sustain a variety of proposals about the kinds of curricula that schools should offer.

Arguments for General Education

The resolution of arguments about whether schools should continue to stress general education in technological societies depends, in a theoretical sense, on the relative weight to be given to grounds arising from logistic and problematic perspectives. It is, on the one hand, evident that technical advance creates a demand for particular skills and knowledge and that questions must be asked about how far schools should respond to such demands. However, the problematic perspective is less well examined and deserves attention because of the support it lends to claims for the preservation, in the face of technical change, of general education as the key mission of the public schools.

The technological society, we have argued, despite its apparently unique character, can be seen as quantitatively rather than qualitatively different from societies in other times and places. All societies have been technological. The cooperation implied in the idea of society, as opposed to a collection of individuals, centers on ways of mastering the environment by means of tools and artefacts. But technical mastery is not simply a matter of the invention and use of these: it also and crucially depends on processes of initiation into the cultural web[11] which determines who shall use them, on what occasion, for what purpose, and with what accompanying observances and rituals. A symbiosis exists between the beliefs and practices of a society and its significant artefacts. Thus, aspects of technology become invested with meaning over and above that which inheres in their instrumental utility. At one level they may become tokens of wealth and of the status of individuals and groups; at another they may carry a rich symbolism of how a society sees itself or what it aspires to. For example, clocks were highly valued in the Middle Ages in spite of their notorious inaccuracy and unreliability (later to be cured by the invention of the pendulum-based regulating mechanism). They constituted, it has been claimed, a "defining technology, . . . always available to serve as metaphor, example, model, or symbol."[12]

Within the problematic perspective, much that is claimed to be unique about the technological society is seen to partake of the nature of societies generally. It has always been the case that technologies have had the capacity, or indeed the propensity, for becoming commonplace. Weaving is an example of an ancient technology that was pervasive in its products and applications and, just like the computer technology of today, provided a widely shared pool of commonplaces for thinking about man and nature. In more recent times, factories, steam engines, and cars have intruded just as forcefully into our lives. The new is always striking, especially when it seems to bear a meaning over and above its technical utility.[13] Equally, it may be said, in the face of recent advances in information processing, that there never was a time when this too was not a key element in technology. The instance of the clock has been cited and others are not hard to find, from neolithic lunar observatories to the printing press and the telegraph. No artefact can perform its function in the absence of a database but, even beyond this, technological endeavor has frequently been devoted to the collection and display of information for which there is no obvious use. What is new about recent advances is that they raise in a real and immediate way questions of the order of: How much information is enough? What are the political implications of changes in methods of storing and supplying information?

Finally, what of the argument that the new technology is really new because it replaces human operators? Again, the translation from fantasy into reality of machines with quasi-human capacities forces upon us, with renewed vigor, questions which are, in fact, fundamental and persistent: What does it mean to be human? Can machines learn? Could they become self-replicating systems? For now, however, it remains the case that, though computers can perform intricate tasks at incredible speed, these are tasks they have been programmed to carry out by human agents, just as looms have been programmed for two centuries to produce patterns unaided and mills have turned their sails to the wind and adjusted their pitch without the miller's intervention. What is new is not the fact of machines performing skilled operations better than humans can, but the rapid and seemingly limitless extension of the areas where this can be done. Thus, in the problematic perspective, the "facts" of the case seem relative: technology is intrinsically pervasive; we have questions to think about in relation to the production and use of knowledge, but the basic issues are not new; there are fresh challenges to our view of ourselves and what is unique or commonplace about us, but these are matters that have always been wondered about. *The challenge to education is human as well as technical.*

Far from deriving from the fact of technological advance the conclusion that the curriculum of the school should be designed to engender positive attitudes to technology, arguments from the problematic perspective will lend support to programs that encourage critical appreciation of its role in society. They will point to the need to teach a wide range of methods for understanding cultures and cultural change. The widespread appearance of computers, video display units, robots, and remote control devices will raise the issue of whether, as materials for a curriculum, they are to be seen as pervasive or invasive. Are machines being invited into schools for their instrumental benefits or as a symbol of modernism and aspiration to status (the "defining technology")? Can we ask such questions or teach others to ask them when technology itself seems to be in control of the selection and presentation of the curriculum? The problematic perspective will claim that the urgent demands of the technological society can be handled only by people whose curriculum has taught them to recognize themselves as total personalities with virtues and responsibilities to be exercised in public as well as private domains. It will also urge that the demand for specialized curricula at the school level be looked at critically: that other considerations be entered into the argument when the need for technical expertise to be possessed by some people is translated into an abandonment of the curriculum of general education in favor of differentiated or sharply tracked curricula. The logistic argument has its force, but so do other types of arguments based on aims of equity, justice, and commonality of interest. The problematic view focuses attention back on the core issues of general education as I have defined them: on knowledge maps, on the curriculum as an inclusive rather than exclusive social device, on character as a goal of education, and on the experience of school as a preparation for citizenship. It allows that these issues may be seen in a fresh light as a result of technological advance, but it denies that such a development has diminished their fundamental importance in discussions on the curriculum of the school.

General Education in Modern Societies

I have so far examined the connections made between the character of the technological society and the form of the school curriculum in terms of arguments and justifications independent of the nature of the specific societies in which they are made. How such connections shape what is done in real school systems is, as I suggested at the outset, affected by the particular social contexts within which decision making occurs. For example, connections between the perceived need for technical experts and the structure and content of the curriculum will be mediated by political and cultural traditions which place greater or lesser emphasis on the importance of equality, or understand equality in different ways. Traditions of general education are more likely to be seen as relevant to the development of the technological society where there is a strong commitment to equal citizenship. A recent report from the state of Victoria, Australia, argues for an extension upwards into the post-sixteen age range of the general curriculum of the lower secondary school since, although continued prosperity will in future depend on the development of human resource skills . . ., technological advance could equally well result in the deskilling of a majority of the workforce and the concentration of high skills and power in a minority of highly educated workers.[14]

Similarly, arguments about educational policies are also mediated by the economic circumstances of nations. Economically successful countries such as the United States and Japan tend to ask, in the face of demands that the imperatives of technological development be reflected in the school curriculum, what this might mean for reaffirming traditional areas of learning that have been, it seems, the basis of past success. The U.S. Committee for Economic Development report, *Investing in Our Children: Business and the Public Schools*, concludes that the response of schools to the challenge of technology should be to work harder for a "common curriculum": "We believe . . . that all children . . . should know how to compute and reason mathematically, should understand the basics of science, and should have a common knowledge of history and literature."[15] Similarly, Wellington reports:

The school curricula in Japan are designed to give children a broad and basic knowledge which is necessary in order to grasp and enjoy a wide range of ideas and activities. In the field of science and technology, Japanese children are taught concepts, principles, and laws of basic science and mathematics, which are the basis of industrial technology. Computer technology is not yet considered to be part of the required "basic knowledge."[16]

In contrast, the relative economic decline of the United Kingdom has been interpreted as a consequence of the schools' excessive attachment to a general or liberal curriculum, and official policies have tended to emphasize the need for differentiation of curricula and for skill acquisition through contact with technological artefacts such as computers. Technical education has been reintroduced as a track in the lower secondary school, while such minor reforms to the public examination system as have been undertaken seem unlikely to result in an extension of general education much beyond the higher-achieving group at which it has been historically targeted. Skill-based and "prevocational" curricula are to be provided for lower achievers.[17]

Of course, the current structure of the curriculum in any country will reflect past as well as present experience. Within the problematic perspective these latest adjustments in response to technological change can be seen as yet a further extension of the problem-solving career of the curriculum of the school within national contexts. In the kinds of countries we have been discussing, the curricula of schools at the secondary level represent various kinds of development from the classical liberal curriculum of college preparatory schools of the nineteenth century, with admixtures of other traditions, principally the technical and the elementary. The problems to be solved through the course of this evolution were:

1. *How* to extend the curriculum to include new subjects such as science (in fact, how to accommodate a redrawing of the map of knowledge brought about by the technical and scientific advances of the nineteenth century),

2. *How* to make the curriculum available to wider sections of the population and, as part of that problem, how to relate it to the curriculum of the elementary school, and

3. *How* to enable the curriculum to serve the dual purpose of providing for a complete education for those not now proceeding to higher education and a preparatory course for those who will.

In the United States, a rapid evolution took place around the turn of the century which resulted in the establishment of a credit-based *equivalent* curriculum offering a choice of small components each having equal value from the point of view of successful completion of the program. This solution, as Ringer points out, yields "an amorphous structure" which "disguises realities of stratification."[18] Hence, while on the one hand it reflects a strong aspiration to fulfillment of general educational criteria (a potentially broad map of knowledge, participation for all, the civic focus of the comprehensive high school), on the other hand, it offers widespread opportunities for their circumvention.[19] It is the main charge of recent high-profile reports such as *A Nation at Risk*[20] that schools are failing to provide the appropriate general education that the technological era demands. The solution to this is seen as stronger intervention on the part of states to ensure that schools deliver on existing and widely understood interpretations of the form and meaning of general education. Appeals for intervention have met with a positive response and many states have taken legislative action to enforce reforms. As an example we may cite the Minnesota Plan which is based on the proposition that the "arrival of the postindustrial age and the advent of global economic competition have radically altered what students must learn" and urges that the usual six years of comprehensive secondary education in junior and senior high schools, with their multiplicity of courses and student tracking, should be phased out. Instead, all students should attend a four-year secondary school that concentrates on core academic subjects. Then they should have opportunities to specialize for two years.[21]

The plan asserts that improved *general* education is the way for schools to respond to technological development and that this can only be achieved by rendering the high school a good deal less "amorphous" than it traditionally has been.

Another kind of solution to the problems of developing a system of public secondary schooling was the *integrated* curriculum that emerged in many nations of Europe. In selective secondary schools, the time given to the study of the classics was reduced to make room for the new academic subjects on the knowledge map. In the postwar period, these schemes have been extended in countries such as Sweden to form the basis of the curriculum of a comprehensive secondary school enrolling all children between the ages of seven and sixteen. In terms of depth of study and academic commitment, this type of curricular structure remains truer to the educational spirit of its classical predecessor than the "equivalent" curriculum, and also resembles it in allowing little choice of curriculum to the student before the years corresponding to grades eleven and twelve. At that point, a number of specialist tracks become available, but the core studies of the main academic areas continue to be followed by all students. The Minnesota Plan suggests that some Americans believe that high schools should move in this direction. The drawback of the integrated curriculum is its lack of scope for adjustment to different types of student. Even in countries such as Sweden with relatively homogeneous populations, substantial numbers of students may be designated "remedial" to solve the problem of their failure to engage with the common curriculum.[22] Such a strategy, resulting in the exclusion of some students from a shared experience of the secondary curriculum, would offend against the basic assumptions of the U.S. school reform movement.

The third type of solution is the *alternative* curriculum adopted in England and, originally, in some of the older Dominions. This derives the curriculum of general education from a version of liberal education which held that its aims were to be achieved through the exercise of *faculties* rather than through contact with specific knowledge or knowledge-producing strategies. Thus, the new subjects could be accommodated in the curriculum by offering them as alternatives to the classics rather than as additions to them. This enduring formative idea was implanted in English schools in the late nineteenth century, before the belated attempt to create a national secondary school system on principles of general education through government regulations issued in 1904.[23] Subsequently, these principles have been permanently at risk through the persistence of the alternative curriculum for students in the equivalent of grades eleven and twelve, and through pressures of selection procedures for higher education which admit students directly to specialist academic and professional courses. Until 1951, the interests of general education were preserved in the eleven to fifteen age range in the selective secondary school through a certificate examination which required knowledge of a range of subjects to be demonstrated. After that date, single subjects could be offered and the way was open for specialist tracks to emerge in the lower secondary school. It was this tracked version of the general curriculum which was transmitted to comprehensive secondary schools when these began to be set up in the 1960s. Thus, proposals for differentiated curricula are inherently more likely to take root in English schools than they are in school systems in the United States or Scandinavia.

Equivalent, integrated, and alternative forms of curricular structure represent different kinds of compromise between general educational aims and such contrary demands as the preparation of specialists, the pursuit of academic excellence, the engagement of recalcitrant students, the provision of resources for disadvantaged groups, and so on. The equivalent system provides a capacious structure which can accommodate many interests with little overt conflict. However, because of its diversity, its mapping of knowledge is weak and diffuse and its attempt to provide general education open to subversion. The integrated curriculum embraces criteria of general education in an overt and controllable way, but at the cost of reduced ability to disguise its failures or to adapt to local and individual differences. The commitment of the alternative curriculum is to liberal rather than general education, insofar as liberal education is identified with the preparation of an elite. The ends of liberal education were served in the nineteenth century through detailed and rigorous study of academic subjects, and the notion of "alternatives" avoided the necessity for developing schooled forms of disciplinary knowledge ("subjects") which would be accessible to a broad population. Even in the selective secondary school there were problems about how far the liberal curriculum could become a general one. In the comprehensive school, it fails to engage the broad spectrum of students and is poorly placed to resist demands for curriculum differentiation or for learning dedicated to vocational preparation.[24]

Nations, we may conclude, preserve through the structure of the curriculum different accounts of who they are, what they feel to be the fundamental nature of society, and what future destiny they aspire to. It is these structures, together with the economic and social factors already referred to, that come into play as education systems confront the challenge of the technological society with varying consequences for the ways in which arguments about the forms of general education are formulated and acted upon.

The Technological Society and the Concept of General Education

Arguments from the "facts" of technological development, from political, social, and cultural traditions, from economic performance, and from the nature of preexisting curriculum structures combine in complex ways to shape proposals for the future of secondary education. In many advanced industrial nations adherence to goals of equality together with evidence of past economic success have led to suggestions for reform that are broadly supportive of school systems which see their main goal as being that of general education. Calls are made for such goals to be reaffirmed, or for general education to be extended to wider populations or higher grades. The futurist thrust of technical advance is, as far as the school system is concerned, filtered through a problematic perspective, leaving other parts of the culture— commerce, domestic artefacts, and the media—to bear the burden of signalling subscription to the "defining technology." But in spite of the futurist slant of the arguments, reaffirmation of support for general education is usually made in terms of historic understanding of what the forms of the general curriculum should be. *What look like reforms are often proposals for restoring the curriculum to the shape it would have had if already established goals were being met.* The writers of *A Nation at Risk* are, one feels, not far removed in spirit from the members of the Committee of Ten. But where, as in England, it is held that major change is required, the proposals are not for a problematically understood reformulation of general education, but for a logistically based redirection of education for many students away from general learning and toward specialized, skill-oriented instruction. Might not such movements become more widespread if arguments for the general curriculum fail to move beyond reaffirmation of old established aims and practices? Consideration of the four basic issues of general education to which I have referred suggests that in the technological society, different kinds of translation into form and structure in the curriculum than those which have served in the past are called for.

First of all, can we still reasonably work with knowledge maps that were drawn at the turn of the century? Reflecting the state of enquiry and technology at the time, these were defined by conceptions stressing the accumulation of facts, by textbooks as the medium of communication, and by the nature of universities as major knowledge-producing institutions. The development of information systems has now moved the priority away from mnemonic knowledge structures, away from static, literary modes of transmission, and away from the university as archetypal knowledge source as this function is spread by technical innovations through other types of institutions and beyond institutions to communities and individuals. All of this suggests that the future curriculum of general education should be geared much more to the exploration of knowledge for practical problem solving and less to knowledge acquisition in forms and sequences determined by early twentieth-century models.

Considerations of this kind serve to complicate solutions to the issue of "at what point and for whom can contact with (the new) map of knowledge be considered complete or sufficient?" The old knowledge mappings, encapsulated in textbook form, provided a framework within which curricula could be uniformly paced and offered criteria for marking the completion of stages and units. A more modern translation of general educational principles into curriculum might render the question of completion an individual rather than a collective one and force consideration of where else in school, apart from contact with a sequenced curriculum, the aspiration to shared initiatory experience could be realized.

The character which general education should produce also becomes a matter of reconsideration. Proposals for the reinforcement of the general curriculum tend to assume that sufficient reorientation can be brought about by the addition to the existing program of new subjects of study, for example, in the form of a "new basic" called "computer science."[25] How far will minor adjustments of this kind enable future citizens to face the social, cultural, and political challenges of the technological society? The challenge of widespread literacy and availability of books was not met by courses in typography and librarianship. Technology changes society in ways that are not made manifest by studies limited to appreciation of its operating systems.

And, finally, how does technology alter the way in which we might think about the balance of public and private goals for general education—and the relationship between them? The tendency of many technical innovations is to render public activity less necessary and make it easier for individuals to lead essentially private lives:

Micro-technology will make homes more and more self-sufficient; those activities which previously joined private with public concerns and provided the grounds for the growth of personal knowledge—entertainment, politics, travel, sports, shopping—are beginning to be confined to the home or to be transacted through impersonal institutions. The concomitant danger is loss of public consciousness and public interest so that the individual becomes a prey to manipulations, and communities become politically incapable of responding to needs and threats.[26]

If the "public" role of the public common schools is to be preserved as part of their essential character as deliverers of general education, then their nature as institutions and the way they relate as institutions to publics and to public issues will need to be reexamined. Though, as we have seen, the roots of general education are still strong, the forms of its realization in the curriculum may need to undergo serious reappraisal if it is not, in the longer run, to be displaced by more logistically inspired interpretations of the educational requirements of the technological society.

Conclusion

"Technological society" has become a dominant conception for thinking about education. Examination of two contrasting interpretations of the impact of technology—the logistic and the problematic— shows that the "facts" of the technological society can be construed in different ways with different consequences for how we think about schools and curriculums. In specific instances, decisions of these matters are influenced by political and cultural traditions, economic circumstances, and the nature of existing curriculum structures. In many cases, the initial reaction to consideration of the effects of new technology has been to call for a strengthening of general education in the compulsory secondary school through reaffirmation of established forms and structures. In others, new technology has become a source of logistic arguments for sacrificing general education goals to specialization and vocationalism. But in most cases, it seems, whether policies have favored general education or not, there has been a tightening of control over the curriculum with movement toward standardization of programs and more detailed accountability. This stems from perception of a direct causal link between schooling and economic performance as the speed of technological advance has made nations more aware of international competition for markets and focused attention on yields from investment as a criterion for decision making. Thus, calls for the reinforcement of general education are taking place in circumstances where new thinking on how it might be reshaped to meet technological demands is discouraged and system responses are determined by institutional structures laid down to meet very different conditions. Unless this reinterpretation can be made, general education will, in the longer run, be at risk from the logistic arguments of which the technological society is so fertile a seedbed.

FOOTNOTES

1. See Eva T. H. Brann, *Paradoxes of Education in a Republic* (Chicago: University of Chicago Press, 1979).

2. Quoted in Brann, *Paradoxes of Education in a Republic*, p. 40.

3. Margaret Wolfenstein, "French Parents Take Their Children to the Park," in *Childhood in Contemporary Cultures*, ed. Margaret Mead and Margaret Wolfenstein (Chicago: University of Chicago Press, 1955), pp. 99–117.

4. Adler, for example, argues this point for American high schools. See Mortimer J. Adler, *The Paideia Proposal* (New York: Macmillan, 1982).

5. Sheldon Rothblatt, *Tradition and Change in English Liberal Education* (London: Faber, 1976).

6. Richard McKeon, "The Battle of the Books," in *The Knowledge Most Worth Having*, ed. Wayne C. Booth (Chicago: University of Chicago Press, 1967).

7. "The heart of the problem of a general education is the continuance of the liberal and humane tradition." See Harvard University, Committee on the Objectives of Education in a Free Society, *General Education in a Free Society: Report of the Harvard Committee* (Cambridge, MA: Harvard University Press, 1945), p. viii.

8. The terms are borrowed, with some modification, from Richard McKeon, "Philosophy and Action," *Ethics* 62 (1952): 79–100.

9. John Bowle, *Politics and Opinion in the 19th Century* (London: Cape, 1954).

10. For the idea of a "defining technology," see J. D. Bolter, *Turing's Man: Western Culture in the Computer Age* (Chapel Hill, NC: University of North Carolina Press, 1984).

11. I owe this term to David Hamilton.

12. Bolter, *Turing's Man*, p. 11.

13. In this connection we have to remind ourselves that the curriculum itself is a technology.

14. Victoria Ministry of Education, *Ministerial Review of Post-Compulsory Schooling: Discussion Paper* (Melbourne: Ministerial Review, 1984), p. 6.

15. Committee for Economic Development, *Investing in Our Children: Business and the Public Schools* (New York: Committee for Economic Development, 1985), p. 21.

16. J. J. Wellington, "Skills for the Future? The Language of Vocational Education and the Needs of Technology" in *Skills and Vocationalism*, ed. Maurice Holt (Milton Keynes: Open University Press, forthcoming).

17. See William A. Reid and Maurice Holt, "Structure and Ideology in Upper Secondary Education" in *Education and Society Today*, ed. Anthony Hartnett and Michael Naish (Lewes: Falmer Press, 1986). The development of the curriculum of general education in the English secondary school is traced in William A. Reid and Jane L. Filby, *The Sixth: An Essay in Education and Democracy* (Lewes: Falmer Press, 1982).

18. Fritz K. Ringer, *Education and Society in Modern Europe* (Bloomington, IN: Indiana University Press, 1979), p. 258.

19. See, for example, Arthur G. Powell, Eleanor Farrar, and David K. Cohen, *The Shopping Mall High School* (Boston: Houghton Mifflin, 1985).

20. National Commission on Excellence in Education, *A Nation at Risk: The Imperative for Educational Reform* (Washington, DC: U.S. Government Printing Office, 1983).

21. Paul Berman, "The Next Step: The Minnesota Plan," *Phi Delta Kappan* 67 (November 1985): 188.

22. Daniel Kallós and Ulf P. Lundgren, "Lessons from a Comprehensive School System for Curriculum Theory and Research," *Journal of Curriculum Studies* 9 (May 1977): 3-20.

23. Reid and Filby, *The Sixth: An Essay in Education and Democracy*, chap. 5.

24. These features of the various curriculum structures are reflected in the findings of the IEA Mathematics Studies. For comment on the mathematics curriculum in England, see Committee of Inquiry into the Teaching of Mathematics in Schools, *Mathematics Counts* (London: HMSO, 1982).

25. National Commission on Excellence in Education, *A Nation at Risk*.

26. Roland Meighan and William Reid, "How Will the 'New Technology' Change the Curriculum?" *Journal of Curriculum Studies* 14 (October-December 1982): 358.

CHAPTER VIII

The Arts and Physical Education in General Education: A Canonical Interpretation

ARTHUR D. EFLAND

Questions about the content and purpose of general education typically begin with the assumption that language and mathematics are the basic necessities of the curriculum. Only when these have been mastered do issues arise about the relative importance of the other subjects: the sciences, the arts, social studies, vocational and physical education. In this chapter I am concerned with the ways educational priorities get established with particular emphasis on the teaching of music, art, and physical education, subjects not usually accorded high priority.

I will argue that general education is influenced by *canons* and that the history of recent curriculum movements is one that demonstrates how the priorities of socially influential groups affected the arts and physical education. The movements to be surveyed include those based on the "structure of the disciplines" of the 1960s and on the "accountability" movement of the 1970s. I conclude with some comments on the roles these subjects play in the overall maintenance of balance in the curriculum.

Canons as Institutional Realities

In its original sense a canon is a body of church law, or an officially accepted list of books, a *Bible*. A canon is an authoritative rule by which things and people are judged. It is canonical that in most secondary schools verbal and mathematical studies are required while the arts are electives.

Inquiry into the nature of educational canons is part of a larger inquiry into the social and institutional forces shaping any conception of general education. Here the object is to see whether the policies that have guided recent curriculum reform movements might be comprehended as the partisan expression of particular social groups, and if so, to assess the consequences for general education as a whole.

I will deal with the influence of the scientific community upon the curriculum especially in the late 1950s and early 1960s. In this period, as Popkewitz, Pitman, and Barry have noted:

> The idealized view of science was incorporated into a new curriculum which emphasized disinterested and consensually based practice in which procedures of research were emphasized. The subject matter of the curriculum was to be the scientific disciplines. The new curriculum was not only to provide the knowledge of the professions but was to include the methods of arguing, thinking, and "seeing" the world that were thought to be contained in these disciplined endeavors.[1]

The influence wielded by the scientific community gave the curriculum reform movement of the early 1960s its unique character. In what follows I review some of its history.[2]

Discipline-Centered Curricula of the 1960s

In the decade following World War II, agitation over the quality of schooling had increased. The Cooperative Research Program was established in 1954 in response to these growing concerns. Then, in 1957, the Soviet Union launched the first artificial satellite. Cremin described the "pedagogical soul-searching" that ensued, quoting, among others, Admiral Hyman Rickover, who wrote:

> None of us is without guilt, but now that the people have awakened to the need for reform, I doubt whether reams of propaganda pamphlets, endless reiteration that all is well with our schools, or even pressure tactics will again fool the American people into believing that education can safely be left to the professional educators.[3]

The legislation which followed Sputnik, the National Defense Education Act, emphasized the improvement of mathematics and science teaching. The curriculum initiatives spurred by these congressional acts made use of scholars in the sciences and mathematics to determine instructional content, a practice which underscored the point that the public had lost its faith in professional educators. Bruner put a positive light on this practice when he said that the ideas for the curriculum were to be obtained from "the best minds in any particular discipline. . . . [O]nly by the use of our best minds in devising curricula will we bring the fruits of scholarship and wisdom to the student just beginning his studies."[4] But, in effect,

Rickover's assertion carried the day—education had become too important to be left to educators. Having the scientist and mathematician identify content made sense, for in the 1950s scientists were cultural heroes. They had, after all, shattered the atom and built the bomb which ended the War. Nuclear technology had then promised an unlimited supply of cheap energy. Why should not their intellectual prowess be used to reform the schools?

It was in Bruner's *The Process of Education* that most educators discovered the term "structure of the discipline." The book reported on the Woods Hole Conference which reviewed the reforms in mathematics and science education underway in 1959. The conference was sponsored by a number of groups including the National Academy of Sciences, the American Association for the Advancement of Science, the Carnegie Corporation, and the National Science Foundation (NSF) with funding provided by the NSF, the U.S. Office of Education, the Air Force, and the Rand Corporation.[5] What was lost on that generation of Bruner's readers was this unprecedented blend of federal agencies, private foundations, science organizations, and the military which loaned support to the direction of the new reforms favoring the disciplines. The underlying motive was to improve national defense, a task to be accomplished by no less than a fundamental reform of general education itself. But, though defense was the ostensive reason for the reforms, the long-term benefits were then felt to be inherently worthwhile and long overdue. Few would have regarded the movement as a partisan expression of the "military-industrial complex."

In the late 1950s social power was located in the defense establishment and industries developing the weapons technology to make nuclear deterrence feasible. Public concern over our defensive capabilities empowered this group with monetary and material resources, causing them to have impact upon broad areas of social policy including education. Power was wielded by federal agencies by way of incentives (grants to curriculum developers and schools) which influenced school authorities responsible for educational policy. School teachers and college professors worked on proposals for curriculum development and implementation grants. Prestige accompanied the awarding of such grants, and the emphasis within general education changed, raising the fortunes of science and mathematics.

The scientific community recommended changes in curriculum content and organization and many scientists served as consultants on curriculum development projects. The recommendations of these projects were regarded as unbiased and impartial, and not involved with such temporal matters as national defense. In Popkewitz's characteristic term, these scientists provided a "symbolic canopy" projecting the image of science as an objective and unbiased producer of new knowledge.

As the disciplines became the focus of curriculum reform, a hierarchy was established elevating some studies to the status of disciplines. Others not so designated were relegated to the status of mere subjects. As Philip Phenix asserted, "*all* curriculum content should be drawn from the disciplines, or, to put it another way, . . . *only* knowledge contained in the disciplines is appropriate to the curriculum."[6] In this new environment such subjects as the arts and physical education either had to become disciplines or lose their legitimacy.

By 1961 the canonical nature of the "disciplines" was clear. For example, in his *On Knowing: Essays for the Left Hand*, Bruner speculated that structures of knowledge similar to those of science might be found in the social studies and humanities, demonstrating the prospect that any field might profit from the approach pioneered in the physical sciences. Later, his *Toward a Theory of Instruction* described the social studies program known as *Man: A Course of Study*, an example of a curriculum organized around concepts drawn from such diverse disciplines as linguistics, anthropology, economics, and sociology.[7]

How the Arts and Physical Education Became Disciplines

By 1963 a number of events began to occur which set the stage for testing the universality of the assumption that a discipline-based approach could be brought to the arts. During the brief period of the Kennedy presidency, support of the arts became a matter of public concern. August Heckscher served as special consultant on the arts for the White House in the period between March 1962 and May 1963, with his principle task being that of preparing a report entitled *The Arts and the National Government* (1963).[8] The report dealt with all aspects of federal support for the arts, and for education recommended support in the form of assistance similar to that given to modern languages, mathematics, and science. It discussed facilities, equipment, teacher training, and the possibility of scholarship and fellowship programs for teachers. The will to do something for the arts in general education had materialized. At issue was the question of the form it was to assume.

In the following year the answer was forthcoming. In 1964 the Panel on Educational Research and Development of the President's Science Advisory Committee expressed concern "with the lack of balance in federal assistance to the arts as compared to science" and suggested that "curriculum reform, as it had developed in science education, could be applied to education in the arts." Music was the first of the arts to adopt this approach, in an event known as the Yale Seminar on Music Education.[9]

DEVELOPMENTS IN MUSIC EDUCATION

The Yale Seminar on Music Education took place in April 1963 and was directed by Claude V. Palisca, a musicologist teaching at the Yale School of Music. Jerrold R. Zacharias is credited with instigating this "seminal event."[10] Zacharias had earlier served as an advisor to Bruner as the latter prepared his report on the Woods Hole Conference. Those invited to attend included composers, performers, musicologists, music critics, and college faculty. Professional music educators were not invited.

Palisca's conference report suggests the extent to which these professional scholars were beguiled by the model of curriculum reform provided by science education.

The music class must be recognized as a laboratory whose purpose is to teach by means of physical exposure to music and experimentation with the making of music. The classroom should not be a museum which merely preserves and disseminates correct facts and attitudes.[11]

This conference assailed the preponderant emphasis upon group instruction and performance and it attacked the musical repertoire used in most school systems as being of "appalling quality, representing little of the heritage of significant music." It noted that "the classics of Western music . . . do not occupy a central place in singing, playing and listening," and that "non-Western music, early Western music, and certain forms of jazz, popular and folk music have been almost altogether ignored." It fails to challenge children, "whose potential is constantly underestimated." It condemned "a whole range of songbook arrangements, as weak, derivative, and artificial, labelling these "pseudomusic." It noted that songs are chosen and graded more on the basis of the limited technical skills of classroom teachers than the needs of children or the ultimate goals of improved hearing and listening skills. It also deplored the neglect of composition. Though many of these criticisms were well founded, we cannot help but note Rickover's dictum being applied to music: the subject being too important to be left to music educators.

Four years later, the Music Educators National Conference (MENC) sponsored a second conference on music education held at Tanglewood, Massachusetts, which repeated many of the recommendations made at the Yale Seminar. A number of curriculum development projects supported by funds from the U.S. Office of Education came about as a direct result of these conferences. Murphy and Jones note that at least a dozen or so projects could be traced to the Yale Seminar.[12] They singled out several for special mention, including *The Yale Music Curriculum Project* which had as its goal the development of musical understanding in secondary students. This project was directed by Kenneth A. Wendrich of Yale and used the services of Palisca himself. The new curriculum consisted of eight units and was designed to stimulate the listening capacity of the secondary student through recognition and analysis of musical genres and to expose students to "an academically respectable music-literature course." The materials were tried in twenty schools, and the units were also used with Yale undergraduates. The *Juilliard Repertory Project* was another project proposed by a Yale Seminar participant. It attempted to enlarge the musical repertory for school children between kindergarten and grade six. It broke away from the prevailing practice of classifying repertories by age groups, and used materials ranging from the classical Western composers like Bach and Beethoven to non-Western, jazz, and folk music. The Juilliard Project was first published in 1971 and was endorsed by the MENC.

In the opinion of Murphy and Jones, the most ambitious project inspired by the Yale Seminar was Ronald Thomas's *Manhattanville Music Curriculum Program* (MMCP). This project proposed the development of a music curriculum from the primary through the high school years, together with the training of classroom teachers to use the curriculum. In his final report, Thomas indicated that he set out to create an alternative for music education. The program emphasized student composition, improvisation, and the use of contemporary and nontraditional instruments. The major product of the curriculum was the "MMCP Synthesis," a comprehensive curriculum for grades three to twelve. Murphy and Jones described Thomas's learning theory:

It was indeed the idea of the spiral curriculum and all it entailed (an idea celebrated in those days, notably by Jerome Bruner) that inspired Thomas, and the underlying concept of the seamless fabric of learning: that "intellectual activity anywhere is the same, whether at the frontier of knowledge or in a third-grade classroom," to quote Bruner. Thomas was fascinated by the mathematicians he encountered whose idea of curriculum reform, based on this concept, so paralleled his own.[13]

DEVELOPMENTS IN ART EDUCATION

In October 1964, a conference on education in the visual arts was held at New York University. Directed by Howard Conant and funded by the U.S. Office of Education, the conference was modelled after the Yale Seminar.[14] Zacharias, whose influence was felt at Woods Hole and at the Yale Seminar, was a participant. Unlike the Yale Seminar, however, this conference did not spawn any far-reaching proposals for curriculum reform. Most of its recommendations were addressed to problems of teacher recruitment and education and the improvement of conditions under which art teachers work. In the following year a seminar held at Pennsylvania State University focused on research and curriculum development in art. This seminar was to have far wider influence upon art education.[15]

This event, known as the Penn State Seminar, emphasized the notion that art is a "discipline" in its own right, with goals which should be stated in terms of their power to help students engage independently in disciplined inquiry in art. At this conference Manuel Barkan summarized the curriculum problems facing art education, and pointed to Bruner's concept of structure as a way of solving these problems.

The concept of structure in the context of the structure of a discipline and its meaning for education, as brought into prominence by Jerome Bruner, has stimulated many in art education, including myself, to try to make sense out of art curriculum problems.

Physics—that is, science—has a formal structure of interrelated theorems, rules, and principles so that conceived hypotheses can be put to test rather than judgment through evaluation of relevant data. Hence, there are science disciplines, and scientific inquiry is disciplined. But does the absence of a formal structure of interrelated theorems, couched in a universal symbol system as in science, mean that branch of the humanities called the arts are not disciplines, and that artistic inquiries are not disciplined? I think the answer is that the disciplines of art are of a different order. Though they are analogical and metaphorical, and they do not grow out of or contribute to a formal structure of knowledge, artistic inquiry is not loose.[16]

Two direct consequences of the Penn State Seminar were the development of the Aesthetic Education Program by the Central Midwestern Regional Educational Laboratory (CEMREL), and the publication of a set of guidelines for aesthetic education.[17] But, unlike music, few curriculum development projects received federal funding in the visual arts. This was due, in part, to cutbacks in federal monies brought on by the intensification of the war effort in Vietnam. Also, the U.S. Office of Education favored "aesthetic education," in which curricula in the several arts could be supported by a single omnibus project.[18]

DEVELOPMENTS IN PHYSICAL EDUCATION

In the early 1960s President Kennedy introduced physical fitness and health to the national agenda with the establishment of his Council on Physical Fitness. Obesity and "softness" in American youth were decried, and the establishment of fitness as an educational aim with measurable standards became a movement within physical education. In many respects the movement reiterated themes that were first sounded during World War II and its aftermath, when it was argued that "strength in the masses is necessary for survival of the nation in times of war."[19]

A second direction also emerged at this time: physical education was identified as an academic discipline comprised of several subdomains such as exercise physiology, the biochemistry of exercise, biomechanics, sports psychology and sociology, and the history and philosophy of sports. Indeed a number of attempts were made to rename physical education with terms like "homokinetics," "human movement sciences," or "sports sciences" to reflect its disciplined character, though none of these was widely adopted at the time.[20]

Commenting upon these two directions in 1965, Delbert Oberteuffer said that the "effort toward programming and curriculum evaluation seems almost completely dominated by the 'physical fitness' theme." However, Ann Jewett made several observations in which she took issue with Oberteuffer's analysis.[21] She noted that "the physical education division of the American Association of Health, Physical Education, and Recreation made a commitment in 1964 to a major curriculum effort 'directed toward the identification and evaluation of a conceptual framework for the curriculum in physical education.' "[22] This work was also supported by the U.S. Office of Education.

With the exception of the conceptual framework project, no curriculum development work was supported by federal funding, this in spite of the fact that physical education could claim the social and biological sciences as bases for its standing as a discipline. This was in part due to the presence of conflicting tendencies in the federal initiatives affecting physical education, but the intensification of the Vietnam War had also begun to change educational priorities so as to reflect an interest in physical fitness per se rather than theoretical attempts to define the discipline.

The Accountability Movement of the 1970s

By 1969, American technology had put a man on the moon; the nation's confidence had been restored. The need for scientific knowledge, so keenly felt in the previous decade, subsided. The energy crisis of 1973 produced the fear that unlimited affluence was at an end, that economic opportunities would decline, and that students would have to compete for fewer positions at the top of the social ladder. Anxious parents were increasingly concerned about SAT scores and other measures of the effectiveness of schooling. This increase in uncertainty over the future, made accountability in educational programs a social need.

As accountability became the new watchword, the influence of science in curricular affairs shifted from the consideration of content to the identification of effective devices for measurement. Curriculum *evaluation* eclipsed curriculum *development* as a professional concern. Popkewitz et al. describe this change as a shift from the "productive" aspects of knowledge where the focus is on inquiry and discovery, to the "reproductive" aspects of knowledge where the emphasis was placed upon the monitoring of student performance to measure the mastery of existing facts.

These conflicting social motives of professionalization and science were in the 1960s reforms. Much of the "open classroom" movement and some curriculum materials, such as *Man: A Course of Study*, stressed the *productive* quality of science. The tentativeness of knowledge, the social origin of our understanding and the importance of the community are emphasized. In contrast, the "school accountability" movement gave attention to the *reproductive* aspects of science. A crystallized view of knowledge and procedures was posited as behavioral objectives and criterion-referenced measures defined curriculum.[23]

As the 1960s drew to a close, a gradual, almost imperceptible shift from curriculum initiatives inspired by "the structure of the disciplines" to ones based upon precise formulation of instructional objectives and efficiency began to occur. So gradual was the change that proposals for curriculum reform based on the disciplines sometimes incorporated procedures calling for the preparation of highly specified objectives. For example, at the Penn State Seminar Asahel Woodruff specifically dealt with the problems that would have to be faced in attempting to specify the behaviors taught in a visual arts curriculum based on the disciplines while Elliot Eisner also discussed ways that taxonomic schemes have been developed for organizing educational objectives.[24] Thus some of the language and curriculum procedures that characterized the accountability movement were already in the picture by the middle 1960s.

Only through hindsight had the incompatibility of the "productive" and "reproductive" aspects of the curriculum become clear. By the late 1960s the rhetoric concerning instructional objectives was ubiquitous, and by the middle 1970s, most educators in the arts and physical education talked more about instructional objectives, competency-based teacher education, and evaluation designs than about structures of knowledge. By the middle 1970s many anticipated the widespread acceptance of procedures where instructional objectives would be linked up with budgeting and cost-accounting procedures to evaluate the attainment of goals in terms of their overall cost. The accountability movement was in full swing. At the time Ralph Smith noted:

Many of the essential elements of PPBS were fashioned by the Rand Corporation while studying Air Force deterrence strategies and were later incorporated into Defense Department planning under Robert McNamara, and then by executive order of President Johnson into all governmental agencies including Health, Education and Welfare.

The model that economic theory has devised for thinking about such matters is essentially a model of productive functions in which an attempt is made to increase productivity by calculating as precisely as possible a variety of input-output ratios. ... Again, a PPBS approach offers a model of efficient production as a paradigm for the planning, managing, and evaluating of education, and it derives its image, inspiration, language, and methodology primarily from economic and organization theory, computer science, and military and space technological delivery systems.[25]

One can understand why art and music educators might have been attracted to the idea of the disciplines since proponents like Bruner celebrated the speculative, intuitive aspects involved in the production of knowledge. One would even have predicted resistance to this new approach to curriculum with its emphasis upon precisely described instructional objectives which tended to leave little room for imagination. However, there was a remarkable degree of acceptance of this regimen in both the arts and physical education. This might be explained by the fact that a new generation of arts educators, largely receiving their training in the 1950s and 1960s, were eager to change the image of the field as intellectually soft areas steeped in the philosophies of the child-centered school and self-expression while physical educators were intent upon shedding their "jock" image. The new spirit is seen in the unqualified support these leaders gave for empirical research in such areas as exercise physiology, psychological creativity, visual perception, pitch discrimination, and in the zeal to state teaching objectives in behavioral terms.

A number of music and art educators began to devise curricula based upon behavioral objectives. In many states, such as Michigan and Florida, this practice was mandated by law. MENC put out a monograph entitled *Instructional Objectives in Music: Resources for Planning Instruction and Evaluating Achievement* while the National Art Education Association (NAEA) published *Behavioral Emphasis in Art Education*.[26] A similar movement was afoot in physical education. John Nixon described a program called Project Broadfront in which program management principles adapted from business and industry were utilized to add to the efficiency and quality of the work of eleven curriculum associates in health, physical education, recreation, and outdoor education.[27] His program management system included (a) seven levels of hierarchical behaviors, (b) task schedules, (c) a subsystem for monitoring progress in tasks, (d) performance reports, (e) ways of evaluating quality in task performance, and (f) internal feedback loops to facilitate and maintain normal functioning of all these subsystems. He also described the use of cost-effectiveness analysis techniques to compare two educational programs in physical education.

Criticism of the Accountability Movement

This accountability movement rested on the assumption that behavioral objectives and cost-accounting methods are essentially value-free technologies, and are merely means toward accomplishing the end of providing the best education for the least cost. Writing behavioral objectives was seen as an application of behavior-control technology, and since these were scientific procedures, they were assumed to be value-free.[28] Dennis Nolan critiqued this assumption as it appeared in B. F. Skinner's *Beyond Freedom and Dignity*:

A particular technology at a given stage of development will not be equally efficient at accomplishing all goals. In the absence of an independent basis for specifying goals, the technology is likely to dictate those goals which it can most efficiently accomplish. Such goals are not necessarily ethically neutral.[29]

Writing behavioral objectives for performance skills in art, music, or in physical education is not difficult, but writing objectives that assess increased appreciation for sports, art, or music is difficult: appreciation is not always an observable event. In music, one might measure appreciation by the volume of applause in an auditorium, or in art by the number of visits a student makes to a museum, but then, one is not observing the appreciation directly but actions presumably linked to it. It is also easier to formulate an objective for a skill which is measured by matching a student's performance to an established standard than it is to formulate one asking for an original or imaginative product. Technologies are not able to do all things equally well. Art and music objectives written during the time period moved in the direction where the technology could excel—toward measurable skills and away from imaginative productivity or ephemeral appreciations.

Implications for General Education

Powerful and influential social forces played a key role in giving rise to the discipline movement of the 1960s and the accountability movement which followed in its wake. These movements had to do with social agendas quite removed either from the arts or from physical education. These social concerns greatly expanded the influence of the scientific community in educational matters. Once these movements became established, they became *canonical*, affecting all areas of the curriculum. The disciplined forms of knowledge characteristic of the sciences were imposed upon subjects as though they too were disciplines, when, in fact, many were not.

Though arts and physical educators often subscribed to the tenets of each new canon that arose, the need to accommodate these subjects to forms of thinking and acting belonging to other subjects often occurred at the expense of the intrinsic attributes of the affected subject. This is not to say that there was less art and music than before, but rather that the canons of these periods reduced the legitimacy of the forms of learning. Following the lead of the sciences, art educators began to describe artistic activity as an "inquiry after aesthetic meanings" or as "qualitative problem solving," losing sight of the expressive aspects of artistic activity that involve the imaginative creation of images. Barkan in particular tended to equate artistic activity with scientific inquiry. This is seen in his recommendations to teach art history and art criticism, and his lessened emphasis upon studio art activities.[30] Both art history and criticism treat the work of art as an "object of inquiry" rather than as something to be experienced qualitatively. And similarly, when music educators defined their curricula in terms of performance objectives, they began to lose the qualities of joy and sadness in the music, the feeling-life the music was expressing.

A scientific discipline characteristically approaches its content as an "object of inquiry" as something outside the learner which he or she tries to understand. As a result of the emphasis on the disciplines there was greater emphasis upon "looking" at art and "listening" to music. And while looking and listening are valuable experiences, they are passive when compared with the activities of performing music or working in the studio. The discipline emphasis as it affected teaching in the arts pulled attention away from active participation in artistic creation—an ironic outcome because the emphasis increased the amount of laboratory experience in the sciences. Douglas Sloan describes this approach to learning as involving an "onlooker consciousness":

The world exists "out there," with no integral, essential relation to the subject as knower. It is this sense of separateness from nature, what Ernst Lehrs has called the "onlooker consciousness," of modern man, that has been the characteristic mode of scientific consciousness."[31]

The obvious difficulty with the discipline orientation is that not all learning is a striving for knowledge. Humans also learn to create beauty. They strive for excellence as in the performance of music or in athletics. Similarly, the striving for morality, though it may depend upon a knowledge of right and wrong, is not a striving for greater understanding, but toward the good. What is learned in these situations is not knowledge per se, but self-mastery! And when the canons controlling general education denied these aspects of human striving, they led inevitably to a loss of balance.

The Balanced Curriculum

Plato discussed the necessity of educational balance in *The Republic* when he recalled that the Spartans were schooled "not by gentle influences but by force, for they have neglected her reason and philosophy, and have honored gymnastics more than music." He conceived of educational balance as lying between music and gymnastics. Both subjects included more than the terms mean in our own time. Music included all of the arts and sciences that came under the patronage of the muses. The singing that accompanied the text of the great poets carried the cultural heritage, and expressed the tone and sentiment of the community, what the Greeks called *ethos*. Gymnastics with its concern for athletics reflected the noble, albeit military, character of the Greek aristocratic tradition, but it was also concerned with the care of the body and diet, for the healthy body was the place of habitation for the soul. Music nurtured the soul while gymnastics strengthened the body, and the balance struck between the two was more than Plato's formula for the good life; it was his prescription for cultural survival.

Current notions of general education need to strike a balance among the forms of knowing embodied in the sciences with their powers of generalization and abstraction, while at the same time recognizing the limitations of science seen in its tendency to remove the learner from the object of his or her inquiry. While the scientist makes a virtue of objective detachment and precision, the artist by contrast makes a virtue of affective engagement.

The capacity to be moved by the inner pictures and images, with which the imagination in the artistic experience works, is to find a connection within ourselves to the qualitative dimensions in reality, to the source of life and meaning in the world.[32]

For Sloan, curricular balance is to be found between the rational thinking exemplified in the sciences, the life of feeling as embodied in the arts, and willing as it occurs in participatory learning. On the surface Sloan's view sounds as if it could be a discussion of the cognitive, affective, and psycho-motor domains of learning. Affective learnings were supposed to restore the emotional aspect to learning that had become increasingly dominated by the cognitive emphasis as seen in the curriculum reforms of the 1960s.

But Sloan has been quick to point out that this separation into specific categories tends to reinforce the notion that thinking has nothing to do with feeling, and that these are unrelated to physical action. An unbalanced curriculum might be one dominated by feelings and emotions at the expense of careful, rigorous thought. Yet one that is dominated by reason without feeling is unable to judge the importance of knowledge, or to take enjoyment in new discoveries or to appreciate beauty. The task of general education is not to separate thinking, feeling, and willing but to give play to all the forms of thought through which reality may be apprehended.

FOOTNOTES

1. Thomas S. Popkewitz, Allan Pitman, and Arlene Barry, "Educational Reform and Its Millennial Quality: The 1980s," *Journal of Curriculum Studies* 18, no. 3 (1986): 269.

2. The scientific community has not always enjoyed influence, and is often at odds with powerful elements in society. For example, it has had little or no influence in the area of environmental policy during the late 1970s and 1980s.

3. Lawrence A. Cremin, *The Transformation of the School: Progressivism in American Education 1876-1957* (New York: Vintage Books, 1964), pp. 346-47.

4. Jerome S. Bruner, *The Process of Education* (Cambridge, MA: Harvard University Press, 1960), p. 19.

5. Ibid.

6. Philip H. Phenix, "The Use of the Disciplines as Curriculum Content," in *The Subjects in the Curriculum: Selected Readings*, ed. Frank L. Steeves (New York: Odyssey Press, 1968). Originally published in *Educational Forum* 26 (March 1962): 273-80.

7. Jerome S. Bruner, *On Knowing: Essays for the Left Hand* (Cambridge, MA: Harvard University Press, 1961); idem, *Toward a Theory of Instruction* (Cambridge, MA: Harvard University Press, 1965).

8. August Heckscher, *The Arts and the National Government: Report to the President* (Washington, DC: U.S. Government Printing Office, 1963).

9. Judith Murphy and Lonna Jones, *Research in Arts Education: A Federal Chapter* (Washington, DC: U.S. Department of Health, Education, and Welfare, 1978), p. 3.

10. Ibid., pp. 26-28.

11. Claude V. Palisca, *Music in Our Schools: A Search for Improvement: Report of the Yale Seminar on Music Education* (Washington, DC: U.S. Department of Health, Education, and Welfare, 1964).

12. Murphy and Jones, *Research in Arts Education*, p. 53.

13. Ibid., pp. 58-59. The Manhattanville Music Program is described in R. B. Thomas, *Manhattanville Music Curriculum Program: Final Report* (Purchase, NY: Manhattanville College of the Sacred Heart, 1970).

14. Howard Conant, *Seminar on Elementary and Secondary School Education in the Arts* (New York: New York University, 1965). ERIC ED 002-975.

15. Edward L. Mattil, ed., *A Seminar on Art Education for Research and Curriculum Development*, USOE Cooperative Research Project No. V-002 (University Park, PA: Pennsylvania State University, 1966). ERIC ED 010 000.

16. Manuel Barkan, "Curriculum Problems in Art Education," in *A Seminar in Art Education*, ed. Mattil, pp. 244-45.

17. Manuel Barkan, Laura Chapman, and Evan J. Kern, *Guidelines: Curriculum Development for Aesthetic Education* (St. Louis, MO: CEMREL, 1970).

18. Laura H. Chapman, *Instant Art, Instant Culture: The Unspoken Policy for American Schools* (New York: Teachers College Press, 1982) describes some negative consequences of this policy.

19. Marion A. Sanborn and Betty G. Hartman, *Issues in Physical Education* (Philadelphia, PA: Lee and Febiger, 1983), p. 48.

20. M. Pieron, "Physical Education Programs," in *International Encyclopaedia of Education Research and Studies* (Oxford: Pergamon Press, 1984).

21. Delbert Oberteuffer, *Health Education and Physical Education: New Curriculum Developments* (Washington, DC: Association for Supervision and Curriculum Development, 1965); Ann Jewett, "Implications from Curriculum Theory for Physical Education," in *The Academy Papers #2* (Tucson, AZ: American Academy of Physical Education, 1968).

22. American Association for Health, Physical Education, and Recreation, *Cooperative Development for a Design for a Long-term Research Project Directed toward the Identification and Evaluation of a Conceptual Framework for the Curriculum in Physical Education Grades K-16*, Final Report, Contract No. OEC 2-6-068314-0743 (Washington, DC: American Association for Health, Physical Education, and Recreation, 1968).

23. Popkewitz, Pitman, and Barry, "Educational Reform and Its Millennial Quality." The authors also link the "reproductive" aspects of curriculum to the phenomenon of social reproduction where the unacknowledged function of the curriculum is tied to the maintenance of a social class system.

24. Asahel Woodruff, "The Examined Curriculum," in *A Seminar in Art Education*, ed. Mattil, pp. 259-66; Elliot W. Eisner, "Concepts, Issues, and Problems in the Field of Curriculum," in *A Seminar in Art Education*, ed. Mattil, pp. 222-35.

25. Ralph A. Smith, "Educational Criticism and the PPBS Movement in Education," in *Regaining Educational Leadership*, ed. Ralph A. Smith (New York: John Wiley and Sons, 1975), p. 3. Smith's description of the rise of cost-accounting initiatives during the Johnson administration drew upon Leo Ruth, "Dangers of System-Think in Education," in *Accountability and the Teaching of English*, ed. Henry B. Maloney (Urbana, IL: National Council of Teachers of English, 1972), pp. 67-74.

26. See Florida Department of Education, *Art Pre-Objectives and Performance Objectives 9-12*, Assessment Project in Art No. 720-077 (Tallahassee, FL: Florida Department of Education, 1972); J. J. Boyle, *Instructional Objectives in Music: Resources for Planning and Evaluating Achievement* (Reston, VA: Music Educators National Conference, 1974).

27. John Nixon, "Needed Curriculum Reform," in *The Academy Papers #3* (Tucson, AZ: American Academy of Physical Education, 1969).

28. Douglas Sloan, *Insight-Imagination: The Emancipation of Thought and the Modern World* (Westport, CT: Greenwood Press, 1983) draws upon Frederick Ferre and Jacques Ellul to note that a technology is not merely a system involving machinery; it is any system where calculative intelligence intervenes to design a methodology. Ferre in particular says that such technology is present in the minutely considered lesson plans and behavioral objectives employed in our most advanced schools.

29. J. Dennis Nolan, "Freedom and Dignity: A Functional Analysis," *American Psychologist* 29 (March 1974): 157-60.

30. My forthcoming paper, "How Art as a Discipline Emerged: A Study of Our Recent Past," *Studies in Art Education*, in press, explores this development in Manuel Barkan's writings in greater detail than space allows here.

31. Sloan, *Insight-Imagination*, p. 7.

32. Ibid., p. 222.

CHAPTER IX

Value Goals and Affective Goals in General Education

R. MURRAY THOMAS

Among educational goals, the ones I believe are defined with the least care and precision are those focusing on values and emotions. There are several reasons for this. In the case of values, both policymakers and teachers often have no more than a murky notion of what the domain of values contains. With only a hazy mental map of the domain, they are poorly equipped to specify values as learning objectives. A second reason is that educators often disagree about which values the education system should foster. Some people strongly advocate one value, such as obedience to authority or prayer in the school, while others advocate a contrary one, such as freedom of thought and action. Therefore, to avoid wrangling over such matters, the adversaries may decide to leave the controversial issue of values out of their list of educational goals. Furthermore, not everyone agrees that teaching values is a proper responsibility of the school. There are those who believe the school's job is to teach facts, concepts, and skills, and that such things as values, character development, and personal-social adjustment are the province of the family, the church, and community agencies.

The realm of affective goals has posed similar problems. The domain of the emotions is not easily delineated, so that the number and diversity of human emotions and their interrelationships are not at all well understood. This is partially because emotions, by their very nature, cannot be adequately translated into words. The terms joy, hate, pride, and fear are no more than imprecise symbols of the actual feelings that such words are supposed to convey. As a consequence, it has been difficult for educators to translate feelings into a form appropriate for stating affective goals. A second problem is that educators have not agreed upon which emotions should be promoted by the school. For example, to what extent should education be "fun"? And cannot a modest degree of anxiety or fear serve as a constructive motivator of learning, stimulating students to work hard toward worthy ends that will bring them ultimate satisfaction? In effect, there is a lack of consensus among educators about the role different emotions should be assigned in the educational process.

A further problem with both value goals and affective goals arises at the stage of assessing students' progress. The task of evaluating learners' values and feelings has proven to be far more elusive than the task of evaluating the facts, concepts, and psychomotor skills that the school teaches. As a result, educators have wondered about how profitable it is to set goals focusing on values and feelings when learners' achievement of such objectives cannot be accurately assessed. In writing their original affective version of the *Taxonomy of Educational Objectives*, Krathwohl, Bloom, and Masia stated:

We studied the history of several major courses at the general education level of college. Typically, we found that in the original statement of objectives there was frequently as much emphasis given to affective objectives as to cognitive objectives. Sometimes in the early years of the course some small attempt was made to secure evidence on the extent to which students were developing in the affective behaviors.

However, as we followed some of these courses over a period of ten to twenty years, we found a rather rapid dropping of the affective objectives from the statements about the course and the almost complete disappearance of efforts at appraisal of student growth in this domain. It became evident to us that there is a characteristic type of *erosion* in which the original intent of a course or educational program becomes worn down to that which can be explicitly evaluated for grading purposes and that which can be taught easily through verbal methods (lectures, discussions, reading materials, and the like).[1]

In view of these problems, what aid can educators be offered in deciding what should be done about values and affective goals in general education? The purpose of this chapter is to consider a variety of available answers by focusing on the choices educators face in (a) defining values and affect as goals of education, (b) deciding which values and emotions can profitably become goals of general education, and (c) deciding how value goals and affective goals can most suitably be evaluated. The early, longer portion of the discussion concerns values, while the later, shorter portion concerns affect.

Varieties of Values

As we address the question of values, we can profitably begin by distinguishing among values, theories, and facts. *Facts* are descriptions of either (a) discrete observations and measurements of people, objects, or events or (b) summaries of such observations and measurements. Statements of fact tell what exists, in what amount, and perhaps in what relation to other facts. Facts are publicly verifiable. *Theories*, broadly speaking, are proposals about (a) which facts are most important for a given purpose and (b) how these facts are related to each other. Hence, a theory or a model is a scheme for organizing facts and concepts. The present chapter is such an organizing scheme—a proposal about how the selection of values and affective goals for general education can be perceived. In contrast, *values* are opinions about the desirability or propriety or goodness of something. The "something" may be a person, a group of people, an object, a place, an event, an idea, a kind of behavior, or the like. Statements of value tell whether something is good or bad, well done or poorly done, suitable or unsuitable.

In selecting goals for general education, it is further useful to distinguish among varieties of values, because educators may wish to stress certain varieties and disregard others. For purpose of discussion, values can be divided into six types: (a) aesthetic, (b) moral, (c) social-conventional, (d) personal welfare, (e) technical or functional, and (f) economic.

Aesthetic values involve opinions offered from an artistic viewpoint. Aesthetic values, when applied to a flower arrangement, a poem, a painting, or a dance performance, are reflected in such phrases as "pleasing to the eye" or "nicely turned metaphor" or "delightfully innovative."

Moral values typically refer to the quality of relationships among people. Moral values reflect standards of social conduct. In addition, some people extend moral values beyond the realm of human relations to encompass relationships between humans and a Supreme Being, so that failing to abide by God's laws becomes a moral issue. Moral values may also become further extended so as to encompass nonhuman aspects of nature—animals and plants and even such inanimate objects as lakes and mountains. For those who hold these views, using dogs and monkeys for medical-laboratory experiments becomes a moral issue, as does the killing of whales and infant seals, the destruction of an ancient redwood tree, the industrial development of a lakeshore, and the removal of a mountain during iron ore mining. In summary, there continues to be considerable controversy over exactly what attitudes and behaviors comprise the realm of moral values.[2]

Included in this controversy is the question of whether moral values should be distinguished from *social-conventional values.* Turiel has contended that moral issues are limited to matters of justice, as when the consequences of acts can cause physical or psychological harm to others, violate people's rights, or affect the general welfare. Social conventions, on the other hand, "constitute shared knowledge of uniformities in social interactions and are determined by the social system in which they are formed," with examples being conventional modes of dress, forms of greeting, and rules of games.[3] In Turiel's view, social conventions can be changed by consent of the members of the group without seriously affecting people's welfare, whereas moral precepts cannot. The fact that Turiel's distinction between moral and social-conventional issues is not generally made by curriculum planners, either in Western or in Eastern societies, is suggested by typical lists of moral education topics in various education systems. For example, authors of a 1975 study of moral education in fifteen Asian countries concluded that even though there were divergent views about the whole concept of moral education,

It was agreed that the term moral education would cover all activities in the school or outside that help students to:
1. develop desirable personal and social habits and skills relating to cleanliness, courtesy, punctuality, cooperation, discipline, self-reliance, etc.;
2. develop such social attributes as sympathy, kindness (including kindness to animals and plants), patriotism, dignity of labor, honesty, justice, tolerance, truthfulness, respect for the individual and democratic spirit;
3. acquire knowledge of moral principles and develop the ability of making moral judgments; and
4. discover their true nature, acquire inner peace, and develop strength of character.[4]

In effect, the distinction made by Turiel is an unusual one. Most educators who address their attention to values would include social conventions as part of their definition of *moral.*

Whereas moral values concern the treatment of people other than oneself, *personal welfare* values are self-centered. They concern "my rights and privileges," "what I owe myself," and "what I deserve" rather than "what I owe others" and "the rights and privileges others deserve." Different societies have been contrasted in terms of the emphasis they place on moral values versus personal welfare values. Oriental cultures and socialist governments have been viewed as placing more emphasis on the general welfare of the society, whereas cultures of Western Europe and North America have been viewed as placing greater emphasis on the individual's rights and privileges, that is, on self-centered values. Furthermore, in many Western nations— perhaps most notably in North America—concern for "what I owe myself" has been an increasingly widespread phenomenon as evidenced in rising divorce rates, the advent of encounter groups and assertiveness training, and a growing claim to "the right to do my thing." As a consequence, general education programs can concern themselves with such issues of the relationship of self to society.

Technical or functional values refer to judgments about how efficiently something serves its intended purpose. The application of functional values is reflected in such phrases as "a well designed automobile," "a poorly run committee," and "a clearly written law."

Economic values relate to the monetary worth of something, as suggested in such comments from consumer education parlance as "a real bargain," "your money's worth," "a bad investment," and "a great savings."

In conclusion, values can be of several types. So I am suggesting that educational planners, in selecting value goals for general education programs, can usefully begin by distinguishing different types of values. Then, under each type they can specify values that fall within that variety. The next step is to decide which of these values should be the concern of the school, and particularly of general education.

Values as Educational Goals

In deciding which values should become goals of general education, curriculum planners can be guided by two initial questions: (a) Which values are properly goals of the school? (b) To what degree should the school seek to inculcate values in contrast to teaching processes of decision making?

THE RESPONSIBILITIES OF THE SCHOOL

For the sake of analysis, a society's broad educational goals—or learning objectives—can be divided into three groups: (a) those goals that are chiefly, if not exclusively, the responsibility of the school, (b) those that are the shared responsibility of the school and of such agencies as the family and church, and (c) those that are rarely, if ever, assigned to schools.

Goals that are chiefly the task of the school are represented in the basic categories of the curriculum: mathematics, the natural and social sciences, reading and writing of both the native language and foreign languages, the arts, and vocational preparation. Whereas the principal goals of teaching in these subject-matter fields are ones of fact and theory and skill, values are also typically included. For example, aesthetic values can make up a significant portion of the instruction in the arts and literature, while social values are typically applied in the teaching of history, sociology, and political science. Technical values are taught in vocational education and natural science classes. For all of these fields of study, the school bears the main burden of instruction. The family and community agencies usually do not systematically contribute to students' achievement in these areas.

Goals whose pursuit is shared by the school, home, church, and other community bodies are mainly concerned with work habits, social behavior, and citizenship. Under the category of work habits, youths are expected to accept responsibility, labor diligently at their assignments, acquire increasingly efficient means of carrying out tasks, complete assignments on time, learn from their mistakes, and more. Under social behavior they are expected to treat other people politely, display tolerance for others whose subgroup characteristics differ from their own (differences of age, sex, ethnic origin, language, religion, socioeconomic class), cooperate with others in contributing to the group good, tell the truth, not use others' property without their permission, not denigrate others for purposes of self-aggrandizement, and the like. Under citizenship, students are expected to hold their nation's and community's ideals in high regard, accept the responsibilities that citizens bear (voting in elections, obeying laws, performing jury duty, giving information to police about law-breakers), and such.

The third category—goals for which the school bears no responsibility—continues to be an area of considerable disagreement. The United States, by virtue of its Constitution, has been committed to a separation of state and religion. And because most schools are public institutions, this has meant that religious matters have been considered outside the schools' province. However, how this separation of state and church should be applied in practice continues to be a matter of acrimonious debate, legislation, and law suits at both national and local levels of government. For example, in the teaching of biology, should a creationist version of the origin of animal species (as represented in the Judeo-Christian biblical account) be taught along with Darwin's theory of evolution? And, in terms of values, should textbooks and teachers depict one of these versions as right and the other wrong? Is school prayer a religious act, when directed to a nonsectarian Supreme Being, or is it simply a display of respect for a universal truth about life (that there is a Supreme Power that controls the universe) so that such prayer is a proper variety of nonreligious behavior, in the sense of an ecumenical or nondenominational act?

Additional goals whose placement continues to be a matter of conflict are those bearing on sexual attitudes and actions. In the past, teaching the young about sex was considered the sole responsibility of the home or, to a lesser extent, of the church. However, during the twentieth century, schools have increasingly taken responsibility for sex education. Schools have seldom sought this responsibility but instead have acquired it by default. Widespread social problems (unwanted pregnancy, sexually transmitted disease, prostitution, disrupted family life, personal distress among the youth) have suggested that the family and church were not succeeding in their sex education roles. Therefore, the schools have been asked to step in to meet the unfulfilled need. However, there is no consensus about what specific matters of sex the schools should teach. But it is clear that only a minor portion of the conflict in this realm is over what factual information should be presented to the young. The greater conflict is over what values are to be encouraged. For instance, is premarital sex a desirable or undesirable thing? And are premarital sexual relations with a single partner over an extended period of time all right, but sex relations with successive partners all wrong? Is homosexuality an acceptable alternative way of life, or is it despicable?

For curriculum development, the obvious implication of the foregoing remarks is that planners are obligated to decide which values are the main responsibility of the school, which ones are shared with the family and community, and which are not the business of the school at all.

VALUES INDOCTRINATION VERSUS VALUES CLARIFICATION

The purpose of most values teaching, both in school and out, has been to have students adopt those values espoused by the authorities— teachers, preachers, parents, law-enforcement agencies, and the like. Learners are urged to accept the Ten Commandments, the Golden Rule, the nation's Constitution, the sayings of Confucius, the school's code of student conduct, and the teacher's aesthetic standards as their own guidelines for distinguishing between good and bad, between desirable and undesirable. In other words, most instruction in values has consisted of indoctrination. However, *indoctrination*, as intended here, does not necessarily involve the use of heavy-handed, threatening, punitive instructional techniques. Rather, it can mean the use of logic and kindly persuasion as well. But whatever the instructional approach, the desired result is that the learners come out believing in the instructors' set of values.

In contrast to indoctrination, educators have developed programs emphasizing *values clarification*. The purpose of such programs is to equip students to determine their own values instead of automatically accepting the values urged on them by others. Whereas indoctrination focuses on which values to accept, values clarification focuses on how to go about arriving at one's own value system. Whereas indoctrination focuses on content goals, values clarification is concerned with process goals. So the purpose of the indoctrination program is to have students accept such principles as "Thou shalt not kill, except in self-defense or in patriotic service to the nation." In contrast, the purpose of the values-clarification program is to have students learn a method of deciding under what conditions they should kill.

In the version of values clarification offered by Raths, Harmin, and Simon, the authors proposed that the act of valuing is comprised of three processes—choosing, prizing, and acting. Each process contains two or three substeps:

Choosing:
    1. freely
    2. from alternatives
    3. after thoughtful consideration of the consequences of each alternative

Prizing:
    1. cherishing, being happy with the choice
    2. willing to affirm the choice publicly

Acting:
    1. doing something with the choice
    2. repeatedly, in some pattern of life[5]

A different version of valuing has been offered by Krathwohl, Bloom, and Masia.

The process begins when the attention of the student is captured by some phenomenon, characteristic, or value. As he pays attention to the phenomenon, characteristic, or value, he differentiates it from the others present in the perceptual field. With differentiation comes a seeking out of the phenomenon as he gradually attaches emotional significance to it and comes to value it. As the process unfolds he relates this phenomenon to other phenomena to which he responds that also have value. This responding is sufficiently frequent so that he comes to react regularly, almost automatically to it and to other things like it. Finally the values are interrelated in a new structure or view of the world, which he brings as a "set" to new problems.[6]

As an outline of separate actions, this valuing process assumes the following pattern:

1.0 Receiving (attending)
  1.1 Awareness
  1.2 Willingness to receive
  1.3 Controlled or selected attention

2.0 Responding
  2.1 Acquiescence in responding
  2.2 Willingness to respond
  2.3 Satisfaction in response

3.0 Valuing
  3.1 Acceptance of a value
  3.2 Preference for a value
  3.3 Commitment (conviction)

4.0 Organization
  4.1 Conceptualization of a value
  4.2 Organization of a value system

5.0 Characterization by a value or value complex
  5.1 Generalized set
  5.2 Characterization[7]

A third version of values goals has been labeled a *practical-reasoning* approach. As Coombs explains it:

Practical reasoning is a matter of deciding what one has good and sufficient reasons to do. . . . Practical reasoning is always comparative. A course of action is judged to be more or less desirable in relation to alternative courses of action, including the alternative of doing nothing or of making no change in existing programs.[8]

Proponents of such a practical-reasoning goal for general education seek to teach students standards they should apply in making life's decisions. Students study methods of (a) identifying what constitutes adequate evidence for establishing facts, (b) discovering one's own genuine values, (c) considering reasons for and against as many plausible alternative courses of action as are feasible, (d) collecting information related to the decision at hand, (e) estimating that a chosen alternative does not involve acting immorally, and (f) ensuring that the best consequences will result from a chosen alternative.

In summary, a number of proposals have been offered for equipping learners to decide for themselves the values they will adopt and the ways they can apply these values in daily life.

For educators, one implication of the indoctrination-versus-reasoning distinction is that curriculum planners and teachers need to decide which of the two sorts of goals—indoctrination or reasoning—should guide instruction in their program. As they pursue this task, they may recognize that they wish to have part of their educational program center on indoctrination and part on clarification processes. For example, it is possible for educators to support indoctrination goals in the realm of moral values but advocate clarification goals in the realm of aesthetics. The rationale underlying such a division would be that amicable human relations require that people follow the same standards of conduct so the society will operate justly and with a minimum of tension. However, in the area of aesthetics, individuals can subscribe to values different from those held by other people without violating anyone's social rights.

A second implication of indoctrination-versus-clarification is that instructional methods will be different for the two sorts of goals. For example, the steps the teacher takes to indoctrinate can include: (a) describing situations in which a given value is at stake, (b) identifying which values are in conflict with this initial value, (c) emphasizing the virtues of the preferred value over the others, and (d) citing instances in life in which the favored value has proven to be superior to the less desirable values. In contrast, the teacher who seeks to equip youths with a way of arriving at their own values can adopt such a methodology as that recommended by Raths, Harmin, and Simon:

1. Encourage children to make choices, and to make them freely.
2. Help them discover and examine available alternatives when faced with choices.
3. Help children weigh alternatives thoughtfully, reflecting on the consequences of each.
4. Encourage children to consider what it is that they prize and cherish.
5. Give them opportunities to make public affirmations of their choices.
6. Encourage them to act, behave, live in accordance with their choices.
7. Help them to examine repeated behaviors or patterns in their life.[9]

It should be apparent that this encouragement of free choice in values is antithetical to typical practice in general education. Traditionally, general education programs have been founded on indoctrination convictions which hold that the unifying materials of any culture are the people's shared values. Over the centuries, the wisest in an evolving society have explored the cultural terrain and discovered the gems that most deserve to be treasured. The worth of these gems has been proven by their lasting over the centuries as essential truths. The task of general education is then to pass these truths to succeeding generations. As a consequence, the core of general education becomes mastery of the *classics*, meaning mastery of the key values of the culture as found in the society's great books. And the educator's goal is not simply to describe such traditions but, rather, to win young people's allegiance to those traditions. Beliefs valued by the teacher are to be equally valued by the learner, so the young become loyal defenders of tradition.

In summary, curriculum planners and teachers face the task of deciding (a) which types of values are properly of concern in the school program and (b) to what extent the school should espouse particular values as compared to teaching young people ways of arriving at their own values. In my experience, values clarification programs are rarely if ever pure, with *pure* meaning that the instructor gives no indication of which, among the array of values, he or she prefers. Students usually can tell where on the value scale the teacher stands. As a consequence, programs typically vary in the degree to which they involve indoctrination and values clarification or practical reasoning. But at least at the planning stage when the educational goals are specified, it is profitable to indicate to what extent certain values are to be advocated and to what extent decision-making skills are to be taught.

Values as Goals in General Education

If the goals for general education are defined as the objectives that all secondary school and college students should pursue, then our next step in specifying general education goals is that of distinguishing between which values or valuing processes should be acquired by all students and which are the proper province of special fields of study. The way this decision is made will depend greatly on the conceptual structure of the school's or college's overall general education program.

Most general education programs are organized under broad subject-matter or academic-discipline categories, a plan that can result in such categories as the following four-fold division of studies: *Communication Skills, Human Societies, Science and Technology,* and *The Arts and Recreation.* Then there are different ways that courses within each category can be presented. In some schools, within each broad category a set of required courses is specified for all students to take in common. Hence, the general education program is comprised entirely of required classes that are identical for all students. In other schools, however, the general education plan specifies one or two classes that everyone follows within a category, plus an array of additional more specialized courses from which students are to select two or three that particularly interest them. Or, under a third popular approach, there are no courses within any category which everyone must take in common. Instead, each category is comprised of an array of elective courses from which students are to choose several.

How, then, are values goals assigned to courses in such programs? The most practical way consists of course planners first inspecting the topics or the facts and theories that comprise the content of each course in the program. Then, for each topic or set of facts, theories, and skills the planners describe the values or attitudes they believe students should adopt. Or, if values clarification rather than values indoctrination is the aim of the program, the course planners first identify what significant value issues are involved in the topics that compose the course. Students taking the course are then expected to (a) identify the alternative values that bear on each topic, (b) state the rationale underlying each value position, and (c) clarify their own values commitment on each issue.

Next, as a way of estimating how well they have identified significant values goals by focusing on topics, the program planners can cross-check their decisions by considering such categories of values as those designated earlier in this chapter—aesthetic, moral, social-conventional, personal welfare, technical/functional, and economic. For each topic or cluster of fact/theory goals, they can ask: What values do we expect students to acquire during the study of this topic? The following examples suggest the sorts of values goals that can result from such a procedure. For this illustration, I have used the four areas of general education studies cited in the earlier example. For each area, the facts and theories or skills that might be included as part of the content of a course within that area are first identified. Then, associated values are specified, with the types of value indicated in the parentheses within each statement. In all cases, the goals are cast in the form of the behavior that students should display as a result of their study.

COMMUNICATION SKILLS

Fact/Theory/Skill Goals: Students convey their ideas in speaking and writing.

Associated Values Goals: Students speak and write in a manner which renders their ideas easily understood (technical/functional), readily accepted by the intended audience in terms of style of presentation (social-conventional), and phrased in a manner that the audience regards as pleasing (aesthetic).

HUMAN SOCIETIES

Fact/Theory/Skill Goals: Students (a) identify major changes in methods of education and in the spread of literacy over the centuries and (b) describe ways that the type and extent of education has influenced forms of political and economic organization in various societies.

Associated Values Goals: Students propose educational rights they believe people of various societies deserve (moral) and estimate the effect the provision of such rights will likely exert on the quality of life in those societies (technical/functional).

SCIENCE AND TECHNOLOGY

Fact/Theory/Skill Goals: Students trace a chain of scientific discoveries and inventions that evolved during the Industrial Revolution and describe the way these technological advances altered economic conditions in Western societies.

Associated Values Goals: Students (a) assess changes in production efficiency (technical/functional, economic) that resulted from successive technological advances, (b) appraise advantages and disadvantages of increased industrialization for the quality of individuals' lives (moral, personal welfare), and (c) evaluate changes in artistic taste in architecture and product design that accompanied technological change (aesthetic).

THE ARTS AND RECREATION

Fact/Theory/Skill Goals: Students (a) identify different types of poetic form, (b) relate these types to various historical eras and societal settings, and (c) identify different criteria that can be used in assessing the quality of a poem.

Associated Values Goals: Students (a) adopt or create criteria they wish to use in assessing the quality of poems and offer a rationale to support their criteria (aesthetic, personal welfare, possibly moral or social-conventional) and (b) apply their criteria in judging the worth of different poems (aesthetic).

In summary, values goals can be assigned to general education courses by curriculum planners answering this question: What judgments of *desirable-undesirable* or *proper-improper* should students learn to make in relation to the facts, concepts, theories, and skills they study in general education classes?

Assessing Students' Achievement of Values Goals

As noted earlier, a principal reason that values goals are frequently missing from statements of general education objectives is that instructors have encountered difficulty in assessing how well students reach the goals. By failing to find a satisfactory way to appraise values, instructors eliminate values goals. But this assessment difficulty, I believe, is often seated in the way the goals are stated, so that recasting the statement of learning objectives can provide at least a partial solution to the evaluation dilemma. The line of logic behind this solution runs as follows:

It seems apparent that the ultimate purpose of education, including general education, is to have the learners act wisely when they face life's daily decisions. Therefore, it would appear useful to state learning objectives in terms of how a wise person would behave in each of life's circumstances. Thus, objectives can usefully be stated in terms of the now familiar "expected student behavior" rather than in terms of topics or questions or teacher intent. The contrast among these four ways of stating objectives is illustrated by the following example:

Expected Student Behavior: As a result of their learning, students defend others in their society from prejudicial treatment on the basis of ethnic origin, religion, or gender.

Topic: Defending against ethnic, religious, and gender prejudice.

Question: What defenses can be devised against ethnic, religious, and gender prejudice?

Teacher Intent: To explain ways that people can defend others against ethnic, religious, and gender prejudice.

Although casting objectives in the form of desired student actions has the virtue of focusing attention on the proper outcome of education (changes in the learner's actions), this method poses two difficulties for the task of evaluating students' progress.

First, it is not possible to predict with any precision a great many of the decisions students will face in their future, because times change and the conditions under which people are called upon to act wisely cannot be estimated accurately ahead of time. Therefore, while curriculum planners can estimate in at least a general way some of the kinds of situations people will meet in their lives (such as incidents of intergroup prejudice), they cannot predict a host of others. As preparation for such unpredictable decisions, learners can only be taught facts, theories, skills, and values that may serve as a foundation for successfully facing unexpected problems.

A second difficulty arises not from the unpredictability of the future but, rather, from the inability of teachers to observe students in most of their real-life decision-making situations. For instance, the extent to which a teacher can directly assess students' achievement of the "defense against prejudice" goal is quite limited. Most incidents in students' lives which would relate to prejudice are not available for the teacher to appraise.

In light of these two barriers to the effective assessment of values goals, what assessment options do teachers have available? One feasible solution is to view educational evaluation on three levels—those of *understanding*, of *planning*, and of *real-life action*. As suggested earlier, the preferred way to assess educational outcomes is to assess how people apply their learning in their lives—real-life action. But when it is not feasible to see them in action, we can still discover how they think they should behave in such situations. We can, in effect, assess how they would *plan* to act under specified life conditions. When we evaluate on the planning level, we recognize that what people say they would intend to do is not always what they actually would do in that situation. But by assessing on the planning level, we at least discover how well the learners comprehend facts, theories, skills, and values pertinent to the situation and how they would put this knowledge together in order to act. The following example illustrates a way to state a values objective on the planning level:

The students (a) describe steps they would take when facing situations of prejudicial treatment of individuals on ethnic, religious, or gender grounds and (b) tell what values are the foundation for these steps.

One virtue in casting planning goals in this form is that the statement of the objective defines to a great extent the nature of evaluation items. For instance, the following essay-type item could be used to assess how well high school students have achieved the above objective:

Imagine that you and two other students have been asked to choose a five-member committee to plan the senior class dance. When one of these two students suggests putting Tommy Wilson on the committee, the other students says, "He's a black. I don't think it's a great idea to have him on the committee. Let's pick somebody else."

Your task is, first, to tell how you would answer that suggestion. Then tell why you think your answer is a good one.

Assessing on the planning level can therefore assist us in estimating how learners might act in life situations which we can predict they may meet but which we cannot in any practical sense observe directly. However, what can be done about situations that we cannot foresee ahead of time—incidents that will arise in a murkily perceived future? In such cases, we are left to evaluate at the *understanding level*. We assess students' command of facts, theories, skills, and values which, we trust, they can assemble in proper patterns to solve unexpected problems in the years ahead. For example, we assume that students' unforeseen decisions in the future would be guided by which of the facts they know and which of the values they accept from such an array as the following:

Facts

1. The first amendment to the United States Constitution protects people's rights to practice the religion of their choice, to speak their opinion, to publish in the press, to assemble peaceably, and to petition the government to correct injustices.

2. More than half of the auto-accident deaths over the past decade have been related to the use of alcohol by drivers.

3. At an annual growth rate of 3.5 percent, a country's population will double in 21 years. At 1.5 percent, it will double in 47 years.

Values

1. The reason for punishing criminals should be to prevent them from committing crimes in the future.

2. The purpose of punishment should be to ensure that criminals suffer for the trouble and suffering they caused their victims.

3. Any foreigner who wants to live in the United States should be allowed to do so.

4. Residence in the United States should be available only to foreigners who show real promise of making a positive contribution to the nation's social and economic future.

5. Abortion is the same as murder, so abortion should never be permitted.

6. Family planning measures should be adopted to prevent the birth of children who are likely to be abused, be neglected, or become a financial burden on the government.

For the purpose of setting general education goals, a pair of implications that can be drawn from the foregoing discussion are the following: To prepare learners for making decisions in real-life situations whose nature can be predicted, educators can profitably state learning goals in terms of how a person should act—or should plan to act—in those situations. But to prepare learners for making decisions in life situations whose nature cannot be accurately foreseen, educators can appropriately state objectives in terms of facts, concepts, and value convictions that can be combined to serve as useful guides to decision making on such occasions.

Stating Goals as Actions Is Not Enough

It is useful to recognize that even when types of life situations can be predicted, it is not sufficient for assessment purposes to state the goals only as actions that students should take. It is necessary also to learn their reasons for taking such action. In other words, observing students' behavior or testing them on what they would plan to do in life situations needs to be accompanied by the requirement that students give their rationale for such behavior. The need to ask *why* a person has acted in a given manner arises from the fact that the same behavior—killing, choosing one microcomputer over another, rejecting a particular work of art—can derive from different values in different people. For instance, killing can be motivated by various values—self-defense, greed, patriotism, racial prejudice. Therefore, it is necessary to learn the intention behind the act in order to judge which values motivated the behavior. This necessity is commonly demonstrated in studies of moral development. For instance, the methodology featured in the work of Lawrence Kohlberg involves students first telling whether they agree or disagree with the actions taken by characters depicted in moral-decision anecdotes. The students are then required to explain the reasoning behind their answers. It is this explanation of reasons that enables the researcher to determine on which level a particular student belongs according to Kohlberg's hierarchy of moral values.[10] Without learning the students' reasons for their behavior, the researcher cannot draw an informed conclusion about what values undergird the behavior.

The fact that values often cannot accurately be inferred from observed behavior suggests that when values goals are stated at the action or planning level, the statements can properly include the expectation that students explain why they believe their action or plan for action is appropriate. To illustrate, here is an example of the statement of such a goal which identifies both the desired behavior and the desired value that motivates the behavior. The value is one of human rights.

The learner supports legislation and social movements that promote equal treatment before the law for people of all races, religions, national backgrounds, and socioeconomic classes, with such support based on a commitment to the right of every human to be accorded the same legal protection that any other person receives.

Such a goal is significantly different in its values foundation, though identical in its overt behavior, from a goal stated the following way so as to feature the pragmatic value of not disturbing the existing social system.

The learner supports legislation and social movements that promote equal treatment before the law for people of all races, religions, national backgrounds, and socioeconomic classes, with such support based on the conviction that failing to provide equal treatment will lead to violence that can disrupt the social-class structure of the society.

With these observations, we come to the close of our discussion of values goals for general education. We turn now to the second major concern of the chapter—affective goals in general education.

The Relationship of Affect to General Education

One way to perceive affective goals in general education is to develop a line of reasoning built on the following sequence of assumptions, when the terms *affect, emotions,* and *feelings* are used as synonyms.

The first assumption is that emotions do not stand alone but are attached to such cognitive contents as facts, concepts, skills, and values. For a student in a general education class, the instructor, the subject matter, classmates, homework assignments, discussion sessions, tests, and the grades the students receive will all have feelings attached to them.

Emotions vary in their direction. They can be either positive or negative. A positive emotion is one that causes the individual to seek more of it. Such words as joy, pride, satisfaction, relief, fun, and warmth identify positive emotions. A negative emotion is one that causes the individual to seek less of it—to dispel it or to avoid it. Such terms as fear, hate, shame, anger, and coldness identify negative affect. While most of life's experiences appear to have either positive or negative affect associated with them, some experiences seem to be affectively neutral. For instance, a student may not feel one way or the other about a general education class in art appreciation.

Emotions vary in their strength, from weak to strong. A student can gain either great satisfaction from a class in computer literacy or very little satisfaction. The strength of the emotions that students attach to a general education class influences how diligently or enthusiastically they pursue the class's learning goals.

Emotions that motivate students to study can be of various types—fear, curiosity, anxiety, enthusiasm, shame, pleasure. And the type and strength of emotion that a student feels toward a class, such as fear or pleasure, appear to depend on a variety of conditions. One condition is the extent to which students believe they can satisfactorily perform the class's learning tasks. In one student, a feeling of confidence is a strong motivator, while in another a fear of not succeeding can stimulate diligent study. An additional factor is the instructor-student relationship. An instructor who reacts with sarcasm to student contributions during a class discussion will generate different emotions in the learners than will an instructor who appears to welcome students' contributions. Another factor is the inherent value that students feel the course content holds for their lives. Two further conditions are the attitudes of classmates and the quality of the work they produce. A class that includes numbers of vocal, antagonistic students who are critical of the course and do little work will exert a different influence on other learners' feelings than will a class dominated by enthusiastic learners who produce high-quality work.

Not only is student motivation affected differently by various types of emotions, but the diverse feelings that can be associated with a general education course are not mutually exclusive. Instead, they can appear as mixtures. For example, a student may approach a homework assignment with a combination of anxiety (occasioned by puzzlement about how to do the assignment successfully) and of pleasant exhilaration at the opportunity to pursue the intriguing topic that was assigned. Furthermore, the sequence of emotions generated during the progress of a course can vary over time, a consequence of changes in a student's interest in the topics, in her success with assignments and tests, and in her relationship with the instructor. Hence, feelings of curiosity, amusement, boredom, renewed curiosity, wonderment, and admiration may follow, one after the other, as the class proceeds. But even when several different emotions are attached to a class, oftentimes one or two types are dominant, so that the student associates a particular overriding feeling with the course. This pervading feeling may be fear or boredom or enthusiasm, with the student's achievement of the learning goals significantly influenced by whichever emotion is paramount.

If the foregoing can be accepted as a fair, although simplified, description of emotional factors in schooling, then what affective goals can properly be set for general education to achieve? In response, I would suggest two interrelated aims, one focusing on *motivation* and the other on *ultimate satisfaction*. As for motivation, the emotions generated during the course should be ones that stimulate students to work diligently toward the objectives of the class, that is, to work hard to master the facts, concepts, skills, and values that the course is designed to foster. As for ultimate satisfaction, by the close of the course the dominant affect that students attach to the class should be positive and strong—a feeling of achievement, of success, and of pride in having learned much that is worthwhile.

A conviction underlying the first of these goals is that such positive types of emotion as enthusiasm and pride are very desirable stimuli to learning; however, a modest level of certain kinds of negative affect—such as fear of failing to live up to expectations or shame at not doing well—can also be desirable, if such feelings motivate students to study hard and, consequently, to learn much and gain ultimate satisfaction. In regard to the second goal, the importance of students completing the class with a strong sense of achievement lies, I believe, in the influence this feeling can exert on the students' subsequent use of the facts, skills, and values taught in the class. I am convinced that students will make more confident, effective future applications of learning acquired from a course they finish in a spirit of accomplishment than from a course they complete in a sense of shame, hate, depression, or despair.

If these two affective goals—of motivation and of satisfaction—can be accepted as reasonable ones for general education courses to adopt, then several implications can be drawn about the way students are assigned to such courses and about the way the classes are taught.

To direct the assignment of students to courses, two principles appear to apply: (a) that students' background of skill and knowledge provide them a good chance of succeeding in the class and (b) that the content of the course be new and not just a repetition of much the class members learned earlier in their school career. These two principles can likely be fulfilled most adequately in general education programs that provide some options among courses students can take to meet general education requirements. The principles also imply that students will receive adequate faculty advisement in their selection of classes.

As guides to proper methods of teaching general education classes, mastery learning principles seem appropriate.[11] These principles can include (a) setting reasonable learning objectives for students to pursue, (b) stating the objectives as measurable or observable student behavior, (c) informing the students of the goals, (d) dividing the learning sequence into small units or lessons, (e) using multiple means for communicating the learning material to students so as to accommodate to individual differences in learning styles and abilities, (f) providing students with frequent feedback regarding how they are succeeding, and (g) offering them ways to remedy their errors, thus enabling them to master the present goals before they move ahead to the next learning task. Such procedures are intended to maximize the learners' chances of achieving the goals and, in the process, their chances of completing the course with a feeling of pride and accomplishment.

Summary

The aim of this chapter has been to propose values goals and affective goals for general education programs. For the purpose of analysis, the realm of values goals was divided into six types: (a) aesthetic, (b) moral, (c) social-conventional, (d) personal welfare, (e) technical or functional, and (f) economic. I then proposed that curriculum planners and instructors of general education courses could identify values goals suitable for their classes by first inspecting the kinds of facts, concepts, and skills that formed the contents of their courses and then, for each of the six kinds of values, could determine how it could profitably be related to the course contents.

The affective goals proposed as appropriate for general education were ones related to student motivation and to students gaining a strong feeling of accomplishment by the close of each general education class. Suggestions were then offered about methods of assigning students to general education classes and about ways of teaching in those classes to foster the pursuit of the affective goals.

FOOTNOTES

1. David R. Krathwohl, Benjamin S. Bloom, and Bertram B. Masia, *Taxonomy of Educational Objectives—Handbook II: Affective Domain* (New York: McKay, 1964), p. 16.

2. R. Murray Thomas, "Assessing Moral Development," *International Journal of Educational Research* 10, no. 4 (1986): 363-371.

3. Elliot Turiel, "The Development of Social-Conventional and Moral Concepts," in *Moral Development and Socialization*, ed. Myra Windmiller, Nadine Lambert, and Elliot Turiel (Boston: Allyn and Bacon, 1980), p. 364.

4. "Moral Education in Asia," *Research Bulletin of the National Institute for Educational Research*, No. 20 (Tokyo: National Institute for Educational Research, 1981), p. 3.

5. Louis E. Raths, Merrill Harmin, and Sidney B. Simon, *Values and Teaching* (Columbus, OH: Merrill, 1964), p. 30.

6. Krathwohl, Bloom, and Masia, *Taxonomy of Educational Objectives*, p. 33.

7. Ibid., p. 35.

8. Jerrold Coombs, "Practical Reasoning: What Is It? How Do We Enhance It?" (Paper delivered at the International Conference on Thinking at Ohio State University, June 1986).

9. Raths, Harmin, and Simon, *Values and Teaching*, pp. 38-39.

10. Lawrence Kohlberg, *The Psychology of Moral Development* (San Francisco: Harper and Row, 1984).

11. Lorin W. Anderson and James H. Block, "Mastery Learning Model of Teaching and Learning," in *International Encyclopedia of Education*, ed. Torsten Husén and T. Neville Postlethwaite (Oxford: Pergamon, 1985), vol. 6, pp. 3219-3230.

CHAPTER X

Who Can Be Taught What? General Education in the Secondary School

IAN WESTBURY

As several essays in this volume have noted, the traditional language which provides the framework for the discussion of general education is perhaps empty of real meaning but, hallowed as it is by time, it is always worth repeating because of what it stands for. Two samples, separated by over a hundred years, are enough to do the task of context setting for this chapter.

Writing after the passage of the Illinois act of 1845 regulating public education, the then state superintendent of public education explained that:

> The legislature, in prescribing the studies mentioned, assumed and believed them to be fitting for the schools of the people—adapted to the wants and necessities of common life—calculated to promote their material interests, and some of the high interests of the youth of the state, and the commonwealth— designed to aid, encourage and elevate the pupils individually, to promote their success and prosperity in business, and render them better and more intelligent citizens.[1]

The "studies" he referred to were spelling, penmanship, arithmetic, English grammar, modern geography, and the history of the United States. The "schools of the people" were, of course, what we would term elementary schools.

In 1981, writing on the secondary school in the context of a

Some of the research I report here was supported by various funding agencies. The IEA Second International Mathematics Study was supported by U.S. government agencies and by the Spencer Foundation. My research in Australian curriculum thinking was supported by research fellowships granted by the University of Melbourne and the Research Board of the University of Illinois at Champaign-Urbana. The conclusions reflected here are, of course, my own and should not be attributed to these agencies and institutions. I also wish to acknowledge the helpful comments of William A. Reid on an earlier version of this essay.

symposium on "common learning" in the college, Hechinger suggested that general education is:

that part of the baggage that educated men and women should be expected to carry when they leave school. It is the foundation of knowledge and understanding on which people should be able to build for the rest of their lives. It underlies their comprehension of politics and economics; their capacity to stretch their minds through books, as consumers of the arts, as independent thinkers, as guides to their children.[2]

Hechinger does not prescribe a set of studies which might serve to carry out these purposes but he mentions approvingly the general education offered in the lycées, gymnasia, and grammar schools of Europe with their "carefully mapped out curriculum" of history, geography, literature, mathematics, science, and foreign languages. "In the European mode, all of these elements of general education are studied in natural progression by all students."[3]

At one level there is much in common in these statements despite their separation by over a hundred years. Utterances of this kind serve to emphasize a conception of education which has held its own as a core part of all American thinking about the foundations of the work of the school. It is a major part of the purposes of the curriculum to "prepare" students for their lives outside the school, not only in the vocational aspect but also, and perhaps more importantly, in the more general senses of citizenship and culture. This ideal of general education has persisted and developed to control Americans' conceptions of how mass secondary and higher education can be arranged and has set out a sense of purposes which has muted, but not eliminated, the power that the competing ideologies of vocationalism and stratification have over the work of the schools.

At the same time there is a difference between the ways in which our nineteenth-century state superintendent and Hechinger saw and see the context and character of this general education. The state superintendent wrote of the "schools of the people" and derived his sense of the appropriate studies from that context. A century later Hechinger addressed secondary education in a context in which this institution has also become a school for the people but, curiously, the model for an appropriate curriculum which he invokes derives from the still elitist secondary school tradition of Europe. There would seem to be an implicit repudiation in this example of the idea and reality of mass secondary education, the half-century old hallmark of the American educational order. We see here, albeit in the context of what is a throw away sentence, one of the enduring tensions lurking in the idea of general education, a tension which I will be considering in a more specific way later in this essay.

We can, of course, see Hechinger's invocation of the European school as an expression of an ideal that the American school might and should be aspiring to. Ideals are a necessary and critical part of an enterprise like education and are the usual focus of all discussions of this theme. We articulate, in the way that we have seen in my texts, a vision of what might be and seek to prescribe how that vision might or should be enacted in schools of one kind or another—and sometimes our ideals become reality. I will adopt that starting point later in this essay but, at this point of beginning, let me proceed in a different way, by starting with the schools and seeking to infer meaning from what we see on the ground. And, for the purposes of this discussion, let me invoke yet another text defining the tasks of general education. Harold Dunkel, writing in the context of an ambitious attempt in the 1940s to enhance general education in the college, suggested that for his purposes general education is "that minimum of education (in terms of the individual's ability to profit from it) which he must have in our society if he is to live 'effectively' both within himself and in society."[4]

This definition is clearly related to those we considered earlier, but it is also clearly different; and it suggests some questions. What is the minimum of education, seen in terms of an enumeration of subjects, which is mandated as being appropriate to all pupils in secondary schools? What does the minimal curriculum actually taken by pupils in contemporary secondary schools look like? And what might we infer from these data about the working conceptions that schools have about the minimum of education which their graduates must have if they are "to live effectively" both within themselves and in society?

General Education in the High School

In order to answer these questions and provide a springboard for my later discussion let me begin with a listing of state-mandated requirements for graduation from secondary schools. These are, we can assume, the subjects and studies which are thought to be fitting for the "schools of the people." Table 1 presents the requirements that all of the states impose on their schools: typically three or four courses in English and language arts, two or three courses in social studies, two courses in mathematics, one to three courses in science and one course

TABLE 1
State Course Requirements for High School Graduation

State	Total	Language Arts	Social Studies	Mathematics	Science	PE/Health	Electives	Other
Alabama	20	4	3	2	1	3½	6½	
Alaska	19	1	1	1	1	1	9½	½—essentials of the free enterprise system
Arizona	20	4	2	2	2		10	
Arkansas	16	3	1		2	1		
California	13		3	2	2	2		1—fine arts or foreign language
Connecticut	18							
Delaware	19	4	3	2	2	1½	6½	
Florida	24	4	3	3	3	1	9	½—practical arts; ½—fine arts
Georgia	21	4	3	2	2		8	1—fine arts, vocational education or computer technology
Hawaii	20	4	4	2	2	1½	6	½—guidance
Idaho	20	4	2	2	2½	1½	6	1—reading/speech; 1—humanities
Illinois	16	3	2	2	1	4	1	¼—consumer education
Indiana	19½	4	2	2	2	1½	8	
Iowa			1½	2		1		
Kansas	20	4	3	2	2	1	8	
Kentucky	20	3	2	3	3	1	8	
Louisiana	22	4	2	3	2	2	8½	½—free enterprise system
Maine	20	4	1				8	
Maryland			3	2	2	1		
Massachusetts			½			4		
Michigan	15		2					
Minnesota	16	3	2½	1	1	1	8½	
Mississippi	20	3	1	1	1	1		
Missouri		1			1		11	2—English, social studies, math or science; 1—practical arts; 1—fine arts
Montana	16	4	2	2	2	1		1—fine arts; 2—practical arts
Nevada	20	3	2	2	1	2½	2	
New Hampshire	16	4	2	1	1	1	8	
New Jersey	14½	4	2	2	1	4		1—fine, practical or performing arts; ½—career exploration

TABLE 1 (*Continued*)
STATE COURSE REQUIREMENTS FOR HIGH SCHOOL GRADUATION

STATE	TOTAL	LANGUAGE ARTS	SOCIAL STUDIES	MATHE-MATICS	SCIENCE	PE/HEALTH	ELEC-TIVES	OTHER
New Mexico	21	4	2	2	2	1	9	1—practical or fine arts
New York								
Local diploma	16	4	3	1	1	½	6½	
Regents diploma	18	4	3	2	1	½	8½	
North Carolina	20	4	2	2	2	1	9	
North Dakota	19	4	3	2	2	1	7	
Ohio	18	3	2	2	2	1	9	
Oklahoma	20	4	2	2	2		10	
Oregon	21	3	3½	1	1	2	9	½—career development, 1—fine arts or foreign language
Pennsylvania	13	3	2	1	1			
Rhode Island								
General	16	4	1	1	1		9	
College-bound	18	4	2	3	2		4	2—foreign language; ½—arts; ½—computer literacy
South Carolina	20	4	3	3	2	1	7	
South Dakota	18	4	2	2	2		8	
Tennessee	20	4	1½	2	2	1½	9	
Texas	18	3	2½	2	2	2	6½	
Utah	15	3	3	1	1	1½	6½	
Virginia	20	4	3	2	2	2	6	1—additional science or math
Washington	48	9	7½	6	6		16½	3—occupational education
West Virginia	20	4	3	2	1	2	8	
Wyoming	18	4	1	2				
Dist. of Col.								
Comprehensive	20½	4	2	2	2	1½	8	1—foreign language
Career/vocational	23	4	2	2	2	1½	1½	1—foreign language; 9—specialized preparation

Note: Numbers refer to years of instruction.

Source: Education Commission of the States, as quoted in *Book of the States, 1984-1985*, Vol. 25 (Lexington, KY: Council of State Governments, 1984), p. 367.

in physical education plus a group of other miscellaneous requirements in which there is no clear consensus.

Insofar as states are concerned, therefore, the core of an
appropriate general education is found in English/language arts and
social studies, although some, but less, experience must be secured in
mathematics, science, and physical education. However, it needs to be
noted that the kind of listing seen in table 1 contains requirements
which have not yet come into effect in many states because the list
reflects the results of the recent national concern for "excellence." In
some states at least a prescription as broad as those seen in table 1 is a
departure from tradition. In Illinois, for example, the state's current
(1987) requirements include only three years of English with an
emphasis on reading and writing skills, one course in American
history or American history and government, one semester of health
education, thirty clock hours of instruction in driver education, and
eight semester courses in physical education, together with classes
which might be incorporated into several courses to constitute the
equivalent of one quarter of coursework in consumer education. In
addition the state imposes a set of unspecified and unsanctioned
expectations that the schools should teach patriotism, career
education, sex and family life education, conservation education,
honesty, justice, kindness, moral courage, the humane treatment of
animals, and metric education.[5]

In states like Illinois, where state regulation of schools is minimal,
the effective specification of the curriculum is found at the school level
and in the requirements that districts establish as their core
expectations. We must, therefore, look to these school-level
requirements if we are to secure the sense that we want of the
curriculum of general education. Table 2 presents four exemplars
from Illinois of school-level requirements along with some
information which will become important to the arguments that I will
be making later in this chapter.

What we see in these examples are two markedly different sets of
requirements. In the three public schools there is a common core of
three or four courses in English, one or two courses in mathematics,
one and a half or two courses in social studies, and one course in
science, together with the state's requirement of four years of physical
education, driver education, and the like. In the private school (Lake
Forest Academy-Ferry Hall) we see a very different pattern: four
courses in English, three in foreign language(s), three in mathematics,
one in the biological sciences and two in the physical sciences, three in

TABLE 2
High School Graduation Requirements and Plans of Graduates in 1983 for Post High School Years in Four Illinois High Schools

Bloomington High School. Comprehensive school in Bloomington and Normal, population, 80,000. 129 miles south of Chicago; 150 miles north of St. Louis.

Graduation requirements: 17 units, including English 3, mathematics 1, science 1, social studies 2.

Percent of 350 graduates with plans for post high school years

Four-year public college	28
Four-year private college	6
Two-year college	7
Vocational/technical institute	1
Military	1
Employment	50
Other	7
College-bound out of state	8

Cissna Park High School. Small rural school in farming community.

Graduation requirements: 18 units, including English 3, mathematics 1, biological sciences 1, social studies 2.

Percent of 28 graduates with plans for post high school years

Four-year public college	48
Two-year college	24
Vocational/technical institute	10
Military	10
Employment	8
College-bound out of state	7

Lake Forest Academy—Ferry Hall. 30 miles north of Chicago in a community of 18,000.

Graduation requirements: 17 units, including English 4, mathematics 3, biological sciences 1, social studies 3, physical sciences 2, foreign language 3, computer science. Advanced placement: art, biology, chemistry, computer science, English, history, mathematics, physics.

Percent of 350 graduates with plans for post high school years

Four-year public college	34
Four-year private college	66
College-bound out of state	80

New Trier High School. Township north of Chicago.

Graduation requirements: 21 units, including English 4, mathematics 2, science 1, social studies 2. Advanced placement: art, biology, chemistry, French, German, history, Latin, mathematics, physics.

Percent of 1,196 graduates with plans for post high school years

Four-year public college	45
Four-year private college	40
Two-year college	7
Vocational/technical institute	1
Military	1
Employment	4
Other	2

Source: *Guide to Secondary Schools: Illinois* (New York: College Entrance Examination Board, 1984).

social studies, and one in computer science. I will return to the
implications of these clearly different patterns of requirements but,
before doing so let me seek to describe the curriculum of the American
secondary school system in a different way.

Mandates of the kind I have been discussing are, of course,
mandates which prescribe the minimal core curriculum of the
secondary school. To graduate, students must do much more than
meet these minima. What does the core of the actual curriculum taken
by the modal high school student look like? We can assume that this
program represents the more robust conception of the minimum of
education which counselors, parents, and students themselves see as
constituting the core curriculum of the secondary school.

Table 3 reports the findings on course-taking in secondary public
high schools derived from an analysis of the transcripts of a national
sample of graduates who were in school between 1975 and 1981.[6]
The table reports the percentages of all students in the sample taking
each course and includes students who failed. The table also presents
the findings on course-taking by students who identified themselves
as having been in an "academic track."

It is important to note that the rows in table 3 refer to specific
courses whereas the mandates and requirements we considered earlier

TABLE 3

COURSE-TAKING BY HIGH SCHOOL STUDENTS:
PERCENTAGE OF HIGH SCHOOL GRADUATES WHO HAD ENROLLED IN
SPECIFIC COURSES

COURSE	ALL GRADUATES	ACADEMIC TRACK
Physical Education	89.0	89.0
US Government	51.1	47.5
US History I	84.5	83.9
English 1	76.5	76.0
English 2	74.8	75.9
English 3	54.0	55.2
Algebra 1	63.8	72.4
Biology 1	77.1	86.4
Typing 1	67.6	68.2
Driver Education/Safety	58.6	60.7
Geometry 1	—	71.5
Chemistry 1	—	61.1

Note: Only courses which had percentage enrollment rates of over 50 percent are
included in this table.

Source: Clifford Adelman, *Devaluation, Diffusion, and the College Connection: A
Study of High School Transcripts, 1964-1981* (Washington, DC: National Commission
on Excellence in Education, 1982). ERIC ED 228 244.

refer to broad subject areas. A student may meet a particular requirement in, say, mathematics by taking any one of a number of courses the school may offer. Nevertheless, the character of the listing seen in table 3 does resemble the character of the requirements we saw in our set of Illinois schools: the core curriculum for all would seem to consist of physical education, U.S. history, two or three years of English, algebra, and biology, together with one addition, typing. It is also interesting in the light of the requirements of Lake Forest Academy, the private school we introduced earlier, that those students who saw themselves as in the academic track take additional courses in mathematics (Geometry 1) and science (Chemistry 1). I will again postpone a discussion of the implications of this difference until later.

What can we make of the core curriculum that defines the minimum of education that the contemporary high school offers? Let me begin a consideration of this issue by invoking again the texts I quoted at the beginning of this chapter. They suggest that we look outside the school for a rationale for the core curriculum—that we look, to put it crudely, to "life," to the culture, to the "needs" of citizenship, and the like. What sense can we make of a curriculum of three or four years of English, two or three years of social studies (including the ubiquitous American history), one or two years of mathematics, one or two courses in science, and several courses in physical education when seen in these terms?

Of course, the goal of general education embraces more than this minimal curriculum. Much that the school does can be seen as contributing to a general education for students but, even as we recognize this, it is also clear that it is difficult to describe precisely what happens beyond the core curriculum I have been reporting. For many students the patterns of courses they take after completing the more or less coherent academic program of the ninth grade quickly become diffuse and lose all sustained contact with the subject categories that Hechinger saw as the core of the European schools' curriculum—and which are found in the junior high school. For example, in their study of the course-taking patterns of Illinois high school students, Murphy, Hull, and Walker found that enrollments in mathematics dropped by 25 percent of the initial base in each of the four years of high school and that course-taking in science was confined to the ninth and tenth grades.[7] The implication is that, as we saw in table 3, courses like Chemistry I and Geometry I, which are taken by students in the college-preparatory track, are dropped by other students—and are not replaced by alternatives which might be less demanding but are as specific in their focus on science or mathematics. We might well ask what view of the world outside the school informs a core curriculum that does not require all students to devote four years to some study of mathematics and/or science. In the words of Jeremy Bernstein:

We live in a complex, dangerous and fascinating world. Science has played a role in creating the dangers, and one hopes that it will aid in creating ways of dealing with these dangers. But most of these problems cannot, and will not, be dealt with by scientists alone. We need all of the help we can get, and this help has to come from a scientifically literate general public. Ignorance of science and technology is becoming the ultimate self-indulgent luxury.[8]

I will return to this theme of science and technology later but to protect myself against suspicions about my orientation towards the curriculum I must also note that parallel concerns can also be raised about other areas that I would regard as equally central (at least potentially) to an idea of general education. Thus, Murphy, Hull, and Walker found that art was rarely studied in Illinois schools—a finding that parallels the national findings I reported in table 3—and that all of the courses in music they counted made up only 5 percent of the total number of courses taken by the students they investigated.[9] Interestingly there were more artists and commercial artists employed in Illinois in 1982 than there were civil engineers, mathematicians, or social scientists and more musicians than chemists, psychologists, and hospital social workers.[10] Moreover, nationwide one of every four adult Americans plays a musical instrument and secures, one can assume, pleasure in their playing that could only be enhanced by formal experience in school.[11] In other words, like the mythical man from Mars, one can only wonder, in the light of the simpleminded concern for what the tasks of general education might be, why the core curriculum is as it is. Why, for example, do the arts not figure more prominently than they seem to? Why do they receive less attention in the rising mound of literature expressing concern for the curriculum than do, say, foreign languages? My questions are rhetorical, for the answers are clear.

The History of the Curriculum of General Education

The clarity of the answer raises the fundamental question that any attempt to address the idea of general education must face. The curriculum of the high school has remained largely unchanged for almost eighty years. As a consequence the changing definitions of "culture" that have come to pass over those years have largely passed the school by, and where they have affected the school, they have done so in ways that reduced, not enhanced, the contribution the school might make to the ultimate participation of the adults in that culture. This is much less the case insofar as the college is concerned but that is another story.

TABLE 4

PROGRAMS IN NEW TRIER TOWNSHIP HIGH SCHOOL, 1919-20

HOME ARTS COURSE

FIRST YEAR

First Semester	Second Semester
English	English
Algebra	Algebra
Domestic Science	Domestic Science
Freehand Drawing and Design	Freehand Drawing and Design
Elective	Elective
Physical Training	Physical Training
	Physiology (10 wks.)

SECOND YEAR

English	English
Geometry Plane	Geometry
Domestic Science	Domestic Science
Freehand Drawing and Design	Freehand Drawing and Design
French, German, Spanish or Latin	French, German, Spanish or Latin
Physical Training	Physical Training

THIRD YEAR

English	English
Chemistry	Chemistry
Domestic Science	Domestic Science
Freehand Drawing and Design	Freehand Drawing and Design
French, German, Spanish or Latin	French, German, Spanish or Latin
Physical Training	Physical Training

FOURTH YEAR

English	English
American History	American History
Domestic Science	Domestic Science
Freehand Drawing and Design	Freehand Drawing and Design
Elective	Elective
Physical Training	Physical Training

We can see this stability of the curriculum over eighty years very clearly if we compare today's graduation requirements of New Trier Township High School (see table 2) with that school's minimal requirements in 1919-20. Table 4 lays out the required courses from two New Trier programs of that year, the "general" college preparatory program and the "home arts" program. There is one striking difference between the cores of these programs and their successor sixty-five years later: foreign languages have disappeared as a requirement. Otherwise the two programs are essentially similar in the subject categories they mandate as constituting the core curriculum for a four-year program.

TABLE 4 (*Continued*)

GENERAL COURSE

FIRST YEAR

First Semester	Second Semester
English	English
Algebra	Algebra
Physical Training	Physical Training
Choose two five credit subjects	Physiology
	Choose two five credit subjects

SECOND YEAR

English	English
Geometry	Geometry
Foreign Language	Foreign Language
Physical Training	Physical Training
Choose one five credit subject	Choose one five credit subject

THIRD YEAR

English	English
Foreign Language	Foreign Language
*Chemistry or American History	Chemistry or American History
Physical Training	Physical Training
Choose one five credit subject	Choose one five credit subject

FOURTH YEAR

English	English
*Physics or American History	Physics or American History
Physical Training	Physical Training
Choose two five credit subjects	Choose two five credit subjects

*Either Chemistry or Physics and American History are required.

Source: New Trier Township High School, *Yearbook 1919-1920* (Kenilworth, IL: New Trier Township Board of Education, 1919).

The *New Trier Yearbook* for 1919-20 also makes a set of distinctions within the overall curricula offered by the school which resembles the distinction between college-preparatory and "other" curricula that I raised earlier in this essay, but did not address directly. The *Yearbook* notes that over 60 percent of the school's then graduating class entered some institution of higher education and advises parents and pupils to plan programs "so that pupils will be protected in their college preparation." It goes on to note that "most Eastern colleges require three or four years of English, two and one half years to three years of mathematics, four years of Latin, two years of foreign languages, two years of history, and one year of chemistry and physics."[12] Although there have been some significant changes (most notably the elimination of Latin) this college-preparatory curriculum of 1919 resembles the curriculum presently required for graduation from Lake Forest Academy.

What lies unsaid in the distinction between the requirements of the "Eastern colleges" of 1919 and those of New Trier's "general" and "home arts" programs of 1919 (and New Trier's present graduation requirements) is the role of the high school as an agency of economic and social stratification. The "college preparatory" and "general" (and minimal) curricula I have been describing are heavily laden with social, intellectual, and cultural symbolism and, as such, become the bases not only of intellectual and scholastic differentiation, but also of cultural differentiation. However, while this is very clear on the ground and widely recognized, in practice it is mystified ideologically, albeit appropriately in my judgment.

Thus, the ideal of general education is, in the collegiate tradition, closely associated with the notion of liberal arts. In the world of the high school it also has this same association for some, but for others general education is more closely tied to the kind of definition we saw Dunkel articulating. It is a basis for that minimum of education which people must have if they are to live effectively both within themselves and in society. *It is the contest between these two different conceptions of general education that has made it difficult, if not impossible, for the high school to secure a sustained focus on such questions as: What might the core curriculum be? And how might that curriculum serve a goal of general education for all?* And, of course, even if such a discussion of principles were possible, the working out of their implications in the real world of the schools would have to face the press of both the institutional and the organizational forces within and without the school which support the existing curriculum-in-fact if not the curriculum-in-principle. Clearly the most influential of these forces are those associated with the collegiate tradition of liberal education; but I believe that, rather than being a potential saviour in that it can give purpose to the otherwise purposeless enterprise of the modern secondary school, that tradition has been, and most likely will be, pernicious in its consequences for the high school. Let me develop that argument.

General Education and the Collegiate Tradition

In contrast to the universities of many other nations, the American university stands in close proximity to the compulsory secondary school in its intentions at the undergraduate level; in addition, the university has maintained a continuity between the structure of liberal education as this was embodied in the post-Renaissance college with its classical curriculum and the disciplinary curriculum that is the hallmark of all modern universities. This ideological continuity was achieved by transferring to the collectivity of the modern humanities, social sciences, and sciences the notion that *together* they make a contribution to the ideal of liberal or general education by virtue of both the subject matters and themes they address and the forms of thinking and reasoning that they embody. Institutionally this ideology has produced the patterns of collegiate curricula which continue general education into the college years and postpone specialized studies in higher professional fields until the upper division or graduate years. Such curricular practices, and their ideology, have meant that colleges of liberal arts and sciences have assumed a role which, while muted insofar as such fields as engineering are concerned, is central to thinking about the kind of education students should aspire to before entering fields like medicine or law. Furthermore, inasmuch as such culturally central institutions as the "Eastern colleges" and their analogues in other places are, in the main, seen as *only* colleges of liberal arts and science, the hegemony of the liberal arts and sciences has become the more complete.

While it is difficult to generalize across all fields and all institutions, I think it is fair to say that in most colleges of liberal arts and science the values which the faculty, and sometimes even students, invoke to define their work are those associated with what might be loosely called higher culture: intellectualism, cosmopolitanism, socially and ethically responsible professionalism, and the like. And while I must emphasize that I believe that the curricular pattern which has institutionalized these values has enhanced American education and culture in important ways, it has also had consequences which are profoundly deleterious for the schools if not the university. Thus, within the university, faculty members in departments of liberal arts and sciences have been able to differentiate themselves from such undergraduate vocational fields as engineering, agriculture, and the like as well as from such fields as medicine or law by pointing to the "higher" work that they do. As such claims are made, it matters little that in fact the liberal arts are often quite explicitly vocational in their practices and intentions. They (that is, the liberal arts) are seen otherwise and have, by a kind of sleight of hand, succeeded in arrogating the notion of general and liberal education to themselves alone. Thus, architecture, art, music, engineering, medicine, law, and physical education—not to speak of fashion merchandising, criminal justice, and the like—are seen as being outside the canon of fields thought appropriate to, in, and for a general education. And, more important for our theme, it is the kind of work that is or has been done within colleges of liberal arts and science that has been the definer of what should count as valid and legitimate content for schoolwork in these fields.

We can see many aspects of this institutional and cultural context of thinking about the curriculum of the high school, and much of what has happened as the fields associated with the liberal arts have evolved over the past forty years, in *General Education in a Free Society,* an influential report published in 1945 by a Harvard Committee on the Objectives of Education in a Free Society.[13] The problem of "general education," the Report suggests, is "one of combining fixity of aim with diversity in application. ... What is wanted is a general education capable at once of taking on many different forms and yet representing in all of its forms the common knowledge and the common values on which a free society depends." The elements of this common knowledge were defined in the ways we might expect: the areas of "natural science, social studies, and the humanities," and the values that are important are those reflected in the methods of thinking and the traits of mind which should be and perhaps are nurtured by such fields: effective thinking and the communication of the results of thought, judgment, and discrimination among values. The problem, the Report suggests, in planning a framework for general education for the secondary school seen in these terms is one of finding a balance between the demands of a specialized and a general education. Such a balance must acknowledge the presence of diversity and, particularly, the difference between those who are of college calibre and "young people of average intelligence" who might not be suited to the traditional college but can profit from training in agriculture, nursing, and the like. Unity must, therefore, be tempered by the recognition of the reality of difference such that general education "can appeal deeply to each, yet remain in goal and essential teaching the same for all."

To accomplish these purposes, *General Education in a Free Society* recommends a core high school curriculum of eight units: three in English, three in science *and* mathematics, and two in social studies, with the possibility that another course in each area might be added which would be appropriate for those who would not proceed to college. But, as the Report went on to point out, such a prescription should not be taken as implying that all students should take the same courses: "There must be courses of different difficulty and different method in each of the three spheres of general education, and the criterion for membership in these should be neither a student's intentions in life nor his background nor the kind of diploma for which he is aiming, but simply whether or not a given course is the best for him—which is to say, a criterion of ability."

Such sentiments are unexceptionable. However, the way in which they are worked out in the Report reveals what I believe is the essential problem in all applications of the collegiate ideal of liberal education to the school. Thus, when discussing the place and nature of the treatment of science and technology in the curriculum, the Report makes it clear that in the view of its authors, "science is not technology. Its prime end is *knowing* rather than *doing*." A program in science for high school must be based on the laboratory and must acknowledge the form of reasoning which is associated with science, mathematization, and place these at the center of a science program. But given the difficulties which the Report sees such a program posing for less able students (students of average intelligence?), science for all can only consist of two courses: one in general science which should begin to "segregate for [the student] the differences in point of view and approach which are the basis of the division of the sciences into separate disciplines" and a course in biology, a subject "which can be dealt with in a largely descriptive way."[14]

We see the same kind of issue arising in the discussion of mathematics. "We must recognize . . . that for the mathematically less gifted pupils in the ninth grade there is little straightforward mathematics available beyond elementary instruction in arithmetic and informal geometry." Moreover, "it is probably true that any considerable softening of instruction in algebra and demonstrative geometry, to bring them within the compass of the mathematically inept, serves no useful purpose. It makes a contribution of very doubtful value to the slow students at the very real expense of the more acute." As the Report goes on to conclude, weaker students should be directed to courses in "shop math" as a disguise for simple arithmetic and its application to practical problems, for "when a student has reached the limits of his tolerance of handling abstractions, his *general* education in mathematics must also come to an end."[15]

The logic of *General Education in a Free Society* is curious. General education was defined as "the common knowledge and the common values on which a free society depends" but, having asserted this, it turns out that it is impossible in practice to offer the components of such a general education to "young people of average intelligence." The implications of such a commentary may be dismissed with the observation that such flaws in reasoning were to be expected when this Report was written and that *General Education in a Free Society* was but a celebration of a particular view of an older world in which the potentials that might be associated with education were seen as being more narrowly distributed than we might now see them to be. Moreover, it could be argued that, within the limitations of their overall position, the committee authoring the Report did break out of some of the limitations of their context by emphasizing talent over status.

Such arguments would have merit were it not for two things. First, the curriculum of the Report is, of course, the curriculum we saw being reflected in the minimal graduation requirements we discussed above; it was also the curriculum which, as we have seen, long predated the ruminations of the committee. Given this, a case can be made that what we see in *General Education in a Free Society* is not an idiosyncratic statement but is, instead, a testament to what may be thought of as the core ideology of the *institution* of the high school curriculum with all of the confusions that are endemic in such ideologies. Second, the Report spelled out in some detail what was to come to pass, both in the practice and the spirit of the secondary school curriculum, and this was to be different from what had gone before. The curriculum of the Report may have been similar to what had gone before but, within its enumeration of subjects, there was much that was different from what had gone before. And it is with just this difference in the spirit of the curriculum that those who are interested in the idea of general education have to cope.

The authors of the Report were an elite group from an elite university writing *before* what Trow has termed the "second transformation" of the American high school—its passage from an institution of mass secondary education to an institution of mass college-preparatory education.[16] They were, moreover, early and leading members of the new clerisy of professional academics, professional scientists, and engineers who were to dominate the imagination of both elites and the public at large in the postwar years of opportunity; there were in this world hitherto unimaginable opportunities for the talented in old and new professions, including both university and public school teaching. Moreover, increasing national wealth created opportunities to participate both directly and indirectly in the cosmopolitan worlds toward which the socialization and enculturation associated with the ideology of the traditional liberal arts colleges was directed, with the result that these ideals became more meaningful, and more relevant and accessible than they had ever been. Resources of students, money, and status poured in on universities and colleges and permitted their faculties to begin to realize possibilities that could only have been imagined in earlier years. Revolutions in the assumptions of fields like engineering were occurring and were making new demands on undergraduate instruction. In all fields research and graduate instruction became much more important than they had ever been in prewar years and were institutionalized as activities in the host of new graduate schools being developed in these years. Thus, in its emphasis on abstraction and mathematization, *General Education in a Free Society* was reflecting the character of new forms of both scholarship and teaching and was projecting the demands of these new forms onto the schools. This was but a glimmer in the eyes of some at the time of the writing of the Report but ten or so years later this possibility was to become a real movement of "curriculum reform."

Martin Trow's "second transformation" of the secondary school provided the context in which all this was to occur. In prewar years the eastern colleges dominated because, as Daniel Bell puts it, they *reflected* the status structure of the society. In the postwar years the university was increasingly to *determine* status by conferring the expertise that was required for role in a new order.[17] With this came symbolic power as well as the power that came from the creation of elites; and with all this came a new concern for articulation between the school and the college. College and preparation for college became birthrights if not of all, certainly of the middle classes, and the new kinds of school curricula symbolized by such NSF-sponsored programs as "new math," PSSC *Physics*, and the like became programs that might not be wanted but were *needed* by a significant plurality because they reflected the new world of the university.

Several related developments accompanied the emergence of these new programs, and were foreshadowed by *General Education in a Free Society*. The place of the academic, college-preparatory track within the high school was reinforced; as a corollary the rhetoric which had accompanied Trow's "first transformation" of the secondary school— from an elite college preparatory to a mass terminal institution—was devalued.[18] And while the Vietnam era which followed was to split the single-minded focus on investment for entry to a world of university-based professionalism as the end of the school, the embrace of pluralism and consumption of experiences and ideas which followed did not bring about a robust alternative definition of the task of the school.[19] There was a related skirmish in the 1960s and 1970s with the then "new" ideologies of multiculturalism and diversity, but these were also to fail as potential rationales for the curriculum, to be replaced by the kind of reaffirmation we have seen in the recent past of the ideals of the 1950s and early 1960s.

But perhaps even more important than these changes in the context of the curriculum were the changes that took place in the curriculum itself, particularly in the sciences and mathematics. Fensham has, for example, plotted the emphases in Australian textbooks in chemistry— texts that were closely based on the NSF-supported American models—and found that the period since the reforms of the 1950s and 1960s has seen the virtual elimination from texts and courses of the kind of historical and applied topics that had marked earlier periods. Accompanying this, he discerned an emphasis on formalism, both in the curriculum itself and its presentation. The focus is on theoretical knowledge of chemistry as a "science" with the presentation being sequential and without any obvious focus in chemical reality. Such courses are marked by instruction which in Fensham's words "expects the learner to be motivated to the theoretical knowledge of the discipline of chemistry or by the fact that chemistry is a required subject for his or her vocational goals." And, as he goes on to note, when adaptation of such courses has been attempted to meet the needs of a broader group of students, the approach has been one of reduction of the content that is required but not a reconceptualization of that content.[20]

What have been the consequences for school science of a reform that moved science in the direction Fensham describes? In his words, such courses "require a persistence of interest and intellectual achievement in learners that many are not likely to maintain. . . . [As a result] if the success of present courses has been improvement of the education of a minority *in* chemistry, their failure is the education of the majority *through* essentially similar sorts of chemistry." The "needs" of the 20 percent or so of the population who will enter college programs in the sciences and applied sciences may be being met by such courses, but at the expense of the 80 percent who will "live in societies and cultures that are inextricably influenced by and dependent upon the chemical and other sciences." Such courses do not and cannot support the need to develop "an informed populace who will support, or withhold support from, those developments that are possible because of technologies." Such courses cannot support the "purpose [of schooling] that relates to assisting *individuals* in all sorts of ways to share in and respond to the great human endeavors we associate with chemistry." These purposes, the purposes which Fensham suggests are *not* being met by most existing courses, are of course those I would associate with general education. They are the purposes which relate to acquisition of that minimum of education which people must have if they are to live effectively within themselves and in society in the contemporary world.

A "Theory" for General Education

The problem with the line of questioning which Fensham opens— and he makes it clear that he sees school science in general sharing the problems he identifies in chemistry—is that neither of the starting points that dominate discussion of the curriculum leads inevitably in the directions that his concerns would seem to foreshadow. These concerns do not emerge from arguments about the curriculum of the secondary school which start from the presumed needs of the college when these are seen in terms of the liberal arts tradition. They do not emerge as themes from a tradition of curriculum theory which has in many ways stood within public education as the countervailing tradition to the collegiate tradition. Thus, while teaching in the real world of the mass secondary school has demanded that the problems which follow from a single-minded preoccupation with the collegiate tradition be faced, the answers that most curriculum theories offer have led in yet another direction: they accept the implicit hierarchies of status that are built into the traditional curriculum while seeking to mute the inevitable centrifugal forces which follow by emphasizing those tasks of the school and aspects of curriculum that might be accessible to all, at least in principle. General education becomes defined in this tradition in terms of the "values, understandings, and skills" which can be taught to all at some level through a variety of subject matters.[21] There is thus no need for a curricular canon and no direction is given about the specifics of what might be taught in the name of general education.

While this "values, understandings, and skills" approach to the curriculum can be seen as merely symbolic in both character and consequences, such approaches dominate much curricular thinking at this time and, as rhetorics of justification for a curriculum, can be conveniently linked with the formalizing aspects of the competing ideology of the liberal arts we saw being evoked in the Harvard Report to create a powerful, albeit messy, rationale for what schools and colleges should be attempting in the name of general education. However, in some recent essays written from within the tradition of the liberal arts and sciences, Hirsch has condemned such "formal" approaches in principle, and in doing so, has offered a starting point for thinking about general education which has great merit. Thus, Hirsch has proposed that the curriculum should be concerned with what he terms "canonical information" or "cultural literacy," which he further defines as the lexicon of "words" that high school graduates should acquire as the outcome of their secondary schooling. And while Hirsch, a professor of English, draws most of his examples of such "words" from the humanities, his suggested lexicon does include DNA.[22]

Hirsch's argument is embedded in a conception of community and a conviction that "a certain extent of shared, canonical knowledge is inherently necessary to a literate democracy." Such a democracy requires, in Hirsch's view, a body of common, tacitly shared background knowledge of the kind that would reflect the culture of the community to support conversation and debate within the community. It could be, he suggests, the task of a possible National Board of Education to define the lexicon that would encapsulate this culture, although he recognizes that such a Board is unlikely to be established.

Hirsch's conception and approach seem right in principle and direct thinking about the role and tasks of general education in the secondary school in a way that a concern with a body of abstracted "values, understandings, and skills" can never do. And even the idea of a general education conceived along these lines raises issues which other approaches do not, and in so doing suggests possibilities which are intriguing if not immediately practicable. Thus, as I have implied in the preceding discussion, it is unlikely that any lexicon of the kind that Hirsch foreshadows would match in its emphasis, and omissions, the profile of the curriculum that I described earlier. That century-old curriculum, which even in its beginnings rejected the cultural significance of the engineering, architecture, manufacturing, and social organizing which Kenneth Clark has suggested were the creative points of the civilization of the nineteenth century,[23] has remained largely unchanged for its century of existence. While it may have been appropriate in the context of the schools of a century ago to value knowing over doing, today it is harder to believe that knowing about doing—mathematical modeling, applied ethics, agriculture and horticulture, health, and so forth—is less significant in some ultimate sense than knowing about knowing—biology, chemistry, mathematics, and the like. Likewise, it is difficult to see how the social forms that controlled the distribution of knowledge thought appropriate a century ago are still appropriate today; mathematics and science are, for example, too important and too significant to be seen as the reserves of the "talented" or of elites and/or as mechanisms for winnowing those who will have a comfortable home in the higher reaches of the educational system and in the range of learned professions. The world has become too small and too interdependent for the nation to be the exclusive focus for the social studies that the majority experiences. A lexicon of the words that would be a starting place for a curriculum for all must surely include terms like development, industrialization, Sahel, China, Latin America, the USSR, rain forests, Islam, and the like as well as enlightenment, separation of powers, Civil War, and New Deal.

But this raises another issue which is again a focus of Fensham's concern. In several places he proposes a list of "umbrella topic fields for a basic minimum core of science education," which fit into a lexicon of the kind Hirsch advocates, such topics as the universe, the human body, health, nutrition and sanitation, food, and so forth. But, as he notes, if the courses in which such topics are covered are introduced into a curriculum in such a way that they must *compete* with a traditional biology, physics, chemistry, and the like with all of their links with selection and preparation for higher education, they will be perceived as second-rate, as courses which are appropriate for some *but not for all.* This is so inevitable that it must be addressed by curriculum policies so as to *contain* the hegemony of the education which is seen as appropriate for prospective elites. *To ensure that the curriculum of general education is a curriculum for all, the curriculum must be a curriculum for all up to some point in the school—and the core of that curriculum for all must continue to be a curriculum for all to the termination of mass education,* in the United States, perhaps to grade fourteen.

On its face this prescription of Fensham's seems bold and even utopian. But, the problem that he identifies is perhaps more pervasive in American schools than it is in most other school systems. Thus, the mathematics curriculum of the American school begins selection of students in grade eight—and, as the curriculum unfolds, offers less and less to the majority after grade nine—and nothing to the overwhelming majority of those remaining in school to grade twelve.[24] Such early differentiation would seem on its face to deny too much to too many and, although this is the subject of another essay, does not result in outcomes which compare well with school systems which are, on their face, less rigorous in their tracking of students. *American schools, for example, teach their rigorously selected students much less mathematics than is taught in the schools of other nations and enroll fewer students in their mathematics programs.* We enroll 12 to 13 percent of the grade twelve age group in courses in a low-level advanced mathematics as compared to, say, Ontario, where 19 percent of the age group are enrolled in significantly more advanced courses.[25] One can all too easily ask how necessary the kind of elitist differentiation of courses and students is and why, in the face of the different structures of other nations, it persists.

Moreover, such differentiation, with its implications that most students do not experience mathematics, science, and the like after grade ten, would seem paradoxical in the face of the expectation that students in community colleges will, after two or so years of no work in these areas, revisit them in the name of general education and, in so doing, repeat work that could have been done in secondary school were the expectations and curricula different. And, curiously, more often than not such courses are seen as meriting college credit!

I offer this last observation only as a seeming paradox. It clearly raises a host of complex issues that bear on both the tasks of the school and the practicalities of a curriculum for general education. I am not sanguine that, however desirable it may be to think in the ways that Fensham suggests, the kind of containment he proposes would be easily accepted in the foreseeable future. To envisage such changes, the hegemony of the college, and particularly the hegemony of the "liberal arts," must be broken and replaced by a clearer conception of general education along the lines I have been advocating here. But perhaps I am unduly pessimistic because there do seem to be forces at work within "establishments" which have the capacity to influence the shape of the curriculum to bring about radical change. A Mathematical Sciences Education Board has been established within the National Academy of Sciences. Part of its concern is, if not a mathematics for all, certainly a mathematics for the majority that is very different in character from the mathematics that now dominates the secondary school, and reflects a concern for a general education of the kind that I have been describing here.[26]

If such boldness with its explicit rejection of the past and present is possible even within mathematics, it is surely possible within other areas. There are vast numbers of working scientists, physicians, veterinarians, toxicologists, environmental chemists, and so forth, the products of the eras of the 1950s and 1960s, who would and can envisage different futures for the science curriculum than the one that would follow if we were to do no more than project the past. As I suggested earlier, *General Education in a Free Society* can be seen as a hymn to an older order but there is also a sense in which it can be read as a harbinger of a future which was different from the then past. What is needed is perhaps not one National Board of Education of the kind that Hirsch suggested with tongue in cheek but a series of separate commissions (of the kind that he also suggests) concerned with the various categories which make up the curricular canon. It *is* feasible to imagine asking one or another group to consider what a lexicon focusing on the sciences, the social sciences, and so forth might be, although I suspect that they should use categories (to structure their work) like those used in Southern Illinois University's description of its program of general education: "Man's physical environment and biological inheritance," "Man's social inheritance and social responsibilities," "Man's insights and appreciations," "Organization and communication of ideas," and "Health and physical development." Such "words" communicate intentions and purposes in ways that terms like "science," the "social sciences," and "humanities" do not and are closer to the spirit of general education, and the needs of the mass school, than our present century-old framework of "disciplines" or subjects.

A Final Reflection

I must make one final observation. The forms of rhetoric associated with the traditional rationale for collegiate education that is found in the conception of the liberal arts, and the "general education" associated with it, denote not only the culture of an elite but also an aspiration. As Reid points out in his essay in this volume (and in doing so, he follows the thinking of Rothblatt[27]), the forms of liberal education are never settled and have always been directed toward notions of how people *should* relate to the societies in which they live. In its American version, liberal and general education aspires to forms or transcendence within community. This may seem utopian, just as the suggestions I have made about what a common curriculum might be may seem utopian. It was not so many years ago that the idea of universal literacy would have seemed utopian, but it has come to pass. It was the ambition for literacy that created the educability we associate with literacy, just as it was and is the ambition associated with the collegiate tradition of the liberal arts which has created a different but nevertheless equally pervasive educability on the part of a minority. In both cases a conception of educability and the competence to educate went hand in hand to create atmospheres in which what was at one time unthinkable became thinkable and attainable. As Schwab has written, "It is by similarly making no limiting, a priori assumptions as to who are the educable in respect of sounder views of knowledge and more complete modes of enquiry that we can find out how many can and how many cannot master them."[28] Schwab was writing in the context of the college of the 1950s and 1960s and his concern was different from mine, but that does not gainsay the relevance of his claims to the different issue of general education in the secondary school as I have sketched it here. The sentiments he articulated are appropriate ones as we think about the purposes and possibilities of a general education in the secondary school. The liberal tradition has often contrasted its concerns with "freedom" with the "servile" concern it associated with other forms of education, including even professional education. Unfortunately, this distinction has all too often been institutionalized in our thinking about the curriculum of the secondary school (to create assumptions of competence of the kind seen in *General Education in a Free Society*) and this is the malign legacy of the liberal tradition as it has been and is found in the collegiate tradition. Educability has been associated with social status and/or "aptitude" and for those without the appropriate aptitude and status nothing beyond a servile or elementary education was and is possible. Such a differentiation of a perceived educability undergirds the competing ideologies and curricula I described in the first pages of this essay. But the acceptance of the inevitability of such differentiation denies the very competence both to learn and teach that the ideology of liberal education unleashed. It is this same reality that needs to be created as we think anew about what the secondary school might be or aspire to. What I have tried to do here is show how far we are from such ambitions and what we might do to create a new reality around the secondary school. This reality will be, I have tried to suggest, very different from the secondary school we have inherited.

FOOTNOTES

1. Quoted in Illinois State Board of Education, *Instructional Program Mandates: A Preliminary Report* (Springfield, IL: Illinois State Board of Education, 1982), p. 10.

2. Fred Hechinger, "The High School-College Connection," in *Common Learning: A Carnegie Colloquium on General Education* (Washington, DC: Carnegie Foundation for the Advancement of Teaching, 1981), p. 119.

3. Ibid., p. 121.

4. Harold B. Dunkel, *General Education in the Humanities* (Washington, DC: American Council on Education, 1947), p. 4.

5. Illinois State Board of Education, *Instructional Program Mandates*.

6. Clifford Adelman, *Devaluation, Diffusion, and the College Connection: A Study of High School Transcripts 1964-1981* (Washington, DC: National Commission on Excellence in Education, 1982). ERIC ED 228 244.

7. Joseph Murphy, Thomas R. Hull, and Allan Walker, "Academic Drift and Curriculum Debris: Analysis of High School Course-Taking Patterns and Their Implications for Local Policy Makers," *Journal of Curriculum Studies*, in press.

8. Jeremy Bernstein, "Science Education for the Nonscientist," *American Scholar* 52 (Winter 1982-83): 12.

9. Murphy et al., "Academic Drift and Curriculum Debris."

10. Illinois Department of Employment Security, *Occupational Projections 1982-1995: Illinois* (Chicago: Illinois Department of Employment Security, 1986).

11. American Music Conference, *Music USA 85* (Chicago: American Music Conference, 1985), p. 15.

12. New Trier Township High School, *Yearbook 1919-1920* (Kenilworth, IL: New Trier Township Board of Education, 1919), p. 24.

13. Harvard University, Committee on the Objectives of Education in a Free Society, *General Education in a Free Society: Report of the Harvard Committee* (Cambridge, MA: Harvard University Press, 1945).

14. Ibid., pp. 158-59.

15. Ibid., pp. 163-64.

16. Martin Trow, "The Second Transformation of American Secondary Education," *International Journal of Comparative Sociology* 2 (1961): 144-66.

17. Daniel Bell, *The Reforming of General Education: The Columbia College Experience in Its National Setting* (New York: Columbia University Press, 1966), p. 96.

18. Trow, "The Second Transformation of American Secondary Education."

19. For this analysis, see Dennis J. O'Keeffe, "Towards a Socio-economy of the Curriculum," *Journal of Curriculum Studies* 9 (May 1977): 101-110.

20. Peter J. Fensham, "Conceptions, Misconceptions, and Alternative Frameworks in Chemical Education: The Nyholm Lecture," *Chemical Society Reviews* 13 (1984): 203-4. See also, idem, "Science for All: A Reflective Essay," *Journal of Curriculum Studies* 17 (October-December 1985): 415-35.

21. See, for example, Arthur D. Roberts and Gordon Cawelti, *Redefining General Education in the American High School* (Alexandria, VA: Association for Supervision and Curriculum Development, 1984).

22. E. D. Hirsch, Jr., "Cultural Literacy," *American Scholar* 52 (Spring 1983): 159-69. See also, idem, " 'English' and the Perils of Formalism," *American Scholar* 53 (Summer 1984): 369-79. Hirsch's *Cultural Literacy: What Every American Needs to Know* (Boston: Houghton Mifflin, 1987) provides a major development of the arguments outlined in his earlier papers.

23. Kenneth Clark, *Civilization: A Personal View* (New York: Harper and Row, 1969), chap. 13.

24. Curtis C. McKnight et al., *The Underachieving Curriculum: Assessing U.S. High School Mathematics from an International Perspective* (Champaign, IL: Stipes, 1987).

25. These observations derive from my work with the IEA Second International Mathematics Study. See also, Peter Damerow and Ian Westbury, "Mathematics for All: Problems and Implications," *Journal of Curriculum Studies* 17 (April-June 1985): 175-84, and Ian Westbury and Nongnuch Wattanawana, "Mathematics Achievement: A Comparison in Middle- and High-Income Nations," *Pacific Education* 1, no. 3 (1987): 23-39.

26. Mathematical Sciences Education Board, *Curriculum Framework for K-12 Mathematics* (Washington, DC: Mathematical Sciences Education Board, 1987).

27. Sheldon Rothblatt, *Tradition and Change in English Liberal Education* (London: Faber, 1976). See also chap. 2 in this volume.

28. Joseph J. Schwab, "Science and Civil Discourse: The Uses of Diversity," in Joseph J. Schwab, *Science, Curriculum, and Liberal Education*, ed. Ian Westbury and Neil J. Wilkof (Chicago: University of Chicago Press, 1978), p. 148.

Section Four
CURRICULUM "REFORM" AND
ITS PROBLEMS—HIGHER EDUCATION

CHAPTER XI

The Prospects for General Education
in American Higher Education

PHYLLIS FRANKLIN

The current revival of interest in that part of the college curriculum not subsumed by the major, the part described as "liberal arts" or "general" education, is now well established. That some configuration of courses should be required of undergraduates seems self-evident on campuses throughout the country. The question before us here concerns prospects: How long is the current commitment to requirements likely to last and how effective are the new courses and programs likely to be? The major problem in trying to speculate about the future of these requirements centers on assessing the role that national political pressures may have played in shaping them. Once largely an "academic" question, the character of general education became a matter of consequence outside the academy in the 1980s, affecting attitudes toward higher education at the federal level and raising questions about faculty control of the college curriculum. Since changes imposed on institutions, especially changes that conflict with, or attempt to redefine, institutional missions and cultures, are easily subverted, the survival of these requirements is likely to depend on the extent to which they reflect institutional values. Similarly, the effectiveness of an institution's general education program is likely to

I wish to acknowledge my debt to Deborah Brown, who conducted the survey, analyzed the data, and assisted in the writing of the descriptions of the programs included in this chapter.

198

depend on the strength of a faculty's commitment to it and the institution's willingness to provide resources for it and to recognize the work of those who teach in it.

Arguing strongly in favor of both the continuation and effectiveness of this revival of requirements in the curriculum is the fact that reform began within the academy. Indeed, even as the movement away from course requirements was spreading through higher education, concern about the trend emerged. As early as 1971, the president of Yale University, Kingman Brewster, appointed a committee to consider *"a coherent, purposive articulation of the goals of [undergraduate] education at Yale,"*[1] and the president of Harvard University, Derek Bok, observed in his annual report for 1971-72 *"that there was no general understanding at Harvard—or indeed at other American colleges—of what young men and women could expect to gain from a liberal arts education."*[2] Although the report of the Yale committee, which was completed in 1972, was not adopted by the university and received relatively little notice at the time, Harvard's plan for a core curriculum, developed during the mid-1970s under the leadership of Henry Rosovsky, was widely discussed. The plan was approved in 1978 and some of the new courses were in place by 1979, the same year that George W. Bonham edited *The Great Core Curriculum Debate: Education as a Mirror of Culture*, a volume that presented both the Harvard and Yale reports, evaluations of the reports, and an account of a meeting of educators who considered the need for, and shape of, a core curriculum.

By 1979, according to Bonham, "hundreds of academic institutions [were] tackling these central questions concerning the vitality of their educational offerings."[3] By spring of 1984, according to a survey of the American Council on Education's (ACE) Higher Education Panel, "between 50 and 60 percent of the four-year institutions in the United States were either engaged in some stage of restructuring or had just completed restructuring their general education requirements."[4] Two years later El-Khawas noted in *Campus Trends 1986* that 86 percent of American colleges and universities were "making changes in the curriculum or [had] recently done so." She also reported that "more than half of American colleges . . . currently engaged in curriculum reform . . . are discussing changes in: Writing (mentioned by 85 percent); Other competencies (80 percent); and General education requirements (76 percent)."[5]

Trends and Developments

In order to get a sense of the directions these new general education programs were taking, the Modern Language Association (MLA) asked the twenty-six institutions identified in the *New York Times* as participating in the "new wave of curriculum reform" for descriptions of their programs.[6] Twenty-two institutions responded to this request with bulletin descriptions and internal documents containing the arguments offered on behalf of the new programs. The variations in the details of the revisions make a simple quantifiable summary of these programs almost impossible. One point, however, is clear. The direction of change, as the ACE study of 1985 had reported, was toward limiting student options. Nathanael Greene, vice-president for academic affairs at Wesleyan University, describes what was probably a common sequence of events: "Until the late 1960s Wesleyan . . . had requirements in general education, as well as a number of core courses from which students could choose to meet the requirements." In 1968-69 "guidelines" replaced requirements, and in 1976-77 "expectations" replaced guidelines. As a result of a review of the general education program in 1984, beginning with the graduating class of 1991, Wesleyan students will be expected to take two courses in the humanities and arts, two in the social and behavioral sciences, and two in the natural sciences and mathematics. The courses, sufficient in number so that choice is still possible, will be "designed to introduce students to the language, methodology, and workings of a discipline."[7]

The adoption or revision of distribution requirements was the change reported most frequently in the MLA study. Where requirements were already in place, institutions narrowed the number of courses students could select from and/or added new areas of study. Noteworthy among the areas added is the study of non-Western cultures. Also noteworthy is the emphasis on skills acquisition. Two other types of new programs appear as well: (a) the requirement or recommendation of a single core course or a sequence of core courses or (b) the requirement of one or more core courses coupled with distribution requirements. Among the colleges and universities choosing to establish a single recommended core course was Bucknell University. The course, "Classic Texts in the Humanities," was designed to "create a common experience for . . . freshmen" by exposing them to the "basic intellectual issues" found in the classic texts of Western civilization. Established on a pilot basis in

1983, the course has been sufficiently successful that the university is considering the development of an upper-level sequence of humanities courses that would also be required of all students.[8]

Among the institutions requiring a sequence of core courses is the University of Colorado, Colorado Springs. Established in 1985, the program consists of four multidisciplinary, thematic courses "designed to introduce students to art, music, literature, drama, philosophy, and history from the Renaissance to modern times" and to provide "horizontal linkage" across fields in the humanities. Each course centers on a year: 1492, 1792, 1848, and 1948. The designers of the sequence describe the program as "a real *curriculum* in the truest sense of the word: an organized body of study."[9] The Brooklyn College program differs significantly from the Colorado program in that it includes the sciences as well as the humanities. Since 1981, Brooklyn College has required every student to enroll in ten core courses: "Classical Origins of Western Culture"; "Art and Music"; "People, Power, and Politics"; "The Shaping of the Modern World"; "Introduction to Mathematical Reasoning and Computer Programming"; "Landmarks of Literature"; "Science in Modern Life I: Chemistry and Physics"; "Science in Modern Life II: Biology and Geology"; "Studies in African, Asian, and Latin American Cultures"; and "Knowledge, Existence, and Values." In addition, the college has a foreign language requirement and stresses writing across the curriculum. The Brooklyn College publication *The Core Curriculum* states: "Although much of the integration is left to the individual student, all ten courses have been designed to complement one another."[10]

Another kind of core sequence can be found at Wilson College. Established in 1979, this curriculum consists of four courses: "Ancient and Medieval Cultures," "History and Philosophy of Science and Technology," "Contemporary Comparative Cultures," and "The Preservation of the Planet Earth." These are "designed not only to foster skills—e.g., the use of the English language and a speaking acquaintance with a foreign tongue, skills in computer usage and statistics, along with physical education and women's studies—but also to develop mature responses to the Earth and its various human societies."[11]

The Skidmore College curriculum exemplifies the second pattern, which combines prescribed core courses with distribution requirements. Skidmore has established a four-course core sequence called Liberal Studies I-IV: "Human Experience," "Cultural Traditions and

Social Change," "Artistic Forms and Critical Thought," and "Science, Society, and Human Values." Students may take these integrative courses in any order during their first two years. In addition, they are required to fill fairly traditional distribution requirements in expository writing, quantitative reasoning, the laboratory sciences, the visual and performing arts, foreign languages, and non-Western culture.[12]

Cycles of Change

It is illuminating to examine the various kinds of requirements these institutions have adopted in the light of Kimball's excellent study of the cycles of change in liberal and general education. In *Orators and Philosophers: A History of the Idea of Liberal Education*, Kimball makes clear that revivals of requirements are characteristic of American higher education, a fact that also argues for the survival and effectiveness of the new requirements. The statements of concern about the undergraduate curriculum made by Bok and Brewster in 1971 echo statements made earlier in the century by other university presidents. For example, Kimball notes that in 1907, the president of Cornell University observed that "the college is without clear-cut notions of what a liberal arts education is and how it is to be secured . . . and the pity of it is that this is not a local or special disability, but a paralysis affecting every college of arts in America."[13] Equally reassuring is the fact that calls for courses that synthesize and integrate knowledge were also present earlier in the century. Kimball observes that the chairman of the yearbook committee for the thirty-eighth yearbook of the National Society for the Study of Education, *General Education in the American College* (1939) wrote: "Every program of general education designed to date stresses the *need for integration*. . . . [T]he constant emphasis upon it signalize[s] a *quest* for some sort of *unity* now lacking in education matters."[14] Finally, even the variety in the kinds of revisions institutions have adopted is characteristic of earlier movements.

Describing as reassuring periodic dissatisfaction with general education may, at first glance, seem strange. (Are we to take pleasure in the fact that those who preceded us were no better able than we are to solve these problems?) But Kimball's history of the idea of a liberal arts or general education makes clear that certain recurring tensions have been and remain inevitable. Not only are they characteristic of higher education in this country; they protect our institutions from excess. Conflicting ideals of the nature and purpose of a liberal education and conflicting views of human nature provide the basis for these tensions. Only a brief description of the major debate is possible here.

On one side is what Kimball calls the "*artes liberales* ideal." This view of liberal studies Kimball traces back to the orators of ancient Greece and Rome. As articulated in the Renaissance, the ideal was "bound to an image of a man and his function, to a conception of his place in the world and in society." Thus the *artes liberales* "make men free" as they become "bound by a common bond, with a common culture, members of a more universal *res publica*."[15] At the heart of this ideal, then, is the transmission of a culture and its values; education into the common bonds of a common culture prepares the young for life in the world as it was and presumably will continue to be. As articulated in the twentieth century by Robert M. Hutchins, the *artes liberales* ideal assumed: "Education implies teaching. Teaching implies knowledge. Knowledge is truth. The truth is everywhere the same. Hence education should be everywhere the same."[16]

On the other side is a view of liberal studies that also uses the word *freedom*, but in a different way. This ideal Kimball names the "liberal-free ideal." Here the commitment, as articulated in the eighteenth century, was to "freedom from a priori strictures and standards," to rationality, skepticism, tolerance, "a tendency toward egalitarianism," an "emphasis upon volition of the individual rather than upon the obligations of citizenship," and "the pursuit of knowledge . . . for its own sake."[17] Modified in the nineteenth century by the influence of the German universities, the liberal-free ideal emerged in American colleges and universities as a commitment to "*Lehrfreiheit* (freedom to teach what one wishes) and *Lernfreiheit* (freedom to study what one wishes)." The goal of education was "to widen the bounds of knowledge rather than merely to preserve the store of knowledge undiminished."[18] This kind of education, then, prepares the individual to discover new knowledge or truth rather than to seek to transmit existing knowledge. In the opinion of many, including Kimball, this ideal continues to dominate higher education in the United States.

Kimball acknowledges that in American colleges and universities these ideals rarely exist in complete isolation. He also acknowledges that in their purest forms they have counterbalancing advantages and weaknesses. The *artes liberales* ideal offers "the investigation of the best of tradition and the public expression of what is good and true," but also "tempts dogmatic conservatism in education and culture, tending in the long run toward authoritarianism." The liberal-free ideal values "academic freedom, scholarly autonomy, specialized research," and the discovery of new knowledge, but it can also foster "self-indulgent and nihilistic education and culture, which can lead finally to anarchy."[19] Because Kimball judges that curricular problems arise "whenever one ideal of liberal education has become preeminent and the dialectical balance between the two ideals has been lost,"[20] periodic assessment, debate, and revision of the curriculum seem essential and natural activities in American colleges and universities.

Prospects

Given the fact that reform began within the academy over ten years ago and continues to grow and given Kimball's explanation of the dialectical nature of curricular debate in this country, we might conclude that the current revival is likely to last—at least until the higher education community senses a need to swing in the opposite direction. Before we do this, however, we must also consider some unusual pressures that emerged while the community was conducting its debate and beginning to introduce or reestablish requirements.

One of the interesting findings reported in the ACE survey of *General Education Requirements in the Humanities* concerns the question of who initiated the restructuring of general education requirements. Table 1 shows that, although faculty committees, faculty senates, deans, or presidents largely initiated these changes, 30 percent of the doctoral institutions identified initiators of these changes as other than the faculty or administration as compared to only 7 percent of the comprehensive and 10 percent of the baccalaureate institutions. Furthermore, doctoral institutions are less likely to report change initiated by faculty (35 percent versus 56 percent in the comprehensive institutions and 39 percent in the baccalaureate institutions).

How did it happen that "others" played such a role? Earlier in the century curricular change of the kind we are concerned with here might have received little or no national press coverage, for, as Edward Shils has said, until recently "universities were not news. University teachers were not pundits. . . . The main concern of the public relations office of a university was to keep out of the newspapers, not to get into them."[21] But the reforms of the 1980s did not go forward quietly. In April 1983, Terrel H. Bell, then Secretary of Education, released *A Nation at Risk*. This report on public schools in the United States was the first of many that focused attention on the need for educational reform and encouraged widespread public interest in the schools and in ways of improving them. Between October 1984 and February 1985 three reports on higher education

TABLE 1

Institutions Reporting Restructuring of General Education
Requirements, by Initiator, 1984-85
(Percentage of Institutions)

	Doctorate			Comprehensive			Baccalaureate			Two-year		
	Total (N=102)	Public (N=69)	Private (N=33)	Total (N=219)	Public (N=134)	Private (N=85)	Total (N=361)	Public (N=68)	Private (N=293)	Total (N=585)	Public (N=397)	Private (N=188)
Faculty committee	28	28	29	44	39	52	37	25	39	42	46	35
Faculty senate	7	10	0	12	14	8	2	0	3	0	0	0
Dean	30	31	29	20	10	35	42	38	44	37	26	60
President	5	3	7	18	26	5	9	25	5	5	8	0
Other	30	28	36	7	11	0	10	12	9	16	21	5

Note: Percentage based on institutions reporting a restructuring of requirements.

Source: Nancy Suniewick and Elaine El-Khawas, *General Education Requirements in the Humanities* (Washington, DC: American Council on Education, 1985), p. 19. Reproduced with permission of the American Council on Education.

appeared that addressed issues affecting the undergraduate curriculum. Like the earlier reports on the schools, these reports on higher education received widespread attention both within and outside the academy.

It will be many years before the full impact of these reports on the reform of general education is understood. On some campuses they probably made possible the initiation of curricular reviews or strengthened the efforts of those who were already seeking to reform general education. On other campuses they undoubtedly influenced the thinking of those responsible for designing the new core courses. On a number of campuses, however, the reports have also caused resentment, in part because of the publicity, in part because they attacked faculty members and the liberal-free ideal. Inexplicably, these reports failed to appreciate the seriousness of the reform movement already under way, attacking ghosts from the 1960s.[22]

The first such report, *Involvement in Learning: Realizing the Potential of American Higher Education*, was released in October 1984. Published by the U.S. Department of Education, this study was conducted primarily by specialists in higher education, whose recommendations, on the whole, many academics approved: for example, to restore "liberal education to its central role in undergraduate education," to involve students in their education, to maintain high expectations for students, and to limit the use of part-time teachers. With regard to the curriculum, the authors of this report made recommendations that seem to have been influential: the creation of "learning communities, organized around specific intellectual themes or tasks"; at least two years of liberal education; liberal education requirements that ensure "the development of capacities of analysis, problem solving, communication, and synthesis"; and the integration of "knowledge from various disciplines."[23] More problematic was the report's focus on the need for colleges and universities to "produce *demonstrable improvements* in student knowledge, capacities, skills, and attitudes between entrance and graduation." The authors of the report insist that "adequate measures of educational excellence must . . . be couched in terms of *student outcomes*."[24] Because courses in the humanities do not lend themselves to assessing immediately demonstrable improvements in student learning without limiting how and what is taught, courses designed to respond to this goal may not survive.

A month after the publication of *Involvement in Learning*, William J. Bennett, then director of the National Endowment for the Humanities, issued *To Reclaim a Legacy: A Report on the Humanities in*

Higher Education, which was the work of a study group he had established nine months earlier. Accepting primary responsibility for the writing of the report, Bennett emphasizes the importance of content, focusing particularly on the study of those works that "virtually define the development of the Western mind."[25] He argues that "merely being exposed to a variety of subjects and points of view is not enough. Learning to think critically and skeptically is not enough. Being well-rounded is not enough if, after all the sharp edges have been filed down, discernment is blunted and the graduate is left to believe without judgment, to decide without wisdom, or to act without standards." He concludes that the good humanities curriculum should have both breadth and depth, use original texts, extend throughout the undergraduate experience, "respect areas of faculty competence and expertise," and reflect the "centrality of the humanities."[26]

Bennett's defense of the *artes liberales* ideal of liberal education is not in itself troubling; his opinion is shared by many who teach and do scholarly work in the humanities. But his attack on specialization and on faculty members as the chief cause of a decline in enrollments in the humanities was troubling. Bennett insisted that the steep decline in the number of humanities majors in the 1970s was caused as much by the failure of teachers "to bring the humanities to life" as by students' concern to get "good-paying jobs,"[27] despite the fact that at that time a decline in enrollments occurred in all fields that did not promise clear employment opportunities.

The third report on the undergraduate curriculum, *Integrity in the College Curriculum: A Report to the Academic Community*, was published by the Association of American Colleges (AAC) in February 1985. Written primarily by people who had both taught in a variety of disciplines and served as academic administrators, this report recommended a curriculum based on skills acquisition (inquiry, abstract logical thinking, critical analysis; literacy: writing, reading, speaking, listening; understanding numerical data), "ways of growing and thinking" (historical consciousness; science; values; art; international and multicultural experiences), and study in depth.[28] In the opinion of a number of commentators, this report was the least acceptable to the academic community because it overstated the problem of "curricular disarray"; romanticized the coherence and integrity of the American college curriculum of the nineteenth century; and attacked specialization, research, and departmental organization in so strong a way as to go beyond the dialectical tension Kimball describes as necessary.

By the time the AAC report was released, academics began to realize that charges of curricular incoherence and faculty failure were likely to have serious consequences for higher education. For example, before an audience of representatives of the press, government officials, and college and university administrators and trustees, the authors of the AAC report charged that generations of faculty members, driven by self-interested commitments to their disciplines and departments instead of to students and teaching, had managed to reduce a coherent curriculum to one that was chaotic. Within days of the release of this report, Bennett, by this time Secretary of the U.S. Department of Education, said that colleges were defrauding students and argued against federal support of student loans. At the same time members of college and university governing boards announced their intention to play a more active role in decisions affecting the curriculum. Positive statements about higher education were far less newsworthy during this period. For example, the assertion in the 1985 special report of the Carnegie Foundation for the Advancement of Teaching, *Higher Education and the American Resurgence*, that "the American system of higher education is the best in the world" received little attention.[29] *American Professors: A National Resource Imperiled*, by Howard R. Bowen and Jack Y. Schuster, which described college teaching as an increasingly unattractive career, also received less attention than the reports attacking faculty members.

The political consequences of the reports and the negative publicity that followed them have been significant. For example, Senator Orrin Hatch (R. Utah) used Bennett's charges of failure within the humanities community to defend President Reagan's unsuccessful nomination of Edward Curran to head the National Endowment for the Humanities. Faculty members in the humanities had driven students away from humanities courses and therefore someone from outside the academy was needed to set things right. Academics could not solve their own problems.

Unfortunately, in the 1980s, politically motivated attempts to reduce federal support for higher education have mingled inextricably with campus efforts to reform general education. That this kind of pressure continues can be seen in Bennett's insistence on tying the type and extent of financial aid for students to the quality of education he judges is available at colleges and universities. In the words of Secretary Bennett,

It is by no means clear that the performance of many of our colleges and universities justifies [their] level of expenditure. As I said on the occasion of

Harvard's 350th anniversary, too many students fail to receive the education they deserve at our nation's universities. The real problem is not lack of money but failure of vision. . . . Higher education is not underfunded. It is underaccountable and underproductive. Our students deserve better than this. They deserve an education commensurate with the large sums paid by parents and taxpayers and donors. That our universities are places where students can receive a good education, or at least learn a lot, I have no doubt. But too often our universities leave education to chance—a good professor here and a great course there. There is too little real and sustained attention to education in the broader sense, to making sure that when our students leave after four years they leave as educated men and women.[30]

Such politically motivated attacks on higher education, accompanied by instructions for improvement, raise questions about the degree of institutional commitment to the new requirements. Insofar as the newly established core courses and distribution requirements both grow out of the values and missions of individual institutions and reflect what are inescapable, essential ways of knowing, whether from disciplinary or interdisciplinary perspectives, they will survive and be reasonably effective—until it is time for the next adjustment. I doubt, however, that even this achievement will satisfy our critics, for no general education curriculum or set of core courses—with or without distribution requirements—can impose anything but a temporary and partial order on what is intellectually complex and never wholly known. I take comfort in a comment made by William J. Bouwsma regarding the tension between specialization and traditional ideals of general education. He writes:

What then are we to do? My own view is that there are, sometimes, discontents that cannot be relieved, problems that cannot be solved, which therefore we can only learn to live with, and which the remedies proposed may only aggravate. . . . But it seems to me that our kind of culture, our kind of society, secular, pluralistic, incoherent, and messy, but also rich, lively, free, and creative, already has not only the kind of education it deserves but probably the only kind of education it can now sustain. I see no reason for complacency, but perhaps—all in all and considering the alternative—our condition is not after all so bad.[31]

FOOTNOTES

1. George W. Bonham, *The Great Core Curriculum Debate: Education as a Mirror of Culture* (New Rochelle, NY: Change Magazine Press, 1979), p. 79.

2. Ibid., p. 5.

3. Ibid., p. 4.

4. Nancy Suniewick and Elaine El-Khawas, *General Education Requirements in the Humanities* (Washington, DC: American Council on Education, 1985), pp. 9-10.

5. Elaine El-Khawas, *Campus Trends 1986* (Washington, DC: American Council on Education, 1986), p. 2.

6. Edward B. Fiske, "Wave of Curriculum Change Sweeping American Colleges," *New York Times*, 10 March 1985.

7. Nathanael Greene, Wesleyan University, letter to Deborah Brown, 12 June 1986.

8. Bucknell University, unpublished proposal, n.d., p. 11.

9. University of Colorado, Colorado Springs, unpublished document, n.d., pp. 1-2.

10. Brooklyn College, Faculty Council Committee on Core Curriculum, *The Core Curriculum* (Brooklyn, NY: Brooklyn College, n.d.), p. 6.

11. Harry M. Buck, unpublished document (Chambersburg, PA: Wilson College, n.d.).

12. Skidmore College, *The Skidmore Curriculum: New Horizons in Liberal Education* (Saratoga Springs, NY: Skidmore College, n.d.), pp. 3-15.

13. Bruce A. Kimball, *Orators and Philosophers: A History of the Idea of Liberal Education* (New York: Teachers College Press, 1986), pp. 183-84.

14. Ibid., p. 194.

15. Ibid., p. 115.

16. Ibid., p. 179.

17. Ibid., pp. 119-22.

18. Ibid., pp. 161-62.

19. Ibid., p. 237.

20. Ibid., p. 239.

21. Edward Shils, "The University: A Backward Glance," *American Scholar* 51 (1982): 169.

22. See David Bromwich, "Moral Education in the Age of Reagan: On Some Proposals for a Culture without Criticism," *Dissent* 33 (1986): 464.

23. U.S. Department of Education, Study Group on the Conditions of Excellence in American Higher Education, *Involvement in Learning: Realizing the Potential of American Higher Education* (Washington, DC: U.S. Department of Education, 1984), pp. 10, 33, 41, 43.

24. Ibid., pp. 15-16.

25. William J. Bennett, *To Reclaim a Legacy: A Report on the Humanities in Higher Education* (Washington, DC: National Endowment for the Humanities, 1984), pp. 6, 10.

26. Ibid., p. 8.

27. Ibid., p. 13.

28. Association of American Colleges, Project on Redefining the Meaning and Purpose of Baccalaureate Degrees, *Integrity in the College Curriculum: A Report to the Academic Community* (Washington, DC: Association of American Colleges, 1985), pp. 15-23.

29. Frank Newman, *Higher Education and the American Resurgence* (Princeton, NJ: Carnegie Foundation for the Advancement of Teaching, 1985), p. xiii.

30. William J. Bennett, "Our Greedy Colleges," *New York Times*, 18 February 1987, A31.

31. William J. Bouwsma, "Specialization, Departmentalization, and the Humanities," *ACLS Newsletter* 36 (1985): pp. 8-9.

CHAPTER XII

The Prospects for General Education in University Professional Education

LAWRENCE R. MANN

I am not arguing against professional education; I am arguing against narrow vocational training. The first is large, expansive, having the spirit of the liberal arts, setting skills as means within larger ends; concerned with not "the job," but with life and with the social goals the profession promotes and the ethical standards it demands. The second is narrow, restrictive, developing specific skills in preparation for routine tasks sometimes very technical or scientific; it involves knowledge for specific ends, raising no questions of larger significance, impervious to social context, oblivious to moral choice. A liberal outlook may be nurtured within the context of professional education. It soon withers in the presence of vocational training.

FRANK H. T. RHODES
Vital Speeches, 15 June 1984

Frank Rhodes makes an important distinction between professional education and vocational training.[1] But how real in fact is that distinction? To what extent is university professional education enriched with the larger perspective of the liberal arts and sciences? Is professional education designed to give students an understanding of social context and value issues, or is it more likely to be narrowly focused vocational training? Should the liberal arts perspective be an integral and required part of the professional curriculum? Does a liberal orientation—or the lack of it—really make any difference to the professions and to society?

The question of integrating liberal studies into the professional school curriculum has been characterized as a "fundamental dichotomy." It is viewed by some as a specific example in several professional fields of the tension—the intellectual gulf which C. P. Snow and others have discussed—between the "scientific culture" on the one hand and the "literary or humanistic culture" on the other. It is seen by others as a distinction between education for immediately practical pursuits versus education as a foundation for learning. To others it is a question of overspecialization versus breadth. I argue, however, that these interpretations are false dichotomies which should not apply to the integration of liberal studies in professional education. The liberal arts and sciences have substantial practical and real-life value. They are essential aspects of professional education in the sense described by Frank Rhodes. Nevertheless, the pressure of professional specialization (not just in professional fields per se but throughout the university) continues as a substantial obstacle to the integration of the two.

Definitions: General and Professional Education

General education and professional education have been defined in a variety of ways. I have settled on the following descriptions which reflect the common intent of the multiple definitions. I also should note that my orientation for this discussion is a highly decentralized, public, comprehensive research university. Thus, the issues associated with general education and professional education in this context are somewhat different from those in a four-year college.

General education (as distinguished from the more inclusive concept of liberal education) is defined by Alan Purves, in his introduction to this volume, as "the purposeful attempt to provide a particular group of students with a common core of knowledge, skills, and values." He suggests, moreover, that such education usually is based on the liberal arts and sciences and that it is "related to the idea of culture, which is something to which people are affiliated as opposed to their natural filiation." I would expand Purves's view of general education, which focuses on a common and liberally based core of knowledge and skills oriented toward a particular culture, to include also an understanding both of science and technology and of cultures and values different from one's own. The goal of general education should be to broaden and "liberalize" perspectives in order to leave the individual as unrestricted as possible in the opportunities for self-fulfillment—after college.

The acquisition and refinement of this common base of understanding should not be grounded, I contend, on a "common core curriculum" of specifically prescribed subjects or courses. It should be based instead on the development of common experiences and abilities which in their specifications give the student considerable freedom of choice. The proposals recently offered by the Association of

American Colleges (AAC) Select Committee on Redefining the Meaning and Purpose of Baccalaureate Degrees capture the essence of what I ascribe to as the appropriate general education which should be a major component of any undergraduate professional curriculum: (1) opportunities which provide students with continuing practice on developing the arts of "inquiry, abstract logical thinking, critical analysis," (2) recurring emphasis on "literacy: writing, reading, speaking, listening," (3) "recognition throughout the course of study of the necessity for sharpening the ability to understand numerical data," including numerical interpretation and the misuse of numerical data, (4) the development of "historical consciousness" *across* the course of study, (5) an understanding of "science and technology," including fundamental scientific facts and principles, major scientific and technological developments, and the "human, social, and political implications of scientific research," (6) opportunities throughout the curriculum for considering "values" in order to develop and nurture "the capacity to make informed and responsible moral choice," (7) "appreciation and experience of the fine and performing arts" in order to provide "access to realms of creativity, imagination, and feeling that explore and enlarge the meaning of what it is to be human," and (8) "international and multicultural experiences" which "take students into a world beyond themselves, make them again and again outsiders, so that they may return and know themselves better."[2]

Experiences such as these, suggested as the components of a *general* education, should not be studied in isolation. *They should extend into the major area of professional study*—shaping and enriching the study of engineering, education, business, and the like. These several experiences, as envisioned by the AAC Select Committee, with their focus on "methods and processes, the modes of access to understanding and judgment," should be as much a part of the particular professional area of study as they may be of a more "general" course of study.

Professional education, like general education, has been defined in many ways, but the most common element suggests that professions provide something of value to society. Professional education can be defined as that portion of an undergraduate "professional curriculum" which, while influenced and enlarged by the more general course of study, prepares the student to gain particular knowledge and skills that can be applied to benefit society in immediate and direct ways. In this context general education assumes an important position as an integral part of professional education, not something separate and apart from it. This is, I believe, the ideal which both curricula and students should strive to achieve.

However, the distinction between general studies and professional subject matter is not absolute. It depends largely on the student and the program of study. Mathematics taken by a philosophy major, for example, may be a liberating experience consistent with the goal of general education; taken by an engineering student the same course may be a professional subject. Music theory taken by a business student may be a "liberal" course; taken by a budding conductor, it may be a professional course. The same kind of distinction can be made for many courses across the university, and it is for this reason that student choice is particularly important to the goal of general education.

Perspectives on Professional Education

The role of general education—the liberal learning perspective—in the curriculum of the professional school is a perennial issue. It is, has been, and will continue to be a subject of discussion and differing viewpoints. Indeed, as Earl Chiet notes in his study of professional education, the debate concerning what is "liberal" and what is "useful" is one of the oldest issues in education.[3] But the growth in the number of university-based professional programs during the last century has made this debate even more significant. The list of "new professions" is extensive—engineering, business, social work, journalism, pharmacy, education, library science, dentistry, architecture, and so forth. Professional education flourishes in higher education today, and the trend in student interest toward professional programs continues unabated.

Considerations of general education in professional education have assumed a new level of significance in recent years, the result, on the one hand, of the expanding number of professional areas included within the university and the increased number of students who are enrolling in professional fields, particularly at the undergraduate level. The issue is complicated, on the other hand, by the widespread growth of higher education in the decades subsequent to World War II. Higher education has been transformed from the elite system which existed prior to 1940—less than 15 percent of the 18-22 age group attended college—to a system of "mass higher education" in which more than 60 percent of the 18-22 age cohort now attends postsecondary institutions. One result of this transformation has been substantial curricular uncertainty at the undergraduate level and, in particular, the absence of a consensus on what should be learned and how it should be taught.[4] The confusion regarding the role of general education in undergraduate professional education is but one manifestation of this larger curricular uncertainty.

Another characteristic of this transformation is expanded student interest in professional programs of study. But in what ways is this trend a problem and what, if anything, should be done about it?

TABLE 1

NATIONAL CHANGES IN INTENDED AREAS OF STUDY
IN COLLEGE—1975-1984

	1975		1984		
	Number	% of Total	Number	% of Total	% Change
Art	30,890	3.8	29,883	3.4	− 3.3
English/literature	16,258	2.4	11,426	1.3	− 29.7
Foreign language	11,380	1.4	7,031	0.8	− 38.2
Philosophy & religion	5,690	0.7	2,637	0.3	− 53.7
Biological sciences	65,031	8.0	27,246	3.1	− 58.1
Health & medical	121,120	14.9	132,715	15.1	+ 9.6
Physical sciences	22,761	2.8	14,941	1.7	− 34.4
Engineering	54,463	6.7	105,468	12.0	+ 93.7
Undecided	52,837	6.5	38,672	4.4	− 26.8
Mathematics	19,509	2.4	9,668	1.1	− 50.4
Computer sciences/ systems analysis	13,006	1.6	85,254	9.7	+555.5
Business & commerce	93,482	11.5	167,871	19.1	+ 79.6
Communications	21,948	2.7	32,519	3.7	+ 48.2
Education	73,972	9.1	40,430	4.6	− 45.3
History	11,380	1.4	4,395	0.5	− 61.2
Psychology	29,264	3.6	30,761	3.5	+ 5.1
Social science	62,592	5.1	64,160	7.3	+ 2.5

Table 1 includes 17 of 29 categories measured by the College Board. "Total" refers to the total number of respondents cited in this report. It should be noted that, while the number of SAT takers fell by 2.1 percent between 1974 and 1984, the number of students responding to this question increased from 812,813 to 878,904—about 8 percent.

Source: College Entrance Examination Board, *College-Bound Seniors, 1984* (New York: College Entrance Examination Board, 1984).

Data on intended areas of study in college are revealing. College-bound high school seniors taking the Scholastic Aptitude Test in 1975 and 1984 were asked to indicate their intended area of study in college. The results of those surveys reveal a major shift in student interest away from the traditional liberal arts and sciences toward more vocational or professionally oriented fields, especially computer sciences/systems analysis, engineering, business and commerce, communications, and the health sciences. (See table 1.) The number of high school seniors expressing interest in these five professional areas was 37 percent of those responding in 1975 compared with 60 percent in 1984. As striking as those percentages are, the percentage change is even more dramatic; the health fields show a 9.6 percent increase, communications a 48.2 percent increase, business and commerce a 79.6 percent increase, engineering a 93.7 percent increase, and computer sciences/systems analysis a 555.5 percent increase.[5]

Data on undergraduate student majors by subject field for 1969, 1976, and 1984 also reveal the dramatic trend toward professional fields. Between 1969 and 1984, the number of students in the United States majoring in occupational and professional fields increased from 38 percent to 50 percent with the percentage reaching a high of 58 percent in 1976. Over the same time period, the number of students majoring in the traditional arts and sciences areas decreased, especially in the humanities, where the number of majors decreased from 18 percent to 5 percent.[6] If this trend in areas of study in college continues, the number of undergraduate students in the coming decade who will be majoring in professional areas is likely to exceed the 58 percent high of 1976.

What do such data suggest about general education in undergraduate professional curricula? A recent study brings home the point that college students have long been concerned about careers and even the traditional liberal arts and science fields are occupational in the sense that many students have majored in these areas in preparation for careers like teaching or entry into a graduate-level professional school. The key consideration, however, is that "the shift toward occupational and professional majors should not be considered a threat or contrary to past traditions—unless the nation's collegiate institutions fail to give priority to the goals of common learning."[7] The growing number of students majoring in professional fields and the expanded role of the professions in society make it particularly important for professional schools to examine and reexamine the general education component of their curricula. But how does the general course of study measure up in such fields, for example, to the previously discussed set of experiences suggested by the AAC Select Committee?

Recent Reports

The debate about the content of professional education and the relative importance of general education in the professional school curriculum, like many educational questions, ebbs and flows. It has come to the forefront once again as a subject of renewed interest both within the professions and in a number of recent reports which raise concerns about undergraduate education in the United States. These reports are particularly relevant because it is now the norm in many fields for professional education to occur at the baccalaureate level. As a consequence, there are, as William McInnes points out, important new questions and significant practical problems regarding the integration of general education into the professional curriculum. "When professional education was confined to the graduate level, educators could assume (without real evidence) that entrants to law and medical schools had been previously exposed to a humanistic curriculum. When professional training invaded the undergraduate college, that assumption could no longer be safely made. The integration of professional and liberal undergraduate curricula is today a chronic issue for educators."[8]

A central and unifying aspect of the many reports on undergraduate education that have appeared in recent years is their call for renewed attention to the role of the liberal arts and sciences during the undergraduate years.[9] The reports, unprecedented both in number and in commonality of theme, urge higher education's leadership to reassess the quality of the undergraduate experience and to ensure that all undergraduates receive a broad-based education, regardless of the major field of study. Four of the reports speak directly to the matter of general learning as it applies to undergraduate professional education.

The National Institute of Education Study Group on the Conditions of Excellence in American Higher Education recommends, for example, that the undergraduate program of study for all students include "at least two full years of liberal education," recognizing that "in most professional fields, this will require extending undergraduate programs beyond the usual four years." In making this recommendation, the Study Group observed:

When we look carefully at the curricula prescribed for students in . . . [many] professional programs, it is clear that they offer few opportunities to develop the capacities and knowledge that most institutions would expect of baccalaureate graduates. Our objective in expanding those opportunities is to strengthen undergraduate professional degree programs and the future options of students who pursue them. Students are not likely to accumulate in four years both the generalized and specialized knowledge necessary for first-rate performance as professionals. This fact has long been acknowledged in baccalaureate degrees in architecture (most of which require five- or six-year programs) and in many undergraduate programs in engineering (which offer five-year options).[10]

In *America's Business Schools: Priorities for Change*, the Business-Higher Education Forum argues for two-years "devoted to the arts and sciences" in the undergraduate business curriculum,[11] and one of the main conclusions of the Holmes Group's recent evaluation of teacher education, *Tomorrow's Teachers*, is that expanded attention to the liberal arts and sciences in the undergraduate program is essential to the improvement of education for teachers.[12]

The AAC Select Committee takes a similar position on the importance of general education in professional programs in its report, *Integrity in the College Curriculum*. After suggesting nine essential characteristics of an undergraduate education, the Committee turned its attention to the problems of undergraduate professional education.

The danger to intellectual growth in such programs—just the opposite of the disarray in the central disciplines in the liberal arts colleges—is excessive structure and overprescription of training in currently fashionable technique, ephemeral information, and obsolescent technology. Students of professional fields . . . also need . . . [to] learn critical analysis and the capacity to make decisions in uncertain settings with insufficient data; they must gain the ability to write and speak clearly . . . to clients, employees, and professional communities; their future practice must be informed by constant awareness of the environmental and societal impact—human costs vs. political benefits, aesthetic enhancement or debasement—of the work to which they are committing their lives.[13]

In addition to these reports, the recent literature on professional education points to renewed interest in general education in undergraduate professional and preprofessional education in a wide range of professional fields. Although there is far from universal agreement on how best to achieve the integration of liberal and professional education, there is growing consensus that professional programs of study, and many liberal arts majors as well, have become overly specialized at the expense of a broadly defined general studies base.

Common Themes

The literature on general education in professional education demonstrates recurring attention to this subject in several professional areas over the last four decades, especially in law, medicine, engineering, and business. Although the specific considerations differ from field to field, and they are influenced substantially by whether the professional area is focused at the baccalaureate or graduate school level, there are common themes.

1. There is much agreement on, or at least lip service to, the idea that a broad general education is an important part of professional education. There are, at the same time, substantial differences of opinion about what the general education component should entail and how much of it is necessary. The Accrediting Board for Engineering and Technology, for example, claims that the humanities and the social sciences are of great importance to the education of engineers, but it requires, in fact, that only a small proportion of engineering curricula be devoted to these subjects, and many engineering educators and engineering professionals continue to call for greater attention to the liberal arts and sciences. The American Assembly of Collegiate Schools of Business, on the other hand, requires that approximately half of the undergraduate business school curriculum be devoted to studies other than business administration and economics, a requirement which pleases some and annoys others. Despite wide differences of opinion, there is a widely held belief in many professional fields that general education is of fundamental importance and that the amount of time devoted to so-called liberal studies is less than adequate.

2. The role of general education in professional education, especially a broad-gauged understanding of moral and ethical questions and social and public policy considerations, will become increasingly important as professionals assume larger leadership roles in an "information society." This view is held to be particularly important in engineering and related fields where high technology developments are no longer isolated from broader questions of value, social responsibility, and public policy.

3. The traditional liberal arts disciplines also have become increasingly narrow as the professoriate in these fields, too, has become specialized. As a consequence, many of the course offerings in arts and sciences now focus on the research specialties of the faculty.

This development has major implications for general education in both the liberal arts and in professional programs.

Overspecialization is especially problematic in comprehensive research universities where the driving force of research has narrowed many faculty members' interests. As a consequence, there has been a tendency to develop more highly specialized courses in the curricula of all colleges, including Colleges of Liberal Arts and Sciences, and fewer courses that tie concepts from different fields together. There is growing interest, however, in collaborative research activity across disciplines, and some of these new research developments may help bring breadth back into the curriculum.

4. In many professional fields there is a continuing knowledge explosion. As a result, there is considerable discussion about whether the expanding requirements of the professional field and the objectives of general education can still be accommodated within the traditional four-year course of study.

5. There is growing agreement, because of rapid change and new developments in the professions, that it is no longer feasible to view the professional curriculum as a program of study which provides the student with everything he or she will need to know. Indeed, in many professional areas, change is occurring so rapidly that technologies and methods are quickly outmoded, and there is no way to know with certainty the professional requirements of the future. Thus, there is increased discussion about the importance of designing professional study more toward education for adaptability and change which, in the view of those who ascribe to this position, requires greater attention to the development of the skills, attitudes, and modes of thought associated with liberal learning.

6. Despite the widespread advocacy of the importance of general education in professional education, the discussion of the professional school curriculum continues to be influenced to a considerable degree by the long-standing attitude—still widely prevalent in our society—that the "liberal arts" are somewhat superfluous when contrasted with the more useful professionally applied subjects.

But if we look beyond in this literature, it is interesting to note that general education is receiving a new level of support on college campuses across the country. This interest is reflected, for example, in the results of a recent survey conducted by the Carnegie Foundation which indicates that nearly 60 percent of all four-year institutions in the United States are now engaged in systematic reviews of their basic educational requirements.[14] The role of general education in professional education is also a subject of attention in other on-going efforts. Three recent initiatives, the results of which are yet to be determined, illustrate this renewed interest.

Faculty from a wide range of professional fields and representatives of numerous professional accrediting agencies met late in 1986 at the University of Michigan to discuss the integration of subjects from the liberal arts and sciences into the curricula of professional programs. That conference was a prelude to a major new research and outreach program, the Professional Preparation Project, being undertaken by the University of Michigan Center for the Study of Higher and Postsecondary Education.[15] It is anticipated that this study will identify exemplary programs which may be useful to professional schools and professional accrediting groups.

Late in 1985 the Andrew W. Mellon Foundation announced a major grant to the Association of American Colleges to fund a two and one-half year study "to develop new patterns for incorporating humanities and social science courses into undergraduate engineering programs." The intent is to extend the liberal arts perspective throughout the undergraduate experience in engineering, not just to propose additional liberal arts courses.

The American Assembly of Collegiate Schools of Business (AACSB)—the national accrediting agency for the profession—has taken a leadership role over the past two and one-half decades in encouraging business schools, and in fact requiring those it accredits, to incorporate a substantial component of the liberal arts and sciences in the undergraduate business school curriculum. AACSB is currently sponsoring a major study on the future of management education. A portion of that study will focus on the role of liberal learning in the business school program.

Engineering Education

Discussion about the proper mix of liberal and professional subjects in undergraduate engineering curricula is a hardy perennial. It has been discussed and debated within engineering schools and in the engineering profession for decades. Indeed, there is a long history of formal consideration of engineering education which extends at least to the early years of this century, including a number of landmark studies, sponsored by leading engineering associations, which addressed the subject of general and professional subject matter to varying degrees—the Mann Report (1918), the Wickenden Report

(1929), the Jackson Study (1939), the Hammond Reports (1940 and 1944), the Grinter Report (1955), the Walker Report (1968), and the ASEE Report (1975).[16]

Interest in the role of general education in the engineering school curriculum has assumed increased importance, however, since World War II as rapid technological advances have placed ever-increasing pressures on professional specialization and as the growing implications of engineering technology on society have become more and more evident. In 1944 these then emerging developments were articulated by William L. Everitt in his well-known essay, "The Phoenix: A Challenge to Engineering Education." In that essay, Everitt, who would become a leading figure in engineering education in this century, called for a major reevaluation of engineering study and a "synthesis" between liberal and professional studies in engineering education.

Engineering is a way of life for those who pursue it. . . . [It] must be inspired and cannot be taught by rote. . . . However, we lose a golden opportunity . . . if we do not point out to the student the need for high moral principles, and the inspiration which can be drawn in working both with people and the laws of nature. We need also to point out the danger . . . which can result from the improper application of scientific principles. . . .

The definition of engineering given by Webster included . . . "made useful to man." This is extremely important . . . [because] the engineer should understand man as well as matter. . . . Therefore, the curricula should . . . help the young engineer to speak and write fluently and clearly. . . . He should also be taught openmindedness and a survey of other fields of knowledge. . . . And, he should be required to use these principles throughout his course [of study].[17]

Everitt went on to emphasize the impossibility of teaching the engineering student everything he or she will need to know. He argued, therefore, that the aim of engineering education should be to develop in students the desire to continue to learn and to recognize the relationship of engineering knowledge to mankind and society.

The Accrediting Board for Engineering and Technology (ABET), the national certifying agency for collegiate engineering programs, also recognizes the importance of integrating the liberal arts perspective in engineering education, including the humanities and the social sciences, written and spoken communication skills, and an "understanding of ethical, social, and economic considerations in engineering practice."[18] Yet, despite recognition of the importance of these areas of study, when all is said and done, the ABET only *requires* that sixteen hours of a 128 credit-hour program of study be devoted to the humanities and social sciences, and coursework in communication skills and ethical and social and economic considerations of the profession are not specifically required. Thus, in point of fact, a relatively small portion of the coursework in most undergraduate engineering programs is directed toward what is commonly referred to as general education.

The 1968 Walker report, *Goals of Engineering Education*, sponsored by the American Society for Engineering Education, which received widespread attention in the profession, took a strong stand in arguing for breadth in engineering education including greater attention to the humanities and social sciences. It urged, at the same time, experimentation with engineering degree programs longer than four years. And, the ASEE has continued to reiterate its position in support of breadth and education for change, most notably again in 1975 in two publications: *Future Directions for Engineering Education* and *Engineering Education for a Lifetime of Learning*.[19]

Despite such urgings, and despite the goals outlined by the ABET concerning the importance of breadth in engineering education, the curricula of most undergraduate engineering programs continue to focus heavily on professionally oriented subjects. Moreover, the demands of the profession, coupled with rapid advances in engineering knowledge and technology, have produced continuing pressure for even more professional specialization in the curricula.

What might be done to provide greater breadth in engineering curricula? A variety of means have been suggested including lengthening the undergraduate engineering course of study beyond four years, reducing the number of required engineering courses in the traditional four-year course of study to permit greater attention to the liberal arts, and creating a professional school of engineering, similar to law and medicine, where a traditional four-year baccalaureate program is required before the student begins the study of engineering. There are, of course, drawbacks to each of these approaches, but I suggest that the most realistic of these approaches may be to extend the course of study to five years, including two full years of liberal studies along the lines suggested by the Association of American Colleges, coupled with efforts to incorporate into the engineering courses the skills and modes of thought developed during the first two years of general studies. This lengthened course of study would provide breadth without compromising professional standards.

To accomplish this objective it is essential that leadership be provided by the nation's leading engineering schools, coupled with efforts on their part to enlist support from the engineering profession at large. Such extended programs have not flourished in the past, not because the concept was flawed, but because a necessary national leadership and support base was not developed.

Business Education

The role of general education in the curriculum of undergraduate professional education for business has been a subject of continuing attention since the widespread expansion of university-based business schools in the early years of this century. Concerns about the narrowness and the vocational orientation of America's business school programs were first addressed on a national basis in 1959 in two landmark studies of business education—the Gordon-Howell report, sponsored by the Ford Foundation, and the Pierson report, conducted under the auspices of the Carnegie Foundation.[20]

Both of these reports, which received much attention at the time, criticized business schools for being overly vocational, and they called for greater attention to the liberal arts and sciences in both undergraduate- and graduate-level business school programs. They also suggested limitations on enrollment in undergraduate business programs with the focus of business education being at the graduate level.

The Pierson report articulated the importance of a liberal learning perspective in the business school curriculum.

There appears to be no simple method for determining what should be included at the undergraduate or graduate stage of the student's preparation, but three elements seem to be common to all the highly developed professions. First, the tendency to lose sight of the general background and preprofessional subjects poses a serious danger at every stage of the students' preparation. Second, education is largely self-education, and if it is to have any enduring meaning . . . it must be continued throughout life. Third, emphasis should not be placed on mastering the detailed aspects of a given subject but on developing the abilities and methods needed for meeting problems in later life.
. . . If career preparation becomes an end in itself . . . where mastery of a particular job or type of activity is made all important, the most precious element in the college or university experience is likely to be lost.[21]

The Gordon-Howell report took a similar position, stating in part:

Collegiate business education should educate for the whole career and not primarily for the first job. It should view the practice of business professionally in the sense of relating it to what we have in the way of relevant systematic bodies of knowledge. It should emphasize the development of basic problem solving and organizational skills and socially constructive attitudes rather than memory of facts or training in routine skills.[22]

Although the lofty goals for liberal education in the curricula of America's business schools have not been fully met in most business schools, and substantial criticism of business education continues to be voiced by both corporate leaders and business educators,[23] there is much agreement that substantial improvements have been made since the 1959 reports in broadening the knowledge base in many undergraduate business programs. Much of the credit for such improvement is attributed to leadership provided by the American Assembly of Collegiate Schools of Business.[24] The AACSB now requires that at least 40 to 60 percent of the undergraduate program of study in business administration be in areas of study other than business administration and economics, and at least 40 percent of the curriculum in accountancy must be in general education. In its handbook on *Accreditation Council Policies, Procedures, and Standards*, the AACSB states, for example, that the purpose of the business administration curriculum

shall be to provide for a broad education preparing the student for imaginative and responsible citizenship and leadership roles in business and society— domestic and worldwide. The curriculum shall be responsible to social, economic, and technological developments and shall reflect the application of evolving knowledge in economics and the behavioral and quantitative sciences. . . . The objective . . . is to provide a foundation of work in those academic areas necessary for an appropriate combination of descriptive and analytical approaches to the study of business administration. Such foundation work would normally include courses in communications, mathematics, social sciences, humanities, and the natural sciences.[25]

The high priority which is given to general education by the AACSB is significant. However, the expansion of business knowledge and specialization, especially in information systems, is creating new and unprecedented pressures in business education for greater attention to professional studies at the expense of general education. These pressures will continue to grow.

Although the general education goals of the AACSB are not always fully met, it is important that the prominence which general education holds in accreditation standards for business education be retained if collegiate schools of business are to graduate professionals who are able to relate effectively to the social and ethical considerations of the business world. The pressures of specialization in business education are growing and they soon may be similar in degree to those which now exist in engineering. It is likely that collegiate schools of business also will have to confront the difficult question of whether it is possible to continue to meet the growing demands of professional specialization and general education in the traditional four-year time frame. Numerous new approaches to business education are being suggested,[26] and the AACSB and the leading business schools must seriously address this question. They should formulate realistic options which will meet the expanding and changing demands of the profession while, at the same time, ensuring at least two full years of study in the liberal arts and sciences.

A Related Issue: Integrating Science and Technology in the Liberal Arts

A corollary to the topic of general education in professional education is the issue of integrating the study of science and technology into degree programs in the liberal arts. The commanding role which science and technology now play would lead the casual observer of the American academic scene to assume, quite logically, that a basic understanding of science and technology (including the role of computers and their impact on society) would be a major aspect of a modern liberal education for all students, including those majoring in the humanities, the arts and music, and the social sciences. However, despite the pervasive influence of science and technology, their place in the liberal arts curriculum is usually minimal at best and "technological illiteracy" is a widespread and growing national problem.[27]

In recent years, many colleges and universities have organized courses and programs on science, technology, and society. Yet, as desirable as such developments are, relatively few institutions have moved to include such courses as a specific requirement for the bachelor of arts degree. If a liberal education is to provide, in fact, a broad understanding of our culture and society, greater attention must be given to ensuring that all students recognize the important role of science and technology and their impact on our lives.

University presidents and chancellors can play an important leadership role, I believe, in helping to integrate science and technology in the liberal arts program of study. They can serve as catalysts to bring faculty together from the traditional liberal arts and sciences and from engineering and computer science to seriously consider designing courses with a focus on science and technology and their relationship to man and society. Such courses might be added to undergraduate degree requirements in all departments of the university. This effort to provide an integration of science and technology and human values would help transform the traditional liberal arts course of study into a true liberal education well suited to today's scientific realities where an understanding of science and technology is as essential to the definition of liberal education as an appreciation of language and cultural differences.

Conclusion

What are the prospects for general education in professional education? Despite the not inconsequential obstacles of increasing specialization and rapid expansion of knowledge in many professional fields, the present environment appears to present an important opportunity for universities, professional schools, and accrediting agencies to address this important subject. It has been highlighted recently as part of several well-publicized and much discussed national reports on undergraduate education, and it is a subject of some renewed interest within several professions and professional accrediting organizations. Moreover, substantial numbers of students are now enrolling in undergraduate professional and preprofessional programs and, as a result, the subject of general education in the professional school context has assumed a new level of importance.

There are, however, some special problems which need to be addressed. I will mention two of the most difficult ones. In the comprehensive research university setting, where many of the nation's leading professional schools are located, the professional colleges often have substantial autonomy to determine the nature and content of their degree programs, including the general education component. This reality can be a significant limiting factor in achieving the goal of a reasonably broad-based program of general study within the undergraduate professional school curriculum. As long as the professional colleges have complete control, in effect, over the content of their degree programs, limited progress will be made in expanding the role of general studies in undergraduate professional education. There is an institutional or corporate responsibility for general education in the comprehensive research university setting which goes beyond the educational interests of any particular college or professional school. Yet, in far too many instances the comprehensive research university seems to have lost sight of that responsibility. Universities as institutions have a substantial stake in the discussions concerning the role of general education in their professional schools.

Accrediting agencies in most professional fields represent another obstacle to the goal of general education in professional education. In many professions the specialized interests of the particular field—and there are multiple interests in most cases—unintentionally have created an environment where it is difficult, if not impossible, to meet the curricular demands of the profession and the goals of general education within a four-year time frame. Accrediting agencies must continue to serve higher education by setting high standards and demanding quality, but the long-term educational legitimacy of professional requirements should be carefully reviewed on a regular basis. Are all of the professional school requirements essential? Is it still realistic to try to package the professional degree within the traditional four-year time frame? What responsibility should accrediting agencies accept for general education?

Although there is already a good deal of discussion about general education in professional education, I suggest that it might be useful to focus that discussion toward specific improvements in several professional fields. With this goal in mind I believe that a national forum on undergraduate professional and preprofessional education, organized perhaps by the American Council on Education in a fashion similar to the Business-Higher Education Forum, might be a productive vehicle to address a variety of issues in this area on a continuing basis. The participants in this forum would include representatives from the major professional accrediting organizations, faculty and deans from some of the leading professional schools, spokespersons from major disciplinary associations, and practicing professionals from several fields. Certainly, many of the issues addressed by the forum would be common to all of the professional groups, while others would be of primary interest to particular subgroups. The organization of such a forum certainly would present a number of organizational questions, but the common objective of improving general education in the professional school context should be sufficiently important to resolve such organizational questions.

Footnotes

1. Frank H. T. Rhodes, "The Role of the Liberal Arts in a Decade of Increased Technology," *Vital Speeches* 50 (June 15, 1984): 532.

2. Association of American Colleges, *Integrity in the College Curriculum: A Report to the Academic Community—The Findings and Recommendations of the Project on Redefining the Meaning and Purpose of Baccalaureate Degrees* (Washington, D.C.: Association of American Colleges, 1985), pp. 15-23.

3. Earl F. Chiet, *The Useful Arts and the Liberal Tradition* (New York: McGraw-Hill, 1975), pp. 2-3.

4. See, for example, T. R. McConnell, Robert O. Berdahl, and Margaret A. Fay, *From Elite to Mass Higher Education: The British and American Transformations* (Berkeley: Center for Research and Development in Higher Education, University of California, 1973); Martin Trow, *Problems in the Transition from Elite to Mass Higher Education* (Berkeley: Carnegie Commission on Higher Education, 1973).

5. Jan Krukowski, "What Do Students Want?" *Change* 17 (May/June 1985): 24.

6. "Tracking the Undergraduate Major," *Change* 17 (March/April 1985): 31.

7. Ibid., p. 32.

8. William C. McInnes, "The Integration of Liberal and Professional Education," *Thought* 57 (June 1982): 207.

9. Study Group on the Conditions of Excellence in American Higher Education, *Involvement in Learning: Realizing the Potential of American Higher Education* (Washington, DC: National Institute of Education, 1984); William J. Bennett, *To Reclaim a Legacy: A Report on the Humanities in Higher Education* (Washington, DC: National Endowment for the Humanities, 1984); Association of American Colleges, *Integrity in the College Curriculum: A Report to the Academic Community—The Findings and Recommendations of the Project on Redefining the Meaning and Purpose of Baccalaureate Degrees* (Washington, DC: Association of American Colleges, 1985): Southern Regional Education Board, *Access to Quality Undergraduate Education* (Atlanta: Southern Regional Education Board, 1985); Business-Higher Education Forum, *America's Business Schools: Priorities for Change* (Washington, DC: American Council on Education, 1985); Frank Newman, *Higher Education and the American Resurgence* (Princeton, NJ: Princeton University Press, 1985); Education Commission of the States, *Transforming the State Role in Undergraduate Education: Time for a Different View*, Report of the Working Party on Effective State Action to Improve Undergraduate Education (Denver: Education Commission of the States, 1986); Holmes Group, *Tomorrow's Teachers* (East Lansing, MI: Holmes Group, 1986); and Ernest L. Boyer, *College: The Undergraduate Experience in America* (New York: Harper and Row, 1987).

10. Study Group on the Conditions of Excellence, *Involvement in Learning*, p. 41.

11. Business-Higher Education Forum, *America's Business Schools*, pp. 13-17.

12. Holmes Group, *Tomorrow's Teachers*, pp. 46-49.

13. Association of American Colleges, *Integrity in the College Curriculum*, p. 30.

14. "General Education: New Support Growing on Campuses," *Change* 17 (November/December 1985): 27-30.

15. "Educators Discuss Professional Studies," *Higher Education and National Affairs* 35 (November 17, 1986): p. 4.

16. Charles R. Mann, *A Study of Engineering Education, Prepared for the Joint Committee on Engineering Education of the National Engineering Societies*, Bulletin No. 11

(New York: Carnegie Foundation for the Advancement of Teaching, 1918); William E. Wickenden, *A Comparative Study of Engineering Education in the United States and Europe*, sponsored by the Society for the Promotion of Engineering Education (Lancaster, PA: Lancaster Press, 1929); Engineers Council for Professional Development, *Present Status and Trends of Engineering Education in the United States* (New York: ECPD, Committee on Engineering Schools, 1939); Society for the Promotion of Engineering Education, "Report of the Committee on the Aims and Scope of Engineering Curricula," *Journal of Engineering Education* 30 (March 1940): 555-566; Society for the Promotion of Engineering Education, "Report of the Committee on Engineering Education after the War," *Journal of Engineering Education* 34 (May 1944): 589-614; American Society for Engineering Education, *Report on Evaluation of Engineering Education, 1952-55* (Washington, DC: ASEE, Committee on Evaluation of Engineering Education, 1955); American Society for Engineering Education, *Goals of Engineering Education: Final Report of the Goals Committee* (Washington, DC: ASEE, 1968); American Society for Engineering Education, *Engineering Education for a Lifetime of Learning* (Washington, DC: ASEE, 1975); and American Society for Engineering Education, *Future Directions for Engineering Education* (Washington, DC: ASEE, 1975).

17. William L. Everitt, "The Phoenix: A Challenge to Engineering Education," reprinted in *IEEE Transactions on Education*, E-23 (November 1980): p. 181.

18. Accrediting Board for Engineering and Technology, *Criteria for Accrediting Programs in Engineering in the United States* (New York: Accrediting Board for Engineering and Technology, 1986), pp. 5-8.

19. American Society for Engineering Education, *Future Directions for Engineering Education*; idem, *Engineering Education for a Lifetime of Learning*.

20. Robert A. Gordon and J. E. Howell, *Higher Education in Business* (New York: Columbia University Press, 1959); and Frank C. Pierson, *The Education of American Businessmen* (New York: McGraw-Hill, 1959).

21. Pierson, *The Education of American Businessmen*, p. 150.

22. Gordon and Howell, *Higher Education in Business*, p. 127.

23. See, for example, Jack N. Behrman and Richard I. Levin, "Special Report: Are Business Schools Doing Their Job?" *Harvard Business Review* 62 (January/February 1984): 140-47; Edward J. Mandt, "The Failure of Business Education and What to Do about It," *Management Review* 71 (August 1982): 47-52; Robert R. Rehder, "SMR Forum: American Business Education—Is It Too Late to Change?" *Sloan Management Review* 23 (Winter 1982): 63-71; and Roger B. Smith, "Humanities and Business: The Twain Shall Meet—But How?" *Vital Speeches* 50 (August 1, 1984): 632-35.

24. Rehder, "SMR Forum: American Business Education," pp. 65-66.

25. American Assembly of Collegiate Schools of Business, *Accreditation Council Policies, Procedures, and Standards—1985-86* (St. Louis, MO: AACSB, 1985), p. 28.

26. See, for example, Raymond E. Miles, "The Future of Business Education," *California Management Review* 27 (Spring 1985): 63-73; and William H. Newman, ed., *Managers for the Year 2000* (Englewood Cliffs, NJ: Prentice-Hall, 1978).

27. David Saxon, "Liberal Education in a Technological Age," *Science* 218 (November 26, 1982): 7.

Section Five

A PESSIMISTIC CONCLUSION—GENERAL EDUCATION AND THE PUBLIC SCHOOL

CHAPTER XIII

The Fortress Monastery: The Future of the Common Core

MARK HOLMES

The common school, the common program, and general education may be seen as all-embracing ideals, of which the common core is merely a diminutive version. I prefer to see the common core as representing the soul which gives meaning to our cultural continuity as well as the heart which permits cultural survival. It has been beset by the loss of faith that marks the modern age and by the destructive centrifugalism that marks the disintegration of the western democratic empire. A determination must be made, first, whether a common core should be sustained, second, what it will look like and, third, how it can be saved. There is in fact an extant common core but it is not one to light our minds, to give us educational purpose and vision. To rediscover a worthwhile common core to sustain a society wracked with self-doubt we must conserve and rebuild rather than pillage and squander our cultural and spiritual inheritance.

The ABC of Schooling—Basic Functions

There is a common core in contemporary schooling in the developed world and it extends beyond the generally accepted three Rs. Allocation (or social distribution), the basics (the three Rs), and custody together form the necessary triad.[1]

231

ALLOCATION

The division of labor becomes ever more intense. New jobs are created, often requiring highly specialized if sometimes easily learned skills. Highly skilled jobs using new technology open in the upper parts of the labor force. And, at the same time, the demand for unskilled, casual, and part-time labor increases, mainly in service industries. The old industrial and agricultural jobs decline. The net result is a job market both more fluid and more differentiated than in the past.

There are three ways in which young people can be allocated to jobs in a contemporary, democratic society valuing a high degree of individual freedom. Currently, jobs are usually allocated on the basis of earned educational credentials, qualifications sometimes closely related to the job, as in the case of a medical practitioner, and sometimes remotely or not at all, as in the case of a truck driver required to hold a high school diploma.

A second possibility, suggested by Mortimer Adler's *Paideia Proposal* for a uniform, common elementary and secondary education, would postpone the basic stage of allocation from the secondary to the tertiary level of schooling.[2] However, the principle of credentialism would remain untouched. Thus, the idea of postponing job allocation is only peripherally relevant to the common core. If my broad definition of common core as the soul and heart of the cultural inheritance passed on to succeeding generations is accepted, the question of whether the common core extends to age sixteen or age eighteen is not crucial. In contemporary terms, a prior question is whether there should and can be any core at all, the real question today being not whether the common core will last to the end of high school, but whether it will even exist in junior kindergarten.

A more conceptually distinct approach to social distribution, argued by Ivan Illich, is that vocational choices should be formally disconnected from schooling.[3] Instead, employers would determine their own required qualifications to be satisfied by applicants by means of a competitive exercise conducted by the employer. Adoption of this quite different principle would in all probability transform not only the common core but our school system, as Illich intended. If such a proposal came to pass, the common core, if any, would presumably become the lowest common denominator of (a) the common requirements of all jobs within society, (b) the common educational requirements of all parents within society, and (c) the common requirements of all employers other than those that are strictly job-related. It is possible for the common core to turn out in practice and over time to be a null set.

Neither of the two variants seems likely to be adopted in the foreseeable future by the North American and Western European democracies. Illich's proposal for deschooling runs counter to most modern trends and movements. Even the right-wing idea of a voucher system would at least serve to establish the value of schooling, and, by extension, credentials. Left-wing critics would like to integrate schooling more rather than less securely in the fabric of society.[4] Adler's proposal is less functionally inoperable. It merely transfers from rhetoric to the prescribed program the ideal that twelve years of schooling is every child's entitlement. If we leave aside the curricular intent of his proposal, functionally it requires the implementation of the Japanese model within the western world, from where, ironically, that model was first derived. However, despite widespread recognition of the academic success of Japanese schools,[5] there is little sign of an impending movement to provide a more or less common curriculum to the end of high school, thereby postponing the formal differentiation of future status, income, and employment until the age of eighteen. Current trends in the western world lead in the opposite direction.

Right-wing critics often favor a closer integration of secondary schooling and work experience, using the success of West Germany as a model. There is widespread admiration of both the West German and the very different Japanese approaches, not only for their association with steady economic development, but for their apparent ability to provide worthwhile employment for young people. Recent governmental reports in the United States, such as *A Nation at Risk,*[6] are somewhat ambivalent; there is no clear endorsement of either the Japanese or the German model. Liberal critics move part of the way with Adler, approving a ten-year common core and an overall school experience more like the Japanese than the German model.[7]

The implications of James Coleman's examination of private and public high schools in the United States have not been widely accepted. His research has been interpreted as suggesting only that private schools are more effective than public schools as a result of more vigorous employment of "effective schooling," for example, high expectations and standards, direct instruction, universalistic discipline. The more radical implication of his findings, that an undifferentiated instructional environment, without tracking or streaming or a variety of curricular offerings, will produce student achievement characterized by higher standards and lower variance, has not been widely noted.[8] The implication is, of course, that the Japanese model would work well for the United States too. Outside the United States, pressures from business are more unequivocally in favor of movement towards the German model. This is most obvious in Great Britain where the government has completely by-passed the educational bureaucracies to set up new vocational and technical programs in secondary schools by direct contract. In Canada, more tentative moves have been made to encourage cooperative education and joint ventures among vocational colleges, schools, and employers.

On the left, the functional exigency of allocation is considered in the context that it appears to confirm social allocation by race, gender, social class, and ethnic background. As none of the Japanese, German, and deschooling models is seen as changing the allocative tendencies of the "traditional" school with respect to social origin, leftists oppose any move towards their adoption. Such reforms merely distract the public from what they see as the real problems. "Progressive," "child-centered" ideas still retain some currency on the moderate left.[9] Thus, the moderate left and the Marxist radicals join together to oppose proposals asking for more rigor, the one because of dislike for the goals and methodologies implicit in rigorous education, the other because the reports are capitalist in tone and assumptions.

Superficially, the left might be expected to be most receptive to the *Paideia Proposal* as it would postpone curricular and therefore social differentiation. That appears not to be the case. The left is uninterested in an undifferentiated, rigorous, elitist, liberal program; it remembers Adler's association with Robert Hutchins.[10] Adler is not feared but discounted. It may well be that the endorsement of early differentiation of learning and instruction by left-of-center "progressives" runs counter to their hopes for more equal outcomes among social groups; however, illogic is not a barrier to the development of enthusiasm in education.

If some on the right appear to want both the Japanese and the German models, and some on the left want both more differentiation in instruction and more equal outcomes, there is no evident desire or prospect for either a uniform education to the end of twelfth grade or for deschooling. It seems clear that the central function of allocation will remain in the hands of educational institutions, with the secondary school carrying the major load.

I have argued elsewhere that the most beneficial form of social allocation is that based on credentials related to evidence of competence.[11] Like democracy as a political system, competence-based meritocracy may be the worst of all distributive systems, except for all the others. It does provide for a degree of social mobility without destroying the fabric of the social structure. Parents try to help their children, with conspicuous success. But school systems do provide avenues for social change from generation to generation, even if much of that change is based on parental will. It is an unusual family tree that does not reflect significant social variations, within and between generations. Social allocation is likely to be the single most enduring function of schooling, and there seems to be no feasible, desired, and desirable alternative. However, allocation is not dependent on there being a common school, a common program, or even a common core, beyond the ABCs.

THE BASICS

The basics (reading, writing, and the manipulation of number) are an indisputable part of any common core of the school program. Although educators tend to be less enthusiastic than parents, it would be an unusual teacher or principal who would argue publicly that their emphasis should be reduced. One important argument used in their support is that they are required for access to a great many occupations. They are an important part of the legitimacy lying behind the use of educational credentials for social allocation. The fact that many occupations today require few skills in written English or the manipulation of number in no way detracts from parents' wishes for their children. Their own ambitions are for other more demanding occupations. Undemanding jobs are for other people's children. Although most discussion about the value or obsolescence of the basics is based in utilitarian terms, it is important not to forget that the fundamental educational justification for the basics is unrelated to performance on the job.

CUSTODY

Of the three essential components of the common core, custody is the least talked about, the least respectable. Educators are well aware of the public antagonism to professional activity days, early school closing, and long lunch hours. Adding professional activity days, lengthening school vacations, changing the school year, introducing a four-day week are all much more contentious changes than, for example, changing the English curriculum, making cooking compulsory for boys, introducing semestering within the traditional school year, or changing compulsory subjects. If research were to show conclusively that achievement would improve if children had a more concentrated half-day in first and second grade and a longer school day in fourth grade, such a planned change would still, I conjecture, gain little support from parents of first and second grade children, unless the proposed program included enrichment (a euphemism for custodial) activities for the other half-day in the first two grades.

Allocation is generally accepted if not talked about. Only a few brave (or foolhardy) educators would like to degrade the basics. Custody is the last of the ABCs to be recognized and identified. Whereas parents, particularly ambitious middle-class parents are well aware of the importance of success in school for their children's economic future, the roles are reversed in the case of custody. Teachers recognize the custodial reality, parents are loath to admit it.

Current demographic trends reinforce the custodial function of the schools. Increases in the number of nontraditional families and of more traditional families where both spouses work lead to increased reliance on the school for custody. Reduced acceptance by some parents and foster parents of custodial responsibility (for example, for their children's behavior outside the home; for social, spiritual, and medical care) increases the school's custodial responsibility. The two trends interact. Homosexual partners, common-law spouses and transitory, serial partners will, particularly when they are not the biological parents of the children, be unlikely to accept the strong bonds of family responsibility found within the modern, nuclear family. The traditional family of the past survived weak parents by reliance on the extended family of grandparents, siblings, and neighbors. Modern parents carrying out traditional roles must bear the whole burden of upbringing with little community help and frequent community hindrance. Thus even contemporary, traditional parents, may be unable to operationalize their chosen pattern of socialization as peer pressure within the community intensifies.

These essential common core *functions* of schooling should not be compared to the fundamental elements of education. But the three functions are centrally important to an understanding of contemporary schooling. Allocation is important for two reasons. First, society has to have a mechanism to sort its young among a variety of occupational and social futures. Second, the prospect of allocation provides a form of extrinsic motivation that influences nearly every young person. A high level of motivation for schooling, high enough to maintain high participation rates, is necessary if young people, particularly adolescents, are to be kept in situations where they can neither harm others nor be harmed by them. The basics are important because they legitimate the process of schooling. There must be some stuff on which credentials can be based—or appear to be based. Further, the more closely the legitimating stuff is linked to life outside school, particularly if that life is seen in terms of employment, the more legitimate it becomes in our materialistic times. Custody is important because it is insufficient for schools to allocate and to teach the basics. Suppose schools could cover all the stuff required in half the time; the consequences would be unacceptable no matter how the actual time required was arranged. It would be incorrect to infer that custody in school from age six to eighteen is an arbitrary artifact resulting from chance historical origins of modern society. It is not unreasonable to believe that becoming a mature adult in modern society takes at least eighteen years. Thus the ABCs are the necessary lowest common denominator of contemporary schooling in the developed world. But that common denominator is insufficient. The contemporary crisis in education, the loss of faith in education, is at least in part based on the growing recognition that there is not much else to education beyond that common denominator.

Society, Individual, and Group

An examination of functions shows how a social institution, such as formal elementary and secondary schooling, serves as a part of the larger social organization. The fact that the functions of schooling are similar in very different political arrangements (democracy, autocracy, and totalitarianism) suggests that there are characteristics of modern, developed, industrial societies necessitating the pervasive characteristics of contemporary schooling: compulsory attendance, normative ranking, measures of competence related to defined criteria, age grading, universalistic treatment, and division of subject matter. If I am correct in suggesting that it will be difficult to tamper with the ABCs, it does not follow that larger educational purposes are irrelevant or uninteresting. Function and purpose form a dialectic— between what we must be and what we ought to be, between what we are and what we could become, between what we see and what we imagine. But before turning to the educational purposes that should be served by a common core, I should like to examine the context of the contemporary school further. My intent is less to lay out the details of

a preferred common core than to show the context and constraints
which will influence its future development. I am neither predicting
nor choosing but combining both processes. By illustrating the limits
to our choices, I attempt to show that some choices are both more
realizable and more appealing than others. To select what is merely
practical or likely is demeaning; to select the infeasible imaginable is
unwise and frustrating. The functional should be blended with the
desirable.

The units of a social entity are: the *society*, being the structure and
functions characteristic of its human composition; the *group*, being a
coherent subgroup of the population with identifying characteristics
describable by objective criteria; and the *individual*. I do not include
within the concept of *group* unorganized sections of the population
characterized by similar interests, for example, young people. In
contrast, evangelicals, Catholics, and mainstream Protestants all form
groups because each can and does speak with a common voice on some
issues. The jostling interests of the three units form the stuff of
politics. As schools serve to convey a tableau of the society and world
in which children live, conflicts among the three units are abundantly
evident within the school program. By "tableau" I mean a general
picture; it is not at all clear that schools present a microcosm of society
or that they serve the interests of the ruling classes, or that they teach
acceptance and/or rebellion. As the tableau may be and, in any case,
is believed by some to be supportive of and by others prejudicial to the
larger society or some of its groups, the school becomes a
battleground for societal conflict. Much of the conflict results from
competing claims for sensitivity to alleged common characteristics of
the larger society, to the desires of coherent groups and to the asserted
"rights" of individuals, in this case usually individual parents.

People differ as to the priority they accord the three units. Further,
that difference varies with the decision to be made. For example, it is
not irrational to believe both that policing should be carried out by the
state on behalf of society and that grocery selection should be carried
out by the individual. However, whereas there is general consensus in
western democracies about policing and groceries, there is less
consensus about many, specific aspects of education such as morality,
sexual mores, vocational training, choice of appropriate reading
material, and instructional pedagogy. A view of the common core of
schooling derives from one's sense of educational policy.

Society and the Common Core

Most people who think about schools and their purposes have a vision, however vague, of the society they want to bring about. Emile Durkheim believed that schools work towards society's idealized image.[12] While not all French citizens of his time would have shared the details of his secular ideal, his conceptions drew heavily on France's Judeo-Christian heritage and would probably have received widespread acceptance, at least within the public school sector. It is unclear today, in most western societies, that there is a reasonably coherent, consensual vision of society's ideal image. This is the crux of the problem, the more so when translated to the public school, to which individual and group interests are inimical. If the consensus were strong, there would be little need to talk about a common core or general education; we would be doing it.

One of the most powerful beliefs supporting a societal vision of school has been the belief in democratized schooling—with equality of educational opportunity promoting social equality. The road to such equality, it is or was widely believed, is paved with equal opportunities in schools. But that belief, nearly consensual at one time, is increasingly controversial. Access to equal opportunity does not provide social equality—children remain tied by social and cultural constraints.[13] Making postsecondary education available to all qualified applicants does result in a measure of genuine accessibility to both university education and middle-class status to working-class youth.[14] However, as societies become more economically developed, continued equality of educational opportunity is unlikely to contribute much more to increased social mobility, still less to social equality. Thus, government support for postsecondary education in Canada and Britain is increasingly viewed by economists as a tax transfer from the poor to the rich.

There is evidence that the more developed our societies and schools become, the more children's intellectual development becomes dependent on their homes rather than on their school environments. Heyneman made the surprising discovery that educational achievement in Uganda, in stable, pre-Idi Amin days, was scarcely related to home background characteristics at all.[15] Analysis of the other studies showed that there is a general positive relationship between the proportion of variance in achievement explained by the home, as distinct from differences among schools, and the state of economic development of society.[16] There are several hypothetical explanations.

As schools improve, the differences between them decrease. As societies become more complex, the cultural differences among families become greater. Individual scholastic ambition may be both greater and more uniform in school children in less-developed countries. The culture of the home is likely to be foreign to the sophisticated, western culture of the school in less-developed countries. None of these hypotheses gives ground for the expectation that increasing school quality will do much to promote social equality as societies develop. Indeed, current trends suggest that as society becomes more genuinely meritocratic, as material returns are based increasingly on measured competence, schools become increasingly reproductive of social inequality.

Consider how fulfillment of the meritocracy envisaged by Michael Young may come about.[17] Historically, the common school has represented society, notably in the United States and to a lesser but still significant extent in Canada. It did provide, and still does, an avenue of upward mobility for intelligent and ambitious youth. It is important to distinguish between social class and the broader concept of cultural background. Social class (using proxies such as parental jobs, income, and level of education) is a low-level predictor of future success, probably accounting for less than 20 percent of the variance.[18] In other words, economic position in society is far from being a guarantor of economic success for one's children. On the other hand, if we take into account the numerous factors differentiating families, including values, attitudes, expectations, level of control, then we can account for much more of the variance in achievement, and ultimately success.[19] If schools become more alike, as may be happening in Denmark and Sweden, then it is to these family differences we should increasingly look for explanations of individual achievement. If, as frequently happens in socially heterogeneous societies, schools become divided on social class, ethnic, or ideological grounds, we should anticipate that the schools will serve to enhance and recapitulate those family characteristics which provide their guiding purpose. Either way, home backgrounds become increasingly important.

The more equality of opportunity we provide, in terms of access, among races, by geography, between genders, among ethnic groups, the more crucial and the better predictor the home culture becomes. Similarly, the more home backgrounds become differentiated the better they predict success of the children they produce.

The significance of family background is thus heightened by differentiation among families. The new professional, wealthy class is proportionately more wealthy than in the recent past. The male medical practitioner of 1950 supporting a wife and several children is replaced today by a medical practitioner married to a lawyer who together, on a much higher family income, support one or two children. At the other end of the scale, the male, unskilled laborer supporting a wife and family is replaced by an unemployed, single parent raising children on welfare. As the meritocracy becomes fairer, for both males and females, based more on proven merit and less on direct family influence (nepotism), assortative mating increases the chances that the successful parent will pass on advantage to the children; similarly, unsuccessful parents are more likely to pass on their disadvantage. It makes little difference whether the advantage is of genetic or cultural derivation—both are passed on to the children. There may over time be some lessening of the inheritance of privilege from the "regression to the mean" in IQ, that is, two parents of IQ 130 are likely to have children whose IQs average below 130. Similarly, we may find that beneficiaries of ideal cultural circumstances for economic and educational success do not pass on those same ideal cultural circumstances to their children; successful couples are sometimes overcome by self-indulgence and narcissism or they may become overly indulgent to their children in reaction to their own more demanding upbringing. That remains to be seen. At the moment we are living in times of increasing extremes of cultural advantage and disadvantage. In Denmark, where female emancipation and equal opportunity are more advanced than in North America the IQ curve for the child population has changed; there are proportionately more children with both very low and very high IQs.[20]

Ethnicity in the United States and Canada has conflicting effects on this trend. In some parts of those countries (for example, southern Florida, southern California, southern Ontario), the recent influx of immigrants enhances cultural variability. In other parts, where previous immigrants are now becoming assimilated, the opposite effect may be evidenced. Thus one finds regional patterns of cultural differentiation. In stable situations such as those of Vermont, North Dakota, Nova Scotia, and Saskatchewan, the structure and variability in families may be only incrementally different from earlier times— societal changes are offset by ethnic assimilation. In Los Angeles, San Francisco, Miami, and Toronto, where societal and ethnic changes are cumulative, the family structure and environment are radically transformed.

At the same time as families have become more heterogeneous, schools have become more homogeneous, at least in relation to the spectrum of the population. That will appear a strange comment to teachers in Toronto, for example, who see many languages and cultures where they once saw only one. However, fifty years ago the archetypical Canadian and American school was the common school serving a rural community or small town. The school's population, divided primarily on economic grounds, was relatively heterogeneous;[21] the school served almost the entire population, rich and poor. There is no implication here that it served them all equally. Clearly the school, actively or passively, helped the allocative function and in so doing served to pass on social and economic advantage from generation to generation. But there was usually a common school, normally a common program—the school was often too small to provide significant choice—and nearly always, at least at the elementary level, a common core.

Today the school classroom that seems so heterogeneous in downtown Toronto serves a much smaller segment of the total population than did that rural school of fifty, even thirty years ago. Part of the reason is, as I have said, that families are now more varied. The greater the differences among families, the less likely they are to send their children to the same school. There is evidence of this in both the United States and Canada. Integration of blacks and whites seems to work in the suburbs where the black and white families are very similar except in race, and where blacks form a small and unthreatening minority. Integration has usually not worked where middle-class whites are expected to mix with poor blacks. Advantaged parents are likely to seek separate, homogeneous schools for their young when the values of the common or local school are most alien to their own and when that school seems to be unable or reluctant to help them pass on their advantages to their children. Social, cultural, and academic heterogeneity is unlikely to appeal to the advantaged, unless their own interests and culture prevail. I am not here being critical. It seems to me normal for parents to try to help the educational and future economic chances of their children, particularly so in a meritocratic society, where individual merit is cultivated, praised, and rewarded.[22]

It is important to stress that in talking of *homogeneous* schools I am referring to *homogeneity of membership*. The increasing homogeneity of schools within an increasingly heterogeneous society necessarily implies that there is greater differentiation among schools. This does not imply that differences in schools will increasingly explain differences among educational outcomes. It is very likely that the differences in schools result from the families they serve. Thus, less differentiation *within* schools is translated into greater differentiation *among* schools.

It would be misleading to imply that changes in the family patterns or immigration are the sole or major causes of the trend; they are merely the most visible. Perhaps the single biggest cause of the homogenization of schools is the growth of urban and, particularly, suburban conurbations. This development is characterized by social differentiation—there are neighborhoods where houses cost $70,000, others where they cost $200,000. Choice of residential area is reinforced by and reinforces the social distinctiveness of the local school. This is not a new trend, but it is becoming prevalent throughout North America. Geographical mobility, economic restructuring, and the breakdown of the traditional family all enhance it.

What is interesting is that these changes have taken place without much concern or comment among educators; academics applaud or bemoan the changes but school people continue the daily grind. Why should this be so? I think an important reason is that these changes have been accompanied by a centrifugal movement away from society as a unit, towards the individual and towards groups. Educators are part of, if not leaders in, that major change in values. Change in core values legitimates the social changes and gives them additional impetus.

Evidence for this argument is provided by educators' willing embrace of differentiation of instruction to reflect children's individual or group "needs." Partly this stems from their support for "progressive," "child-centered" education, a philosophy much more popular among teachers than among parents.[23] By this philosophy, the demands of an external society, still less the requirements of "obsolete" tradition, are given less heed than "appropriate learning opportunities" in the classroom. The tremendous growth of special education illustrates this trend. At the very least, special education implies differentiated instructional methodology; it usually also means differentiated content. Sometimes it means lengthy periods of withdrawal from the ordinary classroom. At an extreme, as seen in some urban Ontario as well as a few United States school systems, special classes or special schools have been set up for pupils classified as "gifted." Thus simultaneously there is differentiation within classrooms, based on the individual "needs" of children, and differentiation among classrooms and schools.

Various other changes have been introduced which further break down the idea of the common school serving a population reflective of the larger society. Sometimes supported by educators and sometimes opposed, they are rarely opposed on the grounds that they further destroy the common school. In Canada, French immersion is probably the most successful, major innovation in the country's educational history.[24] These programs do not attract heterogeneous populations and are usually not intended for the child experiencing learning difficulties. Secondary school specialization, even schools for the arts based on a model made popular by the television program *Fame,* has also increased. In addition, trends in private school enrollment reflect increasingly individualistic views of education. In Ontario, the proportion of elementary students experiencing significantly segregated schooling has increased, from about one-third to about one-half during the last fifteen years.[25]

These educational changes interact with social changes. Social changes bring about increased separation of children according to social, economic, ethnic, racial, and ideological characteristics. Educational changes enhance these same trends. Thus, instructional differentiation within the classroom permits the children who demand more attention to get more.[26] Special education classes and schools separate the "gifted," who tend to be socially advantaged, from the "learning disabled," who tend to be socially disadvantaged. French immersion appeals to the upwardly mobile middle class.

Of recent educational innovations, only "outcomes-based education," notably mastery learning, counters the move to homogeneity of the group and heterogeneity of available programs.[27] Although there has been considerable comment on a few experimental programs in, for example, Johnson City, Chicago, and Dallas, there has been no widespread adoption.[28] In Ontario, in 1986, there existed not one provincial curriculum guideline based on mastery learning principles and not a single school dominated by that philosophy. Quite the reverse, new guidelines are based heavily on the personal and individual "needs" of children.

We have numerous changes in society at large and in education that have a single result in educational terms: the common school, even for those living in the neighborhood, is dying across large sections of

North America. The common school as a microcosm of the larger
society no longer exists in the most populous and economically
developed regions of the United States and Canada.

THE GROUP, THE INDIVIDUAL, AND THE COMMON CORE

I have illustrated the centrifugal trends away from society as a
source of authority. But where is the new source? The group or the
individual? It is much less easy to demonstrate that either one has
made a net gain, as each has lost to the other as well as making gains
from society.

Increased private school enrollment generally reflects loss of
authority of society balanced by a commensurate gain on the part of
the individual parent. As private schools form alliances (Catholic
schools in the United States, fundamentalist Christian schools in both
the United States and Canada), group affiliation and group loyalty
begin to play an increasingly large part in school enrollment. The
development in Toronto of "heritage language" programs whose
function is to sustain, or to appear to sustain, native language, as
distinct from serving a bridging purpose from native language to
English, represents the loss of authority by society to the group.
Many of the changes reflect a jostling among competing interest
groups and a jostling of individualistic interests.

It is possible that teachers have lost authority individually, but
gained authority collectively. Thus, teachers are increasingly sensitive
to demands from individual parents concerning the treatment of the
individual child. Parents increasingly control children's absence from
school for all but the most unreasonable purposes. They may even
obtain special programs or exemptions from programs considered
compulsory. On the other hand, teachers collectively wield power
over program and evaluation in many jurisdictions. In Ontario,
provincewide testing has been successfully opposed by teachers
despite the desire on the part of two-thirds of the public for its
reintroduction.[29]

One thing seems certain. The strengthening of the authority of
both the individual and the group, even though each may lose
something to the other, weakens the authority of the central society.
And it is only society that can provide the ground for consensus on a
common core.

Left-wing critics argue that society has never formed a consensus
on education in any democratic, representative sense. To them, the
grab for power by individuals and groups is merely a reasonable

reaction to a history of oligarchic hegemony in public schooling. Schooling has always, they argue, been organized for the benefit of the capitalist class and its managers.[30] As the hegemony becomes more evident, a variety of groups, both powerful and powerless become more naked in their assertion of their demands. I leave it to others to dispute this version of educational history, merely noting that it is far from being unanimously accepted as the entire truth. My point here is that there was and to some extent still is, in the less economically developed parts of the United States and Canada, a belief in the institution of schooling, both as a good and fair way of educating all children within a national consensus and as a reasonable way of providing for equality of educational opportunity. It is likely that the virtue of the common school was never unsoiled, was largely myth— in the sense that collective faith in the school represented what people wanted it to be as much as what it was.

My argument here is not that either Canada or the United States has destroyed an excellent system of common schools serving a homogeneous population, replacing it with a system of differentiated schools serving a more heterogeneous population. My argument is that we have, in part deliberately, but very largely by happenstance, destroyed one myth towards which we were working, without replacing it by another. There remains considerable faith in the myth. It was never entirely valid. Increasingly, individuals and groups are, wittingly and unwittingly, acting on preferences which are destructive to the central myth of a common, public education.

The Common School, Common Program, Common Core: The Search For Myth

The three terms of my heading carry much of the same educational and ideological baggage, yet one of the three is particularly distinctive. The idea of the common school is that all children should undergo the experience of a common socialization; the idea of the common program and common core is that all children should achieve, or at least have access to, a degree of common learning. In practice, the ideas merge. The argument for a common core/common program is usually not restricted to the basic skills. Adler proposes a common liberal education for all.[31] Whatever his intentions, there seems little doubt that the result of adopting his prescription would amount to inculcation of the liberal ideal. Fundamentalist Christians, as one example, are not likely to endorse the *Paideia Proposal*.

Let us suppose Adler's proposal for a common general program for all students from age six to eighteen were adopted. Suppose further that it were accompanied by an open voucher system. Under this hypothetical plan, any school, public or independent, would be able to offer the "Paideia program," but only that program. Private schools, based on ability to pay, would continue outside the voucher system. The combination of the two proposals is implausible. Why fund independent schools from public money if they are forbidden to vary the program? And why be so directive about program if the immediate social outcomes would be inconsiderable? The envisaged system would encourage still further departure from the public school as like-minded parents choose schools for children like their own. Many of the strongest supporters for a common program or common core would strongly oppose such a plan.

Despite the obvious distinction between the common school and the common program, in contemporary political terms the concepts are closely allied. The concept of the common school is supported by beliefs about basic ideals, understandings, values, and attitudes that should be shared by all. And so is the concept of the common program. The combination of a voucher plan and a common program is infeasible.

The search for a common core is a search for a residual, societal memory or tradition. So far, I have tried to establish two major points. There is a common core of schooling—it comprises allocation, the basic skills, and custody. Beyond that, the idea of a common process of socialization has been in retreat, particularly over the last two decades. It is not that it has been frontally attacked and defeated, although it has been attacked. Rather it has been undermined by the interpolation of different ideas with which it is fundamentally incompatible. The ideas of individual rights, group rights, separate ethnic development, multiculturalism, the precedence of the "needs" of the individual child in a "child-centered" environment—all, in combination with a variety of centrifugal social trends, enfeeble the cause of common schooling. The public has not come to terms with the requirement for choice. Belief in equal opportunity in public education is often combined with demand for individualization.

Today's crisis in education, most noticeable at the secondary level, derives from the destruction of myth. There is no current, sustaining *myth* to uphold the ideology of a common core of schooling. But I should explain the sense in which I am using the term. Myth is not a false explanation of events. Myth, in my usage, is a traditional narrative which serves to explain, justify, and celebrate social norms and institutions. Far from being false, it is an expression of truth. It is equally important to note that there is no condescension in this usage. There is no implication that the unwashed masses need some security blanket of myth, while we, the educated elite, decide what they deserve and they should believe. As Edward Shils points out, we all need our chart. We all require authority, categories, and rules.[32] We need criteria and judgment. I believe we are each one of us better off if we have some guiding force, religion, or pervasive sense of purpose. I have my own personal myth. My educational myth is an interpretation of that more general, more personal vision.

A myth, as a traditional narrative, is part objective reality, part fancy, part ideology, part feeling, part reconstruction. Myths cannot usefully be graded into six ascending Kohlbergian stages. Indeed, one of the prices sometimes paid for high levels of education, based on cultivation of analytical and other high-level cognitive competence, is the destruction of myth. Myth is holistic; certainly it does not distinguish fact from value. To apply positivist, conceptual tools to it is to destroy it. For example, the noble myth of human equality could easily be destroyed by sustained research into biological and cultural differences among racial and ethnic groups; this may be the one remaining shibboleth immune from attack by contemporary social scientists. To describe the workings of contemporary myths may be functionalist, but it is not necessarily relativist. My purpose is not to suggest that we choose from an assortment of visions by some rational, decision-making matrix. To assert, as I do, that numerous, educational myths contain important aspects of truth is neither to decree they are all equal in ideology, conceptualization, and worth nor to assert that the best can be easily identified. However, I shall argue that one strand of current mythology is particularly crucial for the future of the common core.

Five strands of educational myth can be identified as prevailing in this century in Western society. They are: (a) the technocratic myth; (b) the self-fulfillment myth; (c) the liberal myth; (d) the democratic myth; and (e) the character myth.

The *technocratic myth* is the most prevalent myth of our times. That is to say, the behavior of school people and students is more consonant with it than with the others. To the extent that values denote what we do rather than what we say, it is the most valued. It is the most consistent with the materialistic, utilitarian times in which we live. It is also entirely compatible with the ABCs. The technocratic myth is that school prepares and trains young people for mature functioning in adult life. Every individual should contribute to the larger society and material returns will flow in recognition of that contribution. The school's job is to help every individual find a useful, satisfying place within that larger society.

It is not sensible to look to this myth for the salvation of our common core and the idea of general education. This *is* our myth, but it is insufficient. If we have a crisis in contemporary education it is because this myth, essentially an elaboration of the ABCs, cannot sustain us.

There are three reasons for the failure of the technocratic myth. One is itself technocratic—it is very difficult to make technocratic education work. The United States and Canadian economies are in a time of flux—and the pace of economic change does not seem to be slowing. The division of labor in some highly technical fields is becoming more marked. Even the large, truly comprehensive school (and few exist for the reasons I have given) cannot keep up with changing demands. A second reason is ideological. The other myths have taken a strong emotional hold on North America, particularly among educators both in the university and in the school who do not generally believe their jobs are or ought to be technocratic. Even those who do accept the technocratic reality do so deprecatingly. Parents, too, although their behavior can often be predicted within the technocratic myth, often give different reasons for their particular educational decisions. Thirdly, it is psychically unsatisfying to have one's job reduced in consequence and significance. A physician will not easily become a medical technologist, quite apart from the issue of monetary return. A financial executive would rather become a consultant than a bookkeeper. However much materialistic technocracy represents the daily lives of students in our schools, it is unlikely to become a sustaining myth for education in the United States and Canada. Even students who give material reasons for their conforming behavior in school feel dissatisfied with that rationale, and look outside the school's formal program for sources of satisfaction.[33]

The *self-fulfillment myth* contains within it more fundamental difficulties. Of the five, it is least compatible with the ABCs. The ABCs lead to the familiar regularities of schools—self-contained classrooms, schedules, normative evaluation, attendance checks, codes of behavior, direct and sequenced instruction, universalistic discipline. All of these regularities are incompatible with the notion of self-fulfillment, which I believe explains why Seymour Sarason has replaced his implicit support for functional change with a harsh cry for a retreat from formal schooling.[34]

The self-fulfillment myth is that education provides an opportunity for individual young people to develop, to grow, to test themselves and their environment, and to choose what they want to be, rather than to react to some external demand that they become. First developed by Rousseau, the myth has strong echoes in Dewey and in most treatises on "progressive," "child-centered" education.

There are also three reasons for its failure to seize the hearts and minds of most Americans and Canadians. As I noted, it is not compatible with the regularities of institutional life, with the ABCs. For much the same reason, it is quite antithetical to the dominant, technocratic myth, which requires the imposition of external, industrial demands on the school program. Finally, many parents have quite clear ideas about what they do want their children to learn—whether it be spoken French or problem solving by computer. They are simply unprepared to wait until the chrysalis decides to unfold. Quite simply, the self-fulfillment myth is incompatible with almost everything we mean by the term schooling, as has been discovered by administrators in famous "progressive" schools like Dartington Hall.

The *liberal myth* is well exemplified by the *Paideia Proposal*. It is highly compatible with the ABCs and could be wedded to our technocratic environment. While students would, technocratically, adapt to a world of credits and credentials, educators would enjoy the hard core of substance—the humanities, social sciences, the physical sciences, and aesthetics. While students ostensibly earned credits faintly relevant to some distant job, they would be simultaneously educated in the human and liberal arts. This myth sustains much of the substance of the typical high school program in much of the western world.

The liberal myth is that in the modern age we have outlived the divisive dogmas of past ages and that we can found a new society based on reasoned appreciation of ideas—in literature, in history, in the arts, and by the application of the scientific method to problems in the natural and social sciences. It is a powerful myth among the educated populace and within the university. It lends authority to things possessed by the educated.

Yet if I thought it were sufficient, I would not be writing this essay; there would be no crisis in education. The essential difficulty of this myth lies in its mass application. The university is not beset by the same crisis as elementary and secondary education. It would be

difficult to read any of the recent publications on the secondary school
and remain confident that it is firmly in thrall to the liberal myth.[35]
Some students are unquestionably intellectual in the pursuit of liberal
ideas; but most are not. It is a commonplace to observe that many
teachers neither read nor experience the world of ideas outside the
confines of their work. Mass culture is television and popular music.
My point is not to argue whether or not society is today more or less
"cultured" than it was at some past time. My point is simply to
observe that the hope that mass secondary school would develop a
high-level, mass, liberal culture is as ill-founded as the myth that it
would lead to social equality. "Quality" newspapers, books, and
television remain the preserve of the minority.

The *democratic myth* has its strongest roots in the United States,
but has spread in the heady air of American imperialism to much of the
world. Aspects of it are very compatible with the ABCs; indeed,
insofar as it consists of concepts of equality of opportunity and open,
social mobility, it provides a legitimating rationale for the allocative
function the school must fulfill.

The democratic myth is that the school serves all individuals and
sectors of society equally. In so doing, it both provides equality of
educational opportunity and paves the way towards social equality.
But this myth has lost sustaining influence among the educated
because it is no longer factually accurate. The school may well
provide equal opportunity in terms of accessibility but it does not
provide all children with either equal conditions—there is not a
common school—or equal outcomes, whether measured by individual
or by demographic indicators. I have already noted that there seems to
be no reason why there should be a connection between genuine
equality of educational opportunity and social equality. Indeed, social
inequality can be justified more readily on grounds of differences in
competence than on grounds of differing social origins. The
explanatory power of differences among schools, with respect to
student achievement and subsequent success, is small compared with
the explanatory power of the home culture. It is true that this last
observation is somewhat mitigated by the success of the school
effectiveness movement in showing how schools can be improved to
help the disadvantaged.[36] Nevertheless, the most optimistic hope is
that the school will be able to provide genuine equality of educational
opportunity in terms of access; there is neither prospect nor agreement
that the school will or should provide social equality (that is, a much

smaller gap between the affluent and the poor). That issue must be and is being addressed outside the context of the school.

The *character myth* has been illustrated in nineteenth-century Canada and United States, as well as in English boarding schools.[37] It has been promoted by Urie Bronfenbrenner and Edward Wynne.[38] It has suffered the most from direct ideological attack.[39] It is least consistent with the hedonism and narcissism of contemporary times. The growth of fundamentalist schools can be seen as stemming from the abandonment of this myth by the larger society.

The character myth is that the school task is to produce not primarily self-fulfilled people, not primarily good mechanics, not primarily urbane intellectuals, not primarily equal or even fair distribution of material goods, but good people. The other goals may be secondary consequences from the development of virtue, but the ruling ideal is that children become right-believing, right-thinking, and right-acting adults.

There are two major reasons for the ill repute in which this myth is held. One is that it is fundamentally antithetical to the contemporary belief in secular relativism. C. A. Bowers, for example, illustrates how all modern, liberal, educational ideologies are susceptible to the accusation of nihilism.[40] The term "virtue" is likely to evoke ridicule among modern educators, as is mention of many of the traditional virtues such as purity, sobriety, and humility. The second reason why this myth has not been widely sustained is that it is most often identified with minority groups that are themselves unpopular and unfashionable. The character myth is open to various interpretations, depending on the type of character one wishes to produce. Neither Christian nor Jewish fundamentalism is likely to provide a sustaining myth for the mass of the population. What is left outside the fundamentalist sects is a vacuum. Self-fulfillment cannot fill the vacuum because the technocratic world cannot survive on systematic selfishness. Residual ideas of virtue remain. For example, modern life is dependent on at least some adherence to ideals of honesty and courtesy. But neither these nor any other ideals carry sustaining force.[41]

The five myths are neither exclusive nor discrete; other myths have been promoted. The strands I have identified are often combined in a variety of patterns. However, they are the only strands to which large sections of the population have committed themselves at any time during this century. To find other significant examples, we must look outside the democracies—to authoritarian Germany under Hitler or to totalitarian Russia. Some combination of these strands could conceptually provide a common core beyond the ABCs. For various reasons, none is providing that common core in the United States, in Canada, or in Britain today. The prospect then for a common core is not bright.

The Fortress Monastery

The prospect is bleak for the adoption of a meaningful, common, and general core of education. It is not helpful to accept resignedly that differentiated schooling will fill the vacuum left by the obsolescent common school. It is not helpful to suggest in a simplistic manner that the new common core will be an education for each child according to his or her "needs." Whatever will be the result of such a policy or nonpolicy, it will not be a common core. Differentiated schooling challenges the very purpose of schooling beyond the ABCs.

At the moment, there remains substantial public belief in the idea of the public school. The grounds for that belief are dangerously inconsistent and are being systematically undermined by the growing obsolescence of the common school. If we embrace differentiated schooling, we abandon the ideas of common core and common school and increase the centrifugal and individualistic tendencies of modern times. Yet there is no consensual basis on which we can shore up a significant common core much beyond the ABCs. To be sure, we can add some courses which are uninteresting and uncontentious and of little value. But the public schools become vacuums when vital matters are addressed: the applicability of the scientific method, fundamental values, sexual mores, and political thinking. If we support the common core, we must define some elusive and unimaginable myth. If we move to differentiation, we further destroy the common core.

The beginning and end of a sustaining myth in education must lie in character. If we cannot collectively assert a consensual set of characteristics we would like young people to gain, then mass education is not in the long run sustainable. That is not to say there could not be continued public funding for institutions providing skill training, or funding for groups wanting to sustain their culture in a variety of ways, including the education of their young. But public education requires a societal vision. Materialistic utilitarianism, as is now becoming evident, is insufficient. Not only are there seeds of doubt among teachers and parents, but there is more widespread disenchantment among those students who correctly foresee their futures in subservient roles; to be told that all is fair in a meritocratic world is the more insulting if it happens to be true.

The democratic myth cannot sustain schooling because its original ideas are now seen as being unrealizable. Marxists have changed the definition of "democratic schooling" for their own subversive purposes with which there is little public sympathy.[42] "Democratic" schooling, as the term is now usually used, is far removed from most people's ideas of representative political democracy. None of this is to argue that in a very different and Marxist society, public education would not be an integral part of its democratic vision, as is the case in the USSR. But such societies have to come to terms with or exclude entirely our view of individual freedom; most communist countries have comparatively little difficulty in maintaining a totalitarian, centripetal educational myth—but a high price is paid. The mainstream democratic idea that a common core, common school will bring about social equality is no longer credible.

Self-fulfillment and liberalism pose similar questions—what does one do with one's fulfillment or with one's liberal education? Does it matter? Why does Mother Teresa make a better icon than Madonna? Why is it better to listen to Bach than to Sid Vicious? Satisfactory answers to such questions require a transcendent vision, an idea of the good lying beyond immediate pleasure or satisfaction.

A genuine sustaining myth must have some ultimate, transcendent purpose, some sense of the good, and it is in its expression that we shall find a source for the common core. Prospects for the common core are like those of Christianity at the beginning of the Dark Ages. Just as fortress monasteries survived those times by turning in upon themselves, so the best hope for the common core in today's times is for some schools, public and independent, to synthesize a common core which may once again grow in a more supportive environment.

Such a synthesis, based on character development and reflecting a transcendent good, would draw on other myths. The central characteristic of the new common core is virtue, a search for the good—comprised of such components as truth, courage, justice, friendship, and consideration.[43] But the other strands would also be in evidence—technocracy because our young must be socialized for the material world in which we live; self-fulfillment because free expression provides avenues to expressions of truth; liberalism because its humane, tolerant, and cultivated environment permits truth to flourish; and democracy because it is its underlying strength that allows us to live stable lives in freedom and harmony.

There are contradictions among the five competing myths. Most notably, there is some basic contradiction between the nihilism of self-fulfillment and the authority implicit in a concept of virtue. For that reason, there is no possible synthesis with all five myths making equal contributions. If there is contradiction there must be some authoritative way out. In my view, the dominant ideas must concern the character of the educated person and of the society in which educated people will live—the ideas must be both philosophical and political.

The development and utilization of science and technology; creative expression and appreciation in the arts and humanities; the provision of grounds for intelligent, individual choice—all these sets of ideals and others create the stuff of schooling, and provide grounds for important myths on which the school can be built, developed, and sustained. Transcending these ideas, important as they are, must be some common core of faith—whether it be expressed in terms of the good, or in religious terms, or in terms of a better world.

I have argued that there is little prospect for adoption of such a common core in the western world today for a variety of reasons. Perhaps at the center of our disbelief is Bowers's base of nihilism: the delusion that freedom can form the common core; the failure to recognize that freedom is destructive as well as creative, and that sin is the ultimate proof of freedom.[44] Having analyzed and destroyed our reason for being, we observe with dismay that many of our adolescents have no sense of purpose beyond material well-being. An arbitrary rationality is introduced to fill the vacuum, but rational arguments can be developed for the most destructive forms of self-indulgent behavior.

Perhaps the public school system will be held together by some ramshackle coalition of interests—of educators, of government, of the ABCs. Perhaps it will be gradually replaced by private and semiprivate (for example, religious) alternatives. Either way a universal, common core much beyond the ABCs seems unlikely. That leaves it to a few fortress monasteries, both public and independent, to cherish and nurture a common core founded on the virtue that leads to truth and wisdom, which will integrate the important aspects of our cultural heritage embedded in the myths that have, for a very short period of time, served to sustain public education. The survival of a common core, a moral chart to sustain our civilization, demands that we take advantage of the centrifugal, educational differentiation that is destroying it.

FOOTNOTES

1. Mark Holmes, "Forward to the Basics: A Radical Conservative Reconstruction," *Curriculum Inquiry* 10, no. 4 (1980): 383-418.

2. Mortimer Adler, *The Paideia Proposal* (New York: MacMillan, 1982).

3. Ivan Illich, *Deschooling Society* (New York: Harper and Row, 1971).

4. Samuel Bowles and Herbert Gintis, *Schooling in Capitalist America* (New York: Basic Books, 1976).

5. U.S. Department of Education, *What Works?* (Washington, DC: U.S. Government Printing Office, 1986).

6. National Commission on Excellence in Education, *A Nation at Risk* (Washington, DC: U.S. Government Printing Office, 1983).

7. Ernest L. Boyer, *High School: A Report on Secondary Education in America* (New York: Harper and Row, 1983).

8. James S. Coleman, Thomas Huffer, and Sally Kilgore, *High School Achievement* (New York: Basic Books, 1982).

9. John I. Goodlad, *A Place Called School* (New York: McGraw-Hill, 1984).

10. See, for example, the symposium in the *Harvard Educational Review* 53, no. 4 (1983): 377-411.

11. Mark Holmes, "The Secondary School in Contemporary Western Society: Constraints, Imperatives, and Prospects," *Curriculum Inquiry* 15, no. 1 (1985): 7-36. See also, idem, "Forward to the Basics."

12. Emile Durkheim, *Moral Education* (New York: Free Press, 1961).

13. Christopher Jencks et al., *Who Gets Ahead?* (New York: Basic Books, 1979); John Porter, Marion Porter, and Bernard R. Blishen, *Stations and Callings* (Toronto: Methuen, 1982).

14. Albert H. Halsey, Anthony Heath, and John M. Ridge, *Origins and Destinations: Family, Class, and Education in Modern Britain* (Oxford: Clarendon Press, 1980).

15. Stephen P. Heyneman, "Influences on Academic Achievement: A Comparison of Results from Uganda and More Industrialized Societies," *Sociology of Education* 49, no. 3 (1976): 200-211.

16. L. C. Comber and John P. Keeves, *Science Education in Nineteen Countries: An Empirical Study*, International Studies in Evaluation, Vol. 1 (New York: John Wiley and Sons, 1973).

17. Michael D. Young, *The Rise of the Meritocracy, 1870-2033: An Essay on Education and Equality* (Harmondsworth: Penguin Books, 1961).

18. D. F. Alwin, "Socio-economic Background, College, and Postcollegiate Achievement," in *Schooling and Achievement in American Society*, ed. William H. Sewell, Robert M. Hauser, and David L. Featherman, (New York: Academic Press, 1976).

19. James S. Coleman et al., *Equality of Educational Opportunity* (Washington, DC: Department of Health, Education, and Welfare, 1966).

20. This statement is based on information received from Professor Peter Olson, Royal Institute of Studies in Education, Copenhagen, November 1986.

21. August deB. Hollingshead, *Elmtown's Youth* (New York: John Wiley and Sons, 1949); Robert J. Havighurst, *Growing Up in River City* (New York: John Wiley and Sons, 1962).

22. The natural urge to provide advantage to one's own child poses a dilemma for egalitarian leaders. The fact that prominent British socialist leaders frequently send their

sons to elite boarding schools is frequently commented upon. Even in Canada, where elite private schools are less prominent and less influential, Stephen Lewis, the country's most prominent socialist, sent his own son to Upper Canada College, the country's most elitist private school.

23. In Canada, increased private enrollment is almost entirely in schools that emphasize some combination of discipline, traditional values, and academic emphasis. A recent Gallup Poll in British Columbia differentiated between the "General Public" and "Educational Professionals." Asked what is the main challenge in the next few years, 17 percent of the public, and 10 percent of educators referred to maintaining standards and quality, whereas 5 percent and 16 percent respectively mentioned adapting to society's changing needs. Further, 38 percent and 3 percent respectively believed that "all subjects taught in certain grades should be the same throughout the province": 59 percent and 4 percent thought that "standardized teaching materials" are "very important" and 69 percent and 3 percent believed that "standardized methods" of evaluating students are "very important."

24. For example, enrollment in French Immersion (defined as more than 450 hours per year, between three and six times the amount for regular French) in Ontario was 48,000 in 1984, greater than the total enrollment in private schools.

25. Private enrollment in elementary schools in Ontario grew by 66 percent, from 21,000 to 35,000, between 1971 and 1983. Roman Catholic elementary enrollment increased as a proportion of publicly funded enrollment from 30 percent in 1971 (422,000 out of 1,423,000) to 35 percent in 1982 (425,000 out of 1,213,000). Heritage Language classes, some of which involve segregation within the school day, enrolled 89,000 elementary students in 1983, none fifteen years earlier. In addition, there has been growth in segregated schooling for the gifted. Approximately 48 percent of Ontario's elementary students were enrolled by 1982 in Roman Catholic schools, French Immersion classes, Heritage Language classes, and private schools. Although there is some double counting (many French Immersion and Heritage Language students are in Catholic schools, thereby being doubly segregated), I have not included students in extended French classes, gifted classes, and learning-disabled classes. It is reasonable to assume that close to one-half of Ontario's elementary students are significantly segregated for instruction on the basis of criteria that are closely related to parental income and social status, religion, and ethnicity.

26. Rachel Sharp and Anthony Green, *Education and Social Control* (London: Routledge and Kegan Paul, 1975).

27. Benjamin S. Bloom, *Human Characteristics and School Learning* (New York: McGraw-Hill, 1976).

28. P. Jones, B. Rowan, and R. Burns, "Patterns of Implementation of Outcome-based Education Programs," *Outcomes* 5, no. 4 (1986): 1-4, examined the implementation of outcome-based education. The 140 experts identified, among them, only 89 schools throughout the United States, excluding Johnson City, New York City and Red Bank, New Jersey.

29. D. W. Livingstone, Douglas J. Hart, and Leslie D. McLean, *Public Attitudes toward Education in Ontario, 1982* (Toronto: OISE Press, 1981).

30. Michael B. Katz argues in his *Class, Bureaucracy, and Schools: The Illusion of Educational Change in America* (New York: Praeger, 1971) that genuine educational reform does not take place because the current bureaucratic structure serves the interests of the administrators who control the schools and the affluent members of the public to whose benefit the school's social structure is organized.

31. Adler, *The Paideia Proposal.*

32. Edward A. Shils, *Tradition* (Chicago: University of Chicago Press, 1981), p. 326.

33. Theodore Sizer, *Horace's Compromise: The Dilemma of the American High School* (Boston: Houghton-Mifflin, 1984).

34. Compare Seymour Sarason's, *The Culture of the School and the Problem of Change* (Boston: Allyn and Bacon, 1971) with his *Schooling in America* (New York: Free Press, 1983).

35. See, for example, Goodlad, *A Place Called School* and Sizer, *Horace's Compromise.* See also, Paul Willis, *Learning to Labour* (Farnborough, Hants: Gower, 1977).

36. Michael Rutter, Barbara Maugham, Peter Mortimer, Janet Ouston, and Alan Smith, *Fifteen Thousand Hours: Secondary Schools and Their Effects on Children* (London: Open Books, 1979).

37. Holmes, "The Secondary School in Contemporary Western Society"; David E. Tyack and Elisabeth Hansot, *Managers of Virtue* (New York: Basic Books, 1982); Geoffrey Walford, *Life in Public Schools* (London: Methuen, 1986).

38. Urie Bronfenbrenner, *Two Worlds of Childhood* (New York: Russell Sage, 1970); Edward A. Wynne, *Looking at Schools: Good, Bad, and Indifferent* (Lexington, MA: Lexington Books, 1980).

39. See, for example, Provincial Commission on the Aims and Objectives of Education in the Schools in Ontario, *Living and Learning* (Toronto: Department of Education, 1968) and Central Advisory Council for Education, *Children and Their Primary Schools* (London: Her Majesty's Stationery Office, 1967).

40. C. A. Bowers, "Culture against Itself: Nihilism as an Element in Recent Educational Thought," *American Journal of Education* 93, no. 4 (1985): 465-90.

41. Fundamentalist Christians see the public schools as presenting a secular, relativist view without a conception of fundamental truth. Their schools have grown rapidly in the United States.

42. See, for example, Henry Giroux and Peter McLaren, "Teacher Education and the Politics of Engagement: The Case for Democratic Schooling," *Harvard Educational Review* 56, no. 3 (1986): 213-38.

43. The idea of the good life developed in this section draws on the ideas of Alasdair MacIntyre, *After Virtue: A Study in Moral Theory* (Notre Dame, IN: University of Notre Dame Press, 1981), where Aristotelian ethics are synthesized with the Judeo-Christian heritage, and on Shils, *Tradition,* where it is argued that society and individuals are lost without some guiding chart, a chart to be drawn from cultural traditions. My own position is quite close to neo-Platonism.

44. An elaboration of my comments on Bowers can be found in my "A Response to Bowers, Howard, Stanley, and Soltis," *American Journal of Education* 94, no. 4 (1986): 537-41.

Name Index

259

Subject Index

INFORMATION ABOUT MEMBERSHIP IN THE SOCIETY

Membership in the National Society for the Study of Education is open to all who desire to receive its publications.

There are two categories of membership, Regular and Comprehensive. The Regular Membership (annual dues in 1988, $20) entitles the member to receive both volumes of the yearbook. The Comprehensive Membership (annual dues in 1988, $40) entitles the member to receive the two-volume yearbook and the two current volumes in the Series on Contemporary Educational Issues. For their first year of membership, full-time graduate students pay reduced dues in 1988 as follows: Regular, $16; Comprehensive, $36.

Membership in the Society is for the calendar year. Dues are payable on or before January 1 of each year.

New members are required to pay an entrance fee of $1, in addition to annual dues for the year in which they join.

Members of the Society include professors, researchers, graduate students, and administrators in colleges and universities; teachers, supervisors, curriculum specialists, and administrators in elementary and secondary schools; and a considerable number of persons not formally connected with educational institutions.

All members participate in the nomination and election of the six-member Board of Directors, which is responsible for managing the affairs of the Society, including the authorization of volumes to appear in the yearbook series. All members whose dues are paid for the current year are eligible for election to the Board of Directors.

Each year the Society arranges for meetings to be held in conjunction with the annual conferences of one or more of the major national educational organizations. All members are urged to attend these sessions. Members are also encouraged to submit proposals for future yearbooks or for volumes in the series on Contemporary Educational Issues.

Further information about the Society may be secured by writing to the Secretary-Treasurer, NSSE, 5835 Kimbark Avenue, Chicago, Ill. 60637.

RECENT PUBLICATIONS OF THE NATIONAL SOCIETY FOR THE STUDY OF EDUCATION

1. The Yearbooks

Eighty-seventh Yearbook (1988)
Part 1. *Critical Issues in Curriculum.* Laurel N. Tanner, editor. Cloth.
Part 2. *Cultural Literacy and the Idea of General Education.* Ian Westbury and Alan C. Purves, editors. Cloth.

Eighty-sixth Yearbook (1987)
Part 1. *The Ecology of School Renewal.* John I. Goodlad, editor. Cloth.
Part 2. *Society as Educator in an Age of Transition.* Kenneth D. Benne and Steven Tozer, editors. Cloth.

Eighty-fifth Yearbook (1986)
Part 1. *Microcomputers and Education.* Jack A. Culbertson and Luvern L. Cunningham, editors. Cloth.
Part 2. *The Teaching of Writing.* Anthony R. Petrosky and David Bartholomae, editors. Cloth.

Eighty-fourth Yearbook (1985)
Part 1. *Education in School and Nonschool Settings.* Mario D. Fantini and Robert Sinclair, editors. Cloth.
Part 2. *Learning and Teaching the Ways of Knowing.* Elliot Eisner, editor. Cloth.

Eighty-third Yearbook (1984)
Part 1. *Becoming Readers in a Complex Society.* Alan C. Purves and Olive S. Niles, editors. Cloth.
Part 2. *The Humanities in Precollegiate Education.* Benjamin Ladner, editor. Paper.

Eighty-second Yearbook (1983)
Part 1. *Individual Differences and the Common Curriculum.* Gary D Fenstermacher and John I. Goodlad, editors. Paper.
Part 2. *Staff Development.* Gary Griffin, editor. Paper.

Eighty-first Yearbook (1982)
Part 1. *Policy Making in Education.* Ann Lieberman and Milbrey W. McLaughlin, editors. Cloth.
Part 2. *Education and Work.* Harry F. Silberman, editor. Cloth.

Eightieth Yearbook (1981)
Part 1. *Philosophy and Education.* Jonas P. Soltis, editor. Cloth.
Part 2. *The Social Studies.* Howard D. Mehlinger and O. L. Davis, Jr., editors. Cloth.

Seventy-ninth Yearbook (1980)

Part 1. *Toward Adolescence: The Middle School Years.* Mauritz Johnson, editor. Cloth.

Part 2. *Learning a Second Language.* Frank M. Grittner, editor. Cloth.

Seventy-eighth Yearbook (1979)

Part 1. *The Gifted and the Talented: Their Education and Development.* A. Harry Passow, editor. Paper.

Part 2. *Classroom Management.* Daniel L. Duke, editor. Paper.

Seventy-seventh Yearbook (1978)

Part 1. *The Courts and Education.* Clifford B. Hooker, editor. Cloth.

Seventy-sixth Yearbook (1977)

Part 1. *The Teaching of English.* James R. Squire, editor. Cloth.

The above titles in the Society's Yearbook series may be ordered from the University of Chicago Press, Book Order Department, 11030 Langley Ave., Chicago, IL 60628. For a list of earlier titles in the yearbook series still available, write to the Secretary, NSSE, 5835 Kimbark Ave., Chicago, IL 60637.

2. The Series on Contemporary Educational Issues

The following volumes in the Society's Series on Contemporary Educational Issues may be ordered from the McCutchan Publishing Corporation, P.O. Box 774, Berkeley, Calif. 94701.

Case, Charles W., and Matthes, William A., editors. *Colleges of Education: Perspectives on Their Future.* 1985.

Eisner, Elliot, and Vallance, Elizabeth, editors. *Conflicting Conceptions of Curriculum.* 1974.

Erickson, Donald A., and Reller, Theodore L., editors. *The Principal in Metropolitan Schools.* 1979.

Farley, Frank H., and Gordon, Neal J., editors. *Psychology and Education: The State of the Union.* 1981.

Fennema, Elizabeth, and Ayer, M. Jane, editors. *Women and Education: Equity or Equality.* 1984.

Griffiths, Daniel E., Stout, Robert T., and Forsyth, Patrick, editors. *Better Leaders, Better Schools: Perspectives on School Administration.* 1988.

Jackson, Philip W. *Contributing to Educational Change: Perspectives on Research and Practice.* 1988.

Lane, John J., and Walberg, Herbert J., editors. *Effective School Leadership: Policy and Process.* 1987.

Levine, Daniel U., and Havighurst, Robert J., editors. *The Future of Big City Schools: Desegregation Policies and Magnet Alternatives.* 1977.

Lindquist, Mary M., editor. *Selected Issues in Mathematics Education.* 1981.

Peterson, Penelope L., and Walberg, Herbert J., editors. *Research on Teaching: Concepts, Findings, and Implications.* 1979.

Pflaum-Connor, Susanna, editor. *Aspects of Reading Education.* 1978.

Purves, Alan, and Levine, Daniel U., editors. *Educational Policy and International Assessment: Implications of the IEA Assessment of Achievement.* 1975.

Sinclair, Robert L., and Ghory, Ward. *Reaching Marginal Students: A Prime Concern for School Renewal.* 1987.

Spodek, Bernard, and Walberg, Herbert J., editors. *Early Childhood Education: Issues and Insights.* 1977.

Talmage, Harriet, editor. *Systems of Individualized Education.* 1975.

Tomlinson, Tommy M., and Walberg, Herbert J., editors. *Academic Work and Educational Excellence: Raising Student Productivity.* 1986.

Tyler, Ralph W., editor. *From Youth to Constructive Adult Life: The Role of the Public School.* 1978.

Tyler, Ralph W., and Wolf, Richard M., editors. *Crucial Issues in Testing.* 1974.

Walberg, Herbert J., editor. *Educational Environments and Effects: Evaluation, Policy, and Productivity.* 1979.

Walberg, Herbert J., editor. *Improving Educational Standards and Productivity: The Research Basis for Policy.* 1982.

Wang, Margaret C., and Walberg, Herbert J., editors. *Adapting Instruction to Student Differences.* 1985.

Warren, Donald R., editor. *History, Education, and Public Policy: Recovering the American Educational Past.* 1978.